MODERN GROUP BOOK I

The Origins of
Group Psychoanalysis

BOOKS BY DRS. KAPLAN AND SADOCK

Comprehensive Textbook of Psychiatry
Alfred M. Freedman and Harold I. Kaplan, Editors

Studies in Human Behavior
Alfred M. Freedman and Harold I. Kaplan, General Editors

Modern Synopsis of Comprehensive Textbook of Psychiatry
Harold I. Kaplan, Benjamin J. Sadock, and Alfred M. Freedman

Comprehensive Group Psychotherapy
Harold I. Kaplan and Benjamin J. Sadock, Editors

Modern Group Books
Harold I. Kaplan and Benjamin J. Sadock, Editors

HAROLD I. KAPLAN

Harold I. Kaplan received an undergraduate degree from Columbia University and an M.D. from the New York Medical College. He trained in psychiatry at the Kingsbridge Veterans Hospital and Mount Sinai Hospital in New York and became a Diplomate of the American Board of Psychiatry and Neurology in 1957; presently he is an Associate Examiner of the American Board. He began the practice and teaching of psychiatry and was certified in psychoanalytic medicine at the New York Medical College in 1954 where he became Professor of Psychiatry and Director of Psychiatric Training and Education in 1961. He is Attending Psychiatrist at Metropolitan Hospital Center, Flower and Fifth Avenue Hospitals and Bird S. Coler Hospital. He is the Principal Investigator of ten National Institute of Mental Health training programs, specializing in the areas of undergraduate and graduate psychiatric education as well as the training of women in medicine. He is the author of over seventy scientific papers and co-author and co-editor of the books listed on this page.

BENJAMIN J. SADOCK

Benjamin J. Sadock received his A.B. from Union College and his M.D. from New York Medical College. He trained at Bellevue Psychiatric Hospital. During his military service as an Air Force psychiatrist he was also on the faculty of Southwestern Medical School. Dr. Sadock became a Diplomate of the American Board of Psychiatry and Neurology in 1966 and is an Assistant Examiner for the American Board. Currently Associate Professor of Psychiatry and Director of the Division of Group Process at New York Medical College, Dr. Sadock directs the training program for group therapists and is Chief of Continuing Education in Psychiatry, Chief Psychiatric Consultant to the student health service and co-director of the Sexual Therapy Center. He is on staff of Flower and Fifth Avenue Hospitals, Metropolitan Hospital, and the New York State Psychiatric Institute. Dr. Sadock is active in numerous psychiatric organizations, an officer of the New York County District Branch of the American Psychiatric Association, a Fellow of the New York Academy of Medicine, and has written and lectured extensively in general psychiatry and group psychotherapy. He is co-editor with Dr. Harold I. Kaplan of *Comprehensive Group Psychotherapy* (1971) and co-author with Drs. Alfred M. Freedman and Harold I. Kaplan of *Modern Synopsis of Comprehensive Textbook of Psychiatry* (1972).

The Origins of Group Psychoanalysis

Edited by

HAROLD I. KAPLAN, M.D.

Professor of Psychiatry and Director of Psychiatric Education,
New York Medical College, New York, New York

and

BENJAMIN J. SADOCK, M.D.

Associate Professor of Psychiatry and Director,
Division of Group Process, New York Medical College,
New York, New York

Jason Aronson, Inc.
New York, New York

Library of Congress Catalog Card Number: 72-96928
Standard Book Number: 0-87668-077-5

The editors express their appreciation to the following persons, publishers and publications for permission to reprint portions of the works cited.

Aldine-Atherton, Inc. for "The Marathon Group," by G. R. Bach, reprinted from Hendrik M. Ruitenbeek, editor, *Group Therapy Today* (New York: Atherton Press, 1969); copyright © 1969 by Atherton Press. Reprinted by permission of the author and Aldine-Atherton, Inc.

Bruner/Mazel, Inc. for "The Use of Videotape in the Integrated Treatment of Individuals, Couples, Families, and Groups in Private Practice," by Milton M. Berger, M.D., reprinted from *Videotape Techniques in Psychiatric Training and Treatment*, Milton M. Berger, M.D., editor. Bruner/Mazel, Inc., New York, 1970.

Dr. Herbert Holt for the unpublished essay, "Existential Group Therapy: A Phenomenological Methodology for Psychiatry."

International Journal of Group Psychotherapy for "Sexual Acting Out in Groups," by the members of the Workshop in Group Psychoanalysis of New York: A. Wolf, R. Bross, S. Flowerman, J. Greene, A. Kadis, H. Leopold, N. Locke, I. Milburg, H. Mullan, S. Obers, and H. Rosenbaum. *International Journal of Group Psychotherapy*, Vol. 4, pp. 369-380, 1954.

for "Accelerated Interaction: A Time Limited Approach on the Brief Intensive Approach," by Frederick H. Stoller. *International Journal of Group Psychotherapy*, Vol. 18, pp. 220-235, 1968.

for "Group Therapy and the Small Group Field: An Encounter," by Morris Parloff. *International Journal of Group Psychotherapy*, Vol. 20, pp. 267-304, 1970.

International Universities Press for "Group Therapy with Alcoholics," by A. Stein, M.D. and Eugene Friedman, Ph.D., Chapter III of *Fields of Group Psychotherapy*, S. R. Slavson, editor. International Universities Press, 1956.

American Psychiatric Association for "Phoenix House: Therapeutic Communities for Drug Addicts," by M. S. Rosenthal and D. V. Biase, *Hospital and Community Psychiatry*, Vol. 20, p. 27, 1969.

W. W. Norton & Co., Inc., and the Hogarth Press Ltd. for an excerpt from *An Outline of Psycho-Analysis*, Volume XXIII of Standard Edition of Sigmund Freud, revised and edited by James Strachey. Copyright 1949 by W. W. Norton & Co., Inc., and copyright © 1969 by the Institute of Psychoanalysis and Alix Strachey.

The Williams & Wilkins Co. for an excerpt from "Group Therapy in Married Couples," by Helen Papanek, M.D., reprinted from *Comprehensive Group Psychotherapy*, Harold I. Kaplan and Benjamin J. Sadock, editors. Copyright © 1971 by The Williams & Wilkins Co.

for an excerpt from "Videotape Feedback in Group Setting," by F. Stoller. *Journal of Nervous and Mental Disorders*, Vol. 148, No. 4, pp. 457-466.

Seymour Lawrence/Delacorte Press for an excerpt from *Cat's Cradle* by Kurt Vonnegut, Jr. Copyright © 1963 by Kurt Vonnegut, Jr. A Seymour Lawrence Book/Delacorte Press. Reprinted by permission of the publisher.

Contents

Preface
vi

Introduction
viii

Chapter 1
The History of Group Psychotherapy
E. James Anthony, M.D.
1

Chapter 2
Freud: The First Psychoanalytic Group Leader
Mark Kanzer, M.D.
27

Chapter 3
Psychoanalysis in Groups
Alexander Wolf, M.D. and Emanuel K. Schwartz, Ph.D., D.S.Sc.
41

Chapter 4
Sexual Acting-Out in the Psychoanalysis of Groups
Members of The Workshop in Group Psychoanalysis, New York
Alexander Wolf, M.D. and Associates
92

Glossary
I

Contributors
L

Preface

The emergence of group psychotherapy within the past two decades constitutes one of the most significant and extraordinary developments in the field of psychiatry. Gradually during this period, but particularly within the past five years, group therapy has come to be chosen for the treatment of a widening range of patients with highly diverse problems. Concurrently, professionals and laymen alike see a growing interest in the relationship of group therapy to sociocultural and educational concepts, processes, and systems. Predictably, these theoretical developments are accompanied by the development of myriad therapeutic approaches which vary with respect not only to their underlying philosophy but also to the planning and conduct of treatment.

Psychotherapy is an art as well as a science. What is taught via the lecture hall or seminar room constitutes just one aspect of the teaching curriculum. Training in psychotherapy must also include clinical exercises performed under the supervision of an experienced clinician who acts as a model for the student. The editors' commitment to this project, and its concomitant goals, evolved from their extensive experience as both educators and clinicians. The editors' special interest in group psychotherapy as a treatment technique, and an awareness of the need for more intensive training in this discipline to ensure its continued growth and development, led to the establishment, at the New York Medical College, of the first medical-school-affiliated postgraduate certification program

in group psychotherapy. In addition, they have participated in the organization of training programs in group therapy for workers in other mental health disciplines —psychology, psychiatric social work, and psychiatric nursing.

The stated goal of this series—to provide a survey of current theoretical and therapeutic trends in this field—carries with it the obligation to pursue an eclectic orientation and to present as comprehensive an account of events at every level of its development as is possible. The organization and orientation of this series attempts to provide a comprehensive survey of the theories, hypotheses, and therapeutic techniques which dominate contemporary group practice. There are no final answers, as yet, to the problems and issues which currently face group psychotherapy. But we may help to identify these problems and issues and place them in proper perspective.

This book is one of a series of paperback volumes based on *Comprehensive Group Psychotherapy,* which we previously edited. New articles have been written for each of these volumes and certain subjects have been updated or eliminated in an effort to reach a wider audience. Invitations to participate were extended to those workers who have made major and original contributions to the field of group psychotherapy and who are acknowledged experts in a particular area of theory and/or practice. Thus the preparation of this series afforded the editors a unique opportunity to engage in a stimulating interchange of ideas and to form many rewarding personal relationships. As a result, what would appear to have been an ardous undertaking has in fact been a most gratifying experience.

The editors have received dedicated and valuable help from many people to whom they wish to express their appreciation. For their secretarial and editorial help, we would like to thank Robert Gelfand, Sylvia Houzell, Mercedes Paul, Paulene Demarco, Louise Marshall, and in particular Lois Baken, who coordinated these efforts. Spe-cial thanks are extended to our publishers, E. P. Dutton, and to our outstanding editor, Robert Zenowich.

Finally, the editors wish to express their appreciation to Virginia Sadock, M.D., who acted in the capacity of assistant to the editors and assumed the multitudinous tasks of that office with grace and charm.

HAROLD I. KAPLAN, M.D.

BENJAMIN J. SADOCK, M.D.

Introduction

BACKGROUND

In 1921, the year *Group Psychology and the Analysis of the Ego* was published, Sigmund Freud, the founder of psychoanalysis, turned his attention to group psychology. He wrote, "Group psychology is concerned with the individual man as a member of a race, of a nation, of a caste, of a profession, of an institution, or as a component part of a crowd of people who have been organized into a group at some particular time for a definite purpose."

He then described properties of groups, and differentiated the mob from the small-group. The former, he said, was leaderless and capable of great excesses. It was "impulsive, changeable and irritable . . . It cannot tolerate any delay between its desire and the fulfillment of what it desires. It has a sense of omnipotence; the notion of impossibility disappears . . ." He believed that the latter, the small group which has a leader, offered a climate which diminished anxiety and neurosis and had, thereby, the potential for use as a therapeutic instrument.

GROUP PROCESSES

There are certain processes in the psychotherapy group which can be explained within the framework of theories promulgated by Freud and which form the basis for present-day group psychoanalysis and psychoanalytically oriented group psychotherapy. In brief, the group is seen as re-creating the family. Accordingly, certain members of the group may be viewed as siblings and reacted to as such. When a new member enters the group, feelings similar to that of the birth of a baby brother or sister entering the family may be experienced by some of the members. In a similar way, the leader is most often reacted to as if he were a parent, and participants look to the leader with the same awe as does the young child to his parent, often with the same expectations of omnipotence and omniscience. Group stability results from the members identifying with one another via the common bond they have to the leader and, family-like, with mutualities of love and hate.

HISTORY OF GROUPS

Despite extensive differences in technique and theoretical orientation, all therapy groups share the same historical roots. It follows then that an understanding of the evolution of group psychotherapy as a treatment modality is a prerequisite for the understanding of the current status of groups. This essential background material is provided in the chapter by Anthony, which is an overview of the history of group psychotherapy. His writing extends well beyond the traditional chronological account of events that led to the emergence of group therapy. Rather, he synthesizes these events, forming a cohesive whole, describing and placing in proper perspective the innovative contributions of behavioral scientists to a variety of disciplines.

GROUP DIFFERENCES

Although Freud did not practice group psychotherapy as such, many of his formulations about psychoanalysis in general and in group psychology in particular developed from the study group he organized with his early followers. As a result of differences in theoretical positions which may have been the result of personality clashes between Freud and some of his followers, several split from the "master" and founded their own schools of psychoanalysis. These various schisms and their ramifications are beyond the scope of this book, but one result was that the original Freudian position has come to be referred to as "orthodox" or "classical" psychoanalysis. At the present time one may find other schools of group psychotherapy representing the followers of Jung, Adler, Sullivan, Horney, and others.

THE FIRST GROUP LEADER

The chapter by Kanzer deals with a specific aspect of the historical evolution of group psychotherapy. Freud's concepts of group psychology continue to exert a strong theoretical influence on present-day practitioners. And here, for the first time, is a description of Freud's role as a group leader. The reader is immediately struck by the uncanny similarities between the study groups which Freud's disciples attended each Wednesday evening and certain forms of group therapy which are practiced today. Although Freud's colleagues met to share clinical experiences and to discuss various theoretical problems, members of the group were also encouraged to share the secrets of their inner fantasy life with the group, as are patients in some therapy groups today. The use of the "urn" in Freud's group, to determine who was to speak and to make sure that each member had an opportunity to participate, is remarkably similar to the go-around, an important modern-day group technique.

In the late 1930's Alexander Wolf began his pioneer work in group psychoanalysis in this country. He directly applied the principles and tools of psychoanalysis based on Freudian theory to the group setting. The chapter by Wolf and Schwartz, describing his method, is the most up-to-date, complete, and authoritative exposition available. Wolf uses the major tools of psychoanalytic treatment: free association, in which the patient seeks to verbalize without reservation or censor the passing contents of his mind; dream analysis, which Freud referred to as "the golden road to the unconscious"; the elucidation of the transference, the unconscious phenomenon in which the feelings, attitudes, and wishes originally linked with important figures in one's early life are projected onto current interactions; and the evocation of historical development. The therapy group recreates the family and revives the problems which the patient encountered in his original family group, and which, in this new setting, can be examined more rationally, finally understood, and mastered. Emphasis is placed on the individual patient, and on his relationship to the other members of the group and to the therapist. Wolf also originated the alternate session, during which group members meet on a regular basis without the therapist present. Such a meeting, alternating with a therapist-directed session, facilitates and encourages more intense interactions between members. Their way of responding with and without the therapist can be compared: some patients, it has been found, will be active and verbal in alternate sessions but become withdrawn and quiet in those sessions where the therapist is present. In these cases, one often uncovers a history of a stern, punitive, and intimidating parent.

SEXUAL ACTING-OUT

Depending on the makeup of the group and the rules set forth by the leader, there may be a great deal of sexual activity in a group, almost none at all, or it may be explicitly discouraged. The subject of sexual acting-out is timely for these reasons: sexual mores have changed considerably within the last decade; attitudes are more liberal; and the society as a whole is less repressed. The therapy group, considered by most workers in the field to be a microcosm of society, can be expected to reflect this change. Furthermore, the recent interest in nude group therapy—condemned by the American Psychiatric Association's *Task Force Report on Encounter Groups and Psychiatry*—has definite sexual overtones.

There are, however, no reliable figures available from any source regarding the incidence of sexual activity between members of psychotherapy groups. That it does occur is certain; but the significance, effects, and causes of sexual activity within the group therapy experience are unknown.

After a careful review of the literature, we have selected the statement by the *Workshop in Group Psychoanalysis* as the most comprehensive, thought provoking, and rational on a subject still ambiguous to both professionals and nonprofessionals.

1

The History of Group Psychotherapy

E. James Anthony, M.D.

INTRODUCTION

History can be written in at least two distinctly different ways. The historian can choose to tell it as it really happened (*wie es geschehen ist*, in Ranke's famous phrase) or to reconstruct it in the context of present-day theory and practice. The first method has little dynamic value for the clinical historian, and there is no convincing reason why one should have to contemplate past ideas solely in terms of the *Zeitgeist* prevailing at the time. Moreover, it tends to place history firmly and disjunctively in the past, with little or no bearing on the present except as interest or illustration.

The second historical approach was first opened up by Nietzsche in his *Unseasonable Reflexions* and carried, as so much of his work did, psychoanalytic undertones. According to him, the reconstruction of the past should not be an end in itself but the means of relating the past to the present in a meaningful and operational way. This process could be understood as the historian's equivalent to the transference. This approach assumed that the historian could and should live contemporaneously in the two worlds of the past and the present. In fact, only by linking these two together dynamically could the historical past be made to have both relevance and value in the present. Sometimes surprisingly, the apparently demoded insights of the past could be refurbished for current use. The student of history frequently sees how the present unconsciously plagiarizes the past.

This dynamic viewpoint ensures that history becomes an indispensable handmaiden of on-going life rather than remaining monolithically isolated as a monument to the past. It allows what is now to transact with what was then, and it finds an equal place for both within the continuous historical process. In this crucial scientific dialogue between past and present, the present must take and keep the initiative. The present should in no way become a slave to the past in the manner of tradition; it must be free to make full use of the past for its own evolving purposes.

The essence of the dynamic historical method is to select the significant facts of history and arrange them within a temporal sequence. Inevitably, some manipulation is involved in this selection and arrangement, but there must be no distortion of the facts. The clinical historian must be ready to admit that, although he may have a bias in his arrangement of facts, he is still able to recognize other perspectives, even when they contradict his own thesis. Like the good therapist, he should be able to see in this multiplicity of incompatible perspectives not failure or foolishness but the very richness of life.

The never-ending discovery and rediscovery of past developments by present-day workers are the expression of a dialectic that will last as long as the particular discipline concerned remains viable and growing. On the other hand, the workers who disconnect themselves from the past not only miss out on the enrichment and self-revelation provided by the past but are also fated, if Freud and Santayana are right, to

1

repeat compulsively the past while deluding themselves that they are breaking new theoretical or technical ground. An attentive awareness of past modes of feeling, thinking, and doing—what Meinecke refers to as historicism—helps to safeguard against this proclivity.

It would be a naive conceit on the part of the historian to suppose that he can reduce the conglomerated past to a unified and linear development. In this discipline, as in all other disciplines, there is always an irreducible plurality of operating systems. It is, therefore, important to preserve a wide-angled viewpoint on all the global conspectuses that have existed within the historical evolution—whether actual, factual, mythological, or fantasied—granting to each the recognition of its particularity.

There is another reason for mapping out the topology of the historical field. By doing so, the worker can develop what Whitehead, in a different context, aptly termed graded envisagement. He can become aware of a system of kinship within the general population of ideas belonging to his discipline. For example, the group worker can begin to realize that the disparate concepts of Gestalt therapy and analytic group therapy not only have antecedents in common but are often in close theoretical relationship, separated only by semantic confusion. Since all these ideas fall more or less within the same family system, it is not altogether surprising that intellectual totems and taboos are set up, so that it seems to become something horrendous to mate what are apparently neighboring ideas. Many theorists, having swallowed their own intellectual totems, react to closely related ideas as if they were incestuous.

The ultimate lesson from history, therefore, is that for coherent, logical development in a discipline, one must constantly and consistently remember where he came from and where he is going. The past is conglomerate, complex, confabulatory, and conflictual, but it is incumbent on every worker to resolve these perplexities and complexities for himself and, by so doing, discover his own professional identity and ultimate purpose. Each group psychotherapist must become his own historian and

thread his way with open-mindedness and relative impartiality through the shoals of psychobiologically improbable, mythological, mystical, and paralogical ideas of the past and present, asking his own questions and seeking his own answers within the totality of what is known or imagined. He has to undertake this job for himself, since no one can do it for him.

The scientific mind that is brought up and nurtured on history obtains an equanimity and objectivity that becomes characteristic of the scientist in all his dealings. Bronowski, in describing how scientists communicate, has this to say:

> They do not make wild claims, they do not cheat, they do not try to persuade at any cost, they appeal neither to prejudice nor to authority, they are often frank about their ignorance, their disputes are fairly decorous, they do not confuse what is being argued with race, politics, sex or age, and they listen patiently to the young and to the old who both know everything.

Patience, that essential scientific virtue, can come not only from listening to patients but also from listening to history.

GROUP PSYCHOLOGY

The beginning is always difficult, wrote Schopenhauer. This is true for birth, for writing history, and for history itself. Once, however, one recognizes that the beginning is never really the beginning and that there is always a prehistory antedating every start, the conflict of inertia can be solved. One can deal with group psychology and, by means of it, find his way imperceptibly, if the historical development holds true, into the field of group psychotherapy.

World War I proved to be a great impetus to the development of group psychology and World War II, to the development of group psychotherapy. This relationship to war cannot be regarded as entirely accidental. In war, individual man is forced into groups of all sizes and structures for reasons of survival. In war, he loses much of his identity and becomes better known for fighting, rationing, and security purposes as a number. The understanding and maintenance of group morale becomes a critical factor in the country's struggle for existence. In World War I, various group psychologists stepped forward to meet this pressing need.

A pioneer in this field, and one of the most scintillating intellects of his time, was Wilfred Trotter, a neurosurgeon who, in the middle of World War I, published a remarkable document on the herd instinct in peace and war. Whether there is such an organizing instinct in man has been much debated and is still in dispute, but Trotter developed the insight that it is both logical and biological for human groups to form if one regards the group as a continuation of the multicellular character of all higher organisms. The instinct to come together and develop multifunctional skills for the sake of individual and group survival would be in keeping with evolutionary trends. Later authors also pointed to needs for pairing and fighting as basic elements in group formation, but they gave psychodynamic reasons.

Le Bon and the Popular Mind

It was Le Bon who inadvertently gave the group a bad name to begin with, in 1920. He cannot be blamed for this, since he was careful to specify that his descriptions applied to large groups or crowds that are essentially unorganized or under the mysterious and irresistible influence of charismatic leadership. The capacity of a leader to sway a crowd in the direction of his own purpose—playing on its suggestibility, its exaggerated emotionalism, and its credulity—has never been as subtly portrayed as in Mark Antony's brilliant display of demagoguery in Shakespeare's *Julius Caesar*.

According to Le Bon, the person who joins a group, especially a large group, sacrifices something of his precious individuality. He becomes more suggestible and, therefore, more susceptible to the contagion of neighboring minds. Le Bon's description of the group mind has many of the characteristics of the child, the primitive, and the impulse-ridden psychopath. The group mind is illogical, intolerant, prejudiced, rigid, uninhibited, and submissive to any dominant force that exerts its authority.

If this were even partly true, it would follow that the group is more susceptible to therapeutic influence than the individual and, therefore, a better bet with regard to treatment. Freud, however, pointed out that this detrimental and depreciatory appraisal of the group mind reflects the contempt with which certain thinkers view the masses. This appraisal is certainly not very different from prejudices characteristic of the aristocratic elements of society at all times.

Other critics, such as Kraskovic, held the view that group enthusiasm would bring about the most splendid achievements. The question of who was right gave place, with further consideration, to the view that perhaps both could be right and that the group contained within itself the seeds of both success and failure.

McDougall and the Group Mind

In 1920, McDougall started out from this apparent contradiction and found a solution for it in the factor of organization. In his understanding, there are two psychologies of the group, the one dealing with an unorganized group and the other with a group that is organized.

McDougall's judgment of the unorganized group is as severe as Le Bon's. He, too, saw it as emotional, impulsive, violent, fickle, inconsistent, irresolute, suggestible, irresponsible, and at times almost like a wild beast. But this is not the whole story. A marked change occurs when the group is organized and task-oriented. The collective mental life is then raised to a higher level, and some of the psychological disadvantages of group formation are removed. In addition, the exaltation or intensification of emotion that takes place in every group member and that stirs each one to a degree that they seldom attained under any other conditions can now be used for great achievement.

The "primitive sympathetic response," which is somewhat similar to Le Bon's "contagion," can be harnessed for better purpose if five main organizational conditions are established: group continuity, a system of group relationships, the stimulus of intergroup rivalries, the development of traditions, and the differentiation and specialization of functions. A sixth condition that can be added to these five is the emergence of leadership, a phenomenon that later workers have tended to focus on, since it has special bearing on the therapist's role in group psychotherapy.

The problem for the group psychotherapist using McDougall's frame of reference is how to further the organization desirable for optimal collective life and at the same time make therapeutic use of the primitive sympathetic response that brings with it the mutative affective experience. Throughout the subsequent history of group psychotherapy, workers would be torn between the therapeutic potential of the group mind and the group emotion.

Freud and the Group Leader

In 1921, Freud first outlined a group psychology that was and still is meaningful to the group psychotherapist. One can only conjecture, with regret, what extraordinary developments could have occurred had he been able to follow up on his group psychology and do for group psychotherapy what he did for psychoanalysis. He himself did not feel that the two psychologies are as different as they seem on first glance. He felt that it does not make sense to consider the individual psychologically except in relation to other individuals, so that in a way all psychology is essentially group psychology, and group psychology is the original and older psychology. He was thus able to speak of a group of two, by which means he was able to link individual and group psychology together.

The repercussions of this viewpoint still haunt group psychotherapy. The question of treating the individual through the group or the group through the individual is a perennial one, and one might conclude, in agreement with Freud, that it is largely a pseudoquestion and that the therapist always does a bit of both.

Freud addressed himself to three problems. These are crucial not only for the understanding of group psychology but also for the practice of group psychotherapy: (1) What is a group? (2) How does the group come to exercise such a strong influence over the mental life of the individual? (3) What changes does the group bring about in the mental life of the individual?

Freud indicated that a collection of people is not a group but, given the proper conditions, can develop into a group. A major condition for this to happen is the development of leadership, but to what extent this is dispensable depends on the nature of the group and on the presence of strong group bonds. A leading idea can substitute for an actual leader, especially if it occasions the same strong feeling tones and identifications.

Morphologically, Freud distinguished between transient and permanent groups, homogeneous and heterogeneous ones, natural and artificial ones, and organized and unorganized ones, but his major differentiation was undoubtedly between leadered and leaderless groups.

All these distinctions are still of great importance to the field of group psychotherapy. Therapists are still wondering whether they do better with short-term groups than with long-term groups, whether heterogeneous groups are less therapeutic than homogeneous ones, and whether natural groups, such as families, start off with a stronger therapeutic advantage than artificial stranger groups.

It was Freud's opinion that the mechanism of identification is a basic one in group formations. The group members identify with the leader, whom they view as a father surrogate, and they identify with one another and relate to one another through their common tie to the leader.

A second important mechanism at work in the group is that of empathy, which enables the group members to experience their group life through one another.

By means of these two powerful mechanisms, the one leading to the other, the individual patients in the group are able to obtain an inward experience of another's mental life. Identification not only helps to further positive feeling within the group but also helps in limiting aggressiveness, since there is a general tendency to spare those with whom one is identified.

The psychological cement responsible for group ties is, according to Freud, a composite of cohering elements, such as imitation, identification, empathy, relatedness, sympathy, common purpose, mutual interests, and, more fundamentally, a recognition of something common that is incorporated and shared by all the membership. In its most concrete form, the cohesive element would be eating together; on a more psychological level, it would be taking in and sharing a leader. In the therapeutic group, the feeling of having similar problems, sharing the same therapist, and being together in the same group makes for unification. Some of the narcissism of the members is projected onto the group, so that it becomes something very special, and some of it is projected onto the leader, making him an ego ideal. Under conditions of charismatic leadership, the group may become, as it were, hypnotized, surrendering to the superior power of the leader. The members may then show a marked dependency and submissiveness, a set of circumstances frequently seen in psychotherapeutic groups.

Freud's perception of group formations as being cardinal to the life of the group was indeed an accurate one. To the extent that the members develop into a real group, there is less need for dominant leadership. The more leader-centered the group is, the more regressive does its organization tend to become. For group psychotherapists, the paradox has long been a familiar one. In the words of Lao-tse, the best leader is he who knows how to follow.

When a group with a strong leader loses its leadership, a dissolution of ties rapidly occurs, and, as a result, panic ensues. The members cease to relate to one another in an integrated way, cease to listen to orders, cease to have any concern except self-concern, and become susceptible to the sudden emergence of a gigantic and senseless dread that spreads through them like contagion. Later psychotherapists have substantiated Freud's original observation and have attempted to account for its occurrence. How Freud could develop so much insight into the workings of a group without systematic group experience or experience in a group psychotherapy group remains as much a mystery as how he acquired so much insight into intrapsychic matters

without undergoing a training analysis.

Having coped brilliantly with the questions that he himself raised, Freud confronted himself with still another perplexing problem: What brings the group together?

It has always been recognized that man is a social animal born into a group, living within a group, and usually dying supported by a group. In some religions, it is alleged that he rejoins the group in the afterlife. The instinct theorists, from Trotter on, have postulated some kind of herd instinct that makes the human animal, like other gregarious animals, feel incomplete when he is alone. There is also some sense of security that comes from being with individuals like one's self, the corollary being the sense of threat when associating with individuals unlike one's self.

Freud, although an instinct man, was inclined to reject the theory of a social instinct. For him, man is not a herd animal but a horde animal—that is, an individual brought together with other individuals into a group by a leader. The group is a revival of the primal horde conjectured by Darwin—the herd that is ruled over despotically by a powerful male. What brings the individual members together into the group is the leader, but this is essentially different from what brings the leader into the group. There were thus two basic psychologies within group psychology: the psychology of the individual members of the group and the psychology of the leader of the group. It is these two psychologies, operating in every group psychotherapy group, that makes group psychotherapy twice as complicated as individual psychotherapy.

Deeper forces that keep a group together concerns the erotic impulse, but Freud had less to say about these ties, chiefly because it could not have been possible for him to analyze them without the help of a therapeutic group. However, his hunch was that homosexual love was far more compatible with the maintenance of group ties than was heterosexual love. Both love and neurosis he saw as having a disintegrating effect on the group.

At this point, Freud made one of his most important pronouncements regarding group psychology and group psychotherapy. He pointed out that, where there is a powerful impetus to group formation, neurosis tends to diminish and eventually to disappear, and he felt that it is justifiable to turn this inverse relationship between neurosis and group formation to therapeutic account. He observed that well-organized groups are a powerful protection against the development of neurosis and that, when the individual is excluded from the group, he is compelled to replace group formations with neurotic formations. If Freud had followed up this lead to its logical conclusion, he would have created a complete system of group psychotherapy.

Why did Freud stop at that point? Curiously enough, he did the same thing with the natural group of the family as he did with the artificial stranger group. In his book *Totem and Taboo*, he set out three postulates that could have laid the foundation of systematic family theory and therapy: first, that there is a family psyche whose psychological processes correspond fairly closely to those of the individual; second, that there is a continuity of emotional life in the family psyche from one generation to the next; and third, that the mysterious transmission of attitudes and feelings through the generations is the result of unconscious understanding that makes the latent psychic life of one generation accessible to the succeeding one.

These three postulates could have become the cornerstone of a dynamic and developmental family psychopathology. They presumed a collective psychological life for the family, a process of intergenerational transmission of neurosis, and an unconscious understanding that assimilates neurotic disturbances and generates family pathology.

Why did he stop at these critical points? Who can tell? It is possible that his intense interest in individual intrapsychic conflicts—his own—superseded everything else.

Burrow and Group Analysis

Trigant Burrow gave the name group analysis to the type of behavior analysis first conducted in groups. Since this name led to a great deal of misunderstanding as to what he was doing, he dropped the term and spoke instead of phyloanalysis, which indicated that his interest was in man in his evolutionary status. Although he had a background of psychoanalytic knowledge and working in groups, he did not strongly affect the field of current group psychotherapy. Essentially, he does not belong to the history of group psychotherapy, but one might consider some of his ideas in the light of present-day knowledge. In the first place, he refused to polarize the therapeutic situation into a sick patient needing help on the one side and a well physician giving him help on the other hand. Burrow saw both as elements in a sick society, with both needing to understand the social aberration from which they were suffering. This abdication of the therapist from the leader's role has its current counterpart. In the second place, Burrow stressed the importance of the here-and-now and paid scant attention to genetic aspects. Third, his concern was not with words but with the visible somatic manifestations of stress as they are subjectively or objectively experienced.

What Burrow was searching for was some undiscovered factor within the sphere of man's behavior that belonged to the biophysical bedrock. This factor was observable, physiological, and concrete, with definite localization, and was most manifest in a group setting. To study it, he set up, with his associate, what almost amounted to prolonged sensitivity training groups conducted over many years. Within these groups, he made use of a series of laboratory exercises in an effort to make subjective man objectively appreciative of his own subjective processes. All this sounds as if he were a precursor of the National Training Laboratories at Bethel except for the fact that his frame of reference was radically different.

Since his terminology is often needlessly difficult, it may be helpful to quote a lucid discussion of his approach given in his book *The Social Basis of Consciousness:*

I was led to the idea of an analysis which should take place in a group of persons in which no one individual would hold an authoritative position in relation to the others except in the measure in which his thoughtfulness and intelligence automatically qualified him to act in a responsible capacity. My idea was that each participant would seek to discover the nature of the motivation to the customary expression of his thought and feeling as well as test for himself the nature of the motives to the reactions socially stimulated by him. At the same time he was to register and, in as far as possible, determine in turn the motive to whatever reserve or hesitation or distortion might occur in the spontaneous expression of himself and of others. There was not the slightest interest in hearing about the individual's ideas or opinions as such, or in knowing what he might at any time have thought, said or done. Such reminiscent preoccupations were neither here nor there. Nor was there any concern to know what he planned at some future time to do. *The effort was to reach the organism's immediate motivation in relation to the situation at hand.*

Here is a group in which spontaneity, immediacy, and process are at the heart of things. What Burrow tried to accomplish was a bridging of the gap between words and feelings and a recognition by all the group members that verbal expression is incorrigibly false. He discovered that people in groups exist in a general state of repression and that there is a covert covenant to present one's self in the most acceptable light.

Burrow's training labs discouraged self-consciousness and secrecy and were conducted, as far as possible, nonjudgmentally. The social image or what encounter theorists would call a mask came under close scrutiny in the group experiments. Behind the social image lie Freudian resistances, and behind these resistances lie the bedrock physiological factors continuous through the phylum. Once the group penetrates behind the artificial personality that the individual member created verbally for himself, he is able to function at a more preconscious level that gains expression in a quiet, self-possessed mood.

Burrow can be considered a pioneer of training groups, of the laboratory approach to social neurosis, and of recent work dealing with psychophysiological responses within the group. He progressed from psychoanalysis through group analysis to phylo-analysis, and somewhere along the line, perhaps because of his medical preconceptions, he appeared to take a wrong turn and ended up with an inflated evolutionary theory in which both the individual and the small group were totally lost.

Lewin and Field Theory

Strong primitive forces emanate from groups before they become domesticated by organization. But the controls are never complete, so the life of any group can be plotted in terms of both progressive and regressive outputs.

According to Kurt Lewin, conflict is inherent and inevitable in the group. As he put it, every group contains within it the seeds of its own destruction. In terms of his topological or field theory, each individual member of a group struggles for adequate life space in the way that animals struggle for territory, and it is inevitable that the needs of any particular member conflict in this respect with the needs of the group as a whole. The group situation always demands some sacrifice on the part of the individual member and some limitation on his space for free movement. The amount of conflict generated varies with the amount of restriction imposed by the group as compared with the amount of mutual support and involvement that it gives in exchange.

What the membership does with such group tension depends partly on the structure of the group and partly on its leadership. Two group prototypes in this respect can be described. In the one, the group is poorly organized, weakly integrated, and leaderless; as a result, tension is poorly distributed and tends to rise to disruptive levels. In the contrasting type, the group is well-organized, well-integrated, and well-led; the tension is more evenly distributed, and communications flow more smoothly. Here again, in quite a different conceptual framework, are the two types described by McDougall.

Almost all group behavior may be said to lie somewhere between the two extreme types described. In every group, there is a balance of cohesive and disruptive forces, and the level of tension depends on which factor is paramount. Under benign leadership, the tension within the group remains optimal, allowing for constructive group activity.

As a function of group structure, group leadership, and group interaction, every group develops an atmosphere characteristic of it. The leader may be potent in creating this atmosphere, but the atmosphere, in turn, may create the leader, so that leaders tend to emerge spontaneously from different group situations.

The members of the group also bring into the group with them the status that they habitually occupy and the roles that they normally play. Unless new roles are assigned to them in the group, they will attempt to affirm their usual roles and manipulate other group members into supporting such role activity.

The leadership role is perhaps the most complex of the different roles open to group members and may take different forms. The leader, for example, may be required to coordinate the group's activities, control its internal relationships, symbolize its unity and integration, take the blame for its failures, assume the place of the father in the lives of the members, act as arbitrator in their conflicts, display expertise on all matters, and serve as a model for appropriate attitudes and behavior. In addition to all this, he is expected to take full responsibility for the present and future life of the group, gaining praise for its successes and censure for its failures.

Lewin, despite his profound involvement in social issues and his dedication to action research, had neither the wish nor the capacity to contribute directly to group psychotherapy. He was too much of an experimentalist to be a therapist himself. However, his system of group dynamics and his ahistoric conception of group tensions have been incorporated into several systems, even those with a psychoanalytic structure. The here-and-now is prominent in the encounter groups, but it is also a feature of every group-oriented group where the developmental aspects of the individual are left in abeyance. The psychoanalytic concept of transference has the advantage of linking past and present into a coherent whole and is a more useful tool for the group psychotherapist. The delineation of the leadership role covers most of the functions assumed by the group psychotherapist but omits his representation within the unconscious minds of the group participants. Field theory may complement but never substitute for the more complex and analytic theories.

Bion and the Basic Assumptions

Once the group is civilized and organized, the more primitive elements are largely underground and tend to show themselves only in situations of panic, disrupting tension, and disorganization. The group, like the individual member, functions on both a latent level and a manifest level. Le Bon and McDougall visualized the latent forces as primitive to the point of psychopathy, whereas Bion sees them as psychotic. This latent layer is covered over by the organization that allows the group to become task-oriented. At this manifest level, the group gets to work and occupies itself in ways that are conscious, rational, constructive, and busy. And at this level it needs a leader who can drive the group and direct it. When, however, the group has nothing to do and no leader to lead it, the inner irrational feelings and fantasies become mobilized and rise to the surface, where their presence is felt by a marked increase in tension.

Like Freud, Bion poses some interesting questions and offers some even more interesting answers. He, too, asks why the group comes together in the first place and what keeps it together once it has formed. In addition, he wonders how it deals with its inner tensions, especially when it has been deprived of its leader, and in what way the members get in touch with one another.

At the overt level, the group members are brought together and held together by anything they they have to do together, and, when this is ended, they may disband. They may also continue to work together without a leader, but after a while, unless someone emerges to fulfill this function, the work they do begins to suffer. While they are engaged in legitimate work, the level of interaction rarely deepens. The members communicate mostly in verbal terms and dissipate their tensions in a number of social ways, so that the level of tension never gets to the point of disruption.

Below this overt level, the life of the group is entirely different and has little relationship to reality The group members come together and stay together because of strong basic needs. They want to find and keep a leader who will meet all their dependency needs, assist them in finding a sexual partner, and direct them into fight or flight when danger becomes threatening. The search for a leader, therefore, brings the group members together, and, once they find him, they cannot do without him. If rendered leaderless, they invent a leader in the shape of some predominant idea around which they can coalesce. A leaderless group, consequently, spends a large part of its time searching for a leader, and, depending on the state of the basic assumptions within the group, some kind of leader eventually emerges.

The student of history is intrigued by the fact that similar ideas keep recurring and are always treated as if they were something quite novel. It was once said that there are only seven basic story plots and that storytellers manipulate these with considerable skill to produce new stories for each new generation. The world of ideas may well be similarly impoverished, but theorists become so skillful at putting old ideas into new language that an exhilarating sense of progress is produced. Therefore, the two-group concept has dominated the history of group psychology from the very beginning and is an outcome of the manifest and latent, the conscious and unconscious postulates put forward by psychoanalysis. The two groups within the group perform different activities, have different needs, and speak essentially a different language, since the basic assumption group can communicate nonverbally, empathically, intuitively, and by contagion. Nevertheless, Bion has created, even if only in a limited form, a group psychology

of the unconscious and, by linking this psychology with Kleinian metapsychology, has made it directly available to the group psychotherapist. Furthermore, Bion has raised the important question of how the manifest and latent groups interact. The manifest and latent layers of the mind, as described by psychoanalysis, are in continuous transaction, and one's personality is to a great extent determined by what happens at the interface. Although it may be confounding to extrapolate from the individual member to the group, there is no doubt that the personality of the group may also be a product of a similar interplay. The manifest group tries in all sorts of devious ways to manipulate the latent group, although it keeps an eye on its realistic aims and purposes. If the manifest group becomes disorganized in any way, there is the immediate danger that the basic assumptions will return from the unconscious and take control of the situation, leading to a rise in tension followed by the appearance of primitive drives and feelings.

On the basis of this model, Bion has been able to describe different types of group culture in which some of the basic assumptions are gratified and some frustrated. These cultures represent a transient ascendancy, so that a pairing state may be prominent on one occasion and a fight-flight state on another. This means that one can follow cultural variations over time in the same way as in Lewinian groups; the climate may undergo alteration with any change in leadership.

One can invent a group psychology and not follow it up by making it applicable to group psychotherapy. This happened with Freud and, to some extent, with Bion. He sees himself not as a group psychotherapist but rather as a group investigator.

Whitaker and Lieberman and Focal-Conflict Theory

Focal-conflict theory, thought up by Thomas French, attempts to explain the current behavior of a person as an expression of his method of solving currently experienced personality conflicts that originated very early in his life. The person is constantly resonating to these early focal conflicts. The original solutions and the original feelings are modified by the altered circumstances of later life. The conflicts and their attempted solutions are so much part of the person's way of life that he can hardly do without them, however much he may want to rid himself of them.

In the context of the group situation, Whitaker and Lieberman suggest that each member of the group is affected by some group-focal conflict, as a result of which he tends to behave in a particular stereotyped way. The group conflicts are a threat to the individual member, since they expose him to personal conflicts. The individual member sticks to his pathological solutions because they protect him from the anxiety stemming from unconscious conflicts, and the other group members may respond helpfully or unhelpfully to these lifelong solutions. As the group progresses, the hidden conflict begins to emerge both as a wish and as a fear, and the group may act to reduce the fear and maximize the wish-fulfillment.

This type of group psychology has an artificial ring about it. In the first place, it is an oversimplified adaptation of an individual psychological approach that itself has never gained much general acceptance because of its somewhat schematic nature. The propensity to use borrowed theories has certain pitfalls. As Freud was first to point out, a group does not occur simply by putting a number of people together. Why it comes together and why it stays together are integral parts of how it functions together. Focal-conflict theory has nothing to say about these parts; as a consequence, it lacks the appeal of the conceptual framework put forward by Freud and Bion.

Ezriel and the Common Group Tension

Ezriel, as a psychoanalyst working with groups, also became interested in the interaction between the manifest and latent levels of the group. In the place of Bion's basic assumptions, he postulated an underlying common group problem that gives rise to tension and is a common denominator of the dominant unconscious fantasies of all the group members. In addition, each member projects his unconscious fantasy-objects upon various other group members and then tries to manipulate them accordingly.

This theory is not so difficult to accept. The idea of a collective fantasy may sound Jungian, but then group psychotherapists and group psychologists are always skirting the Jungian unconscious without acknowledging it in any way. The manipulation of the group members in terms of the internal object society is simply an example of group transference and the tendency everyone has of manipulating transference figures.

The emphasis put on insight as an experience leading to change is generally in keeping with the psychoanalytic approach. Others have tended to depreciate the value of insight as an essential therapeutic factor and to accord the leading position to experience.

Foulkes and the Network

What happens in the other 22 or 23 hours of a patient's life when he is not engaged in a psychotherapeutic situation is becoming increasingly important, even to the psychotherapist. Community psychiatry attempts to follow the patient out of the clinic into his world to arrange helpful contacts for him outside of his hour. The more one considers the social orbit of a patient in the framework of the newer ecological approach, the more one becomes aware of the many pathogenic and therapeutic influences at work within it. The idea of a network—that is, the natural group in which the patient lives at the time of his illness and his treatment—was formulated by Foulkes as an adjunct to the fuller understanding of the group analytic situation that he refers to as the group matrix. The matrix and the network together can help to illuminate the understanding of illness as a social process. The matrix is the frame of reference for the interactional context of the group as expressed manifestly, symbolically, symptomatically, effectively, behaviorally, and verbally.

The dynamically interacting network of the patient has, according to Foulkes, a fundamental significance in the production of illness in the patient. And when a significant change occurs in a patient, particularly a change toward greater independence, the other members of the network become active. The network covers not only the nuclear but also the extended family group and can involve friends as well. (It is interesting, in this context, to note that Post found more psychiatric illness within the social orbit of psychiatric patients than one would expect from the distribution of psychiatric illness in the general population.)

The thesis put forward by Foulkes is that illness and related disturbances are due in part to psychopathological processes that involve a number of interacting persons. In the psychoneuroses this multipersonal network of interaction is of central significance, and change in any member of such a network is linked to corresponding changes in other members. Even the nature of individual symptoms may rest on this interdependence. Therefore, the emotional disturbance can no longer be regarded in a vacuum, limited to one individual personality; it is always a function of relationships involving many people. The disturbance is an expression of a disturbed equilibrium in a total field of interaction. The patient is more or less unaware of this fact and may expect changes in himself without concomitant changes in the rest of the network. But it is impossible to change the patient without changing his network. There are, therefore, two important crises in the patient's life. The first period of disequilibrium occurs in the network with the onset of the original disturbance, and the second period of disequilibrium takes place at the cessation of the emotional disturbance. There may be a final re-equilibrium after an enforced readjustment of roles in the various members of the network.

The concept of the network certainly extends the understanding of the group, since each participant enters the group as a representative of his more or less sick network. No doubt the psychotherapist enlarges the scope of his understanding through these twin concepts, but it is difficult to say to what extent the psychotherapy itself gains from this extended viewpoint. Like the researcher, the therapist can easily get bogged down when his variables are multiplied beyond necessity. The psychoanalyst achieves his goal by focusing intensively on the intrapsychic processes. He can widen his focus to include nonverbal behavior. But once he brings in extra-analytic factors, not only does his field of therapy become contaminated, but he may lose his way within the multiplicity of influences at work. Whether the matrix-plus-network perspective is too wide for focused and intensive therapy remains to be investigated.

Moreno and Acting Out

The end of man, said Goethe, lies not in thought but in action, and Moreno has always been action-oriented. This action includes acting, drama, catharsis, spontaneity, creativity. Moreno is essentially an actor who became a therapist, and the role he has set for himself in therapeutic life is to help produce Everyman's drama. He has taken the Shakespearean lines to heart:

All the world's a stage,
And all the men and women merely players.

And he has made use of Aristotle's proposition that the task of tragedy is to produce, through the exercise of fear and pity, a liberation from such emotions; the audience is purged and absolved from the necessity of expressing these emotions in their own lives. Moreno extends this theory. According to him, the playwright, the actor, and the spectators all undergo catharsis.

Moreno coined the term acting out more than 40 years ago, and, oddly enough, it is one of the few things that psychoanalysts have borrowed from him. Psychoanalysts and psychoanalytic group therapists are not generally dramatic men and are not given to dramatizing the emotional struggles going on within their patients. They are more voyeuristic than exhibitionistic, whereas the reverse may be true of the psychodramatist. Furthermore, the individual psychoanalyst and the group analyst are apparently satisfied to reconstruct the conflictual situation presented to them by their patients verbally without making it a flesh-and-blood reality involving all the senses. This objectification, however, is apparently necessary to Moreno's way of doing things; he has to be shown in addition to being told.

The patient, depending on his personality, may derive a certain satisfaction from acting out rather than simply verbalizing his conflicts. For Moreno, acting out represents a great therapeutic maneuver; for the analyst, it is resistance.

The patient is said to gain insight from doing, but catharsis has a tendency to interfere with the acquisition of insight, and the outpouring of emotion may be the patient's only benefit. By training the patient through behavior therapy, the therapist attempts to alter fixed patterns of behavior.

The dramatic enactment of problems may be carried out through psychodrama, in which the patient relives an actual situation or acts out a situation posed by the director, who knows the patient's special problem; through sociodrama, in which the patient is confronted with some concrete social problem that characterizes the society to which he belongs; and through role-playing, in which the patient assumes the role of another person, thus allowing him to try out new types of behavior and new forms of communication in a relatively nonthreatening situation.

The theatre of spontaneous man is a brilliant idea, and it certainly deserves a place in the history and practice of group psychotherapy. But whether all the complex resistances that make up modern civilized man can be dissolved by means of a simple dramatic device is open to question. Is it indeed acting, or is it really acting out in the psychoanalytic sense?

The dramatic approach has spawned a large number of dramatic games that are used to warm up a patient in the initial phase of therapy. These exercises have been incorporated into training groups and other modern departures from classical therapy. In fact, Moreno has claimed with some truth to have pioneered the development of encounter groups, Gestalt therapy, transactional analysis, behavior therapy, and joy workshops. He feels that, together with

Buber, he has been responsible for the existential encounter—the real, concrete, complete experience involving both physical and psychic contact with a convergence of emotional, social, and cosmic factors. He feels that psychodrama is the essence of encounter, since it entails the experience of identity and total reciprocity.

Moreno is a creative, dramatic, spontaneous, and charismatic man whose quasi-religious, dithyrambic style of writing makes him sound at times like a latter-day Nietzsche. His sociometry is a genuine contribution to group psychology and has been widely used by the scientifically oriented who spurn the other side of Moreno, his psychodrama. To many group psychotherapists, he represents a detrimental influence that has split the group world in two, seducing many a group therapist from the careful and patient practice of classical group psychotherapy and leading him into wildly exciting, highly controversial, shortcut methods of treatment.

GROUP PSYCHOTHERAPY

Pioneer Efforts

In 1907, Pratt described what he called a class method of treating tuberculosis in the homes of the poor, and a year later he discussed his results. It was known then, as it is known now, that tuberculous patients are prone to be difficult people and to have emotional problems. Since tuberculous patients, like psychotics, are often herded together and are treated with fear and rejection by the general populace, it seemed appropriate to use group techniques. After Pratt's original efforts, other psychologically oriented physicians have tried to do the same thing.

The psychiatrists in mental hospitals were stimulated by the possibilities of this new technique. Lazell in 1921 and Marsh in 1931 instituted the group method with psychotics.

All these early practices were psychologically naive, and they made little or no use of group dynamics. The instructor lectured to a group of patients on their illness, and sometimes these lectures were broadcast through the hospital by means of loudspeakers. In 1940 Snowden actually gave a course of lectures in which he described the causes of different mental illnesses and then had the patients discuss the lecture in the context of their own illness.

The methods began to grow in sophistication. In 1941 Low and in 1946 Klapman put aside the lecture format and began to use the group as a group.

Burrow. Parallel to these developments in general psychiatry, certain psychoanalysts became interested in group treatment and the possible application of psychoanalysis to it. Trigant Burrow was psychoanalytically minded, but what he did could not really be called group psychotherapy. However, Burrow did note that many of the characteristics of a psychoanalysis could be found in the group. The patients were able to verbalize actual fantasies and family conflicts and even to manifest defense and transference mechanisms—a discovery that has been replicated many times since. Freud had hinted at the same things earlier. Today, it is accepted that groups do have many of the psychological qualities of the individual, although therapists are now as much interested in the differences as in the similarities in the two approaches.

Burrow treated patients in groups because he felt that a patient is less resistant to the treatment process in a group than in individual therapy. Within the setting of the group, the patient becomes aware that he shares many things with others, good things as well as abnormalities. He is no longer alone, his problems are no longer unique, he no longer feels the need for isolation and secrecy, and he is increasingly appreciative of the group support. Burrow felt that, whereas Freud was treating the individual, he was dealing with the human race, but both were using psychoanalytic methods and insights. But Freud put the major emphasis on the past; Burrow stressed the present and eschewed personal reminiscences.

Wender. Wender was probably the first to conduct psychoanalytically oriented groups, and he did so in a hospital setting. In 1936 he combined the group method with individual interviews and made the discovery—also replicated by many others—

that patients involved in group psychotherapy move much more freely and more productively than in the individual situation. However, like the general psychiatrists, he took a didactic line and started each group session with a lecture on the dynamics of behavior and the significance of dreams. Wender, like Burrow, also found that transference relationships develop within the group in relation to both the therapist and other patients. He further found that patients in groups appear to be better motivated than patients in individual psychotherapy.

Wender's work represented a fairly straightforward application of early psychoanalytic theory within a group setting. His observations that the groups themselves did helpful things to patients, apart from lowering their resistances and increasing their spontaneity, were almost incidental to the fact that he was applying his knowledge of psychoanalysis. But psychoanalysts at that time were not well-read in group dynamics (they are not so well-read in group dynamics today), so the significance of the group by itself and in itself did not get any profound consideration.

Schilder. During the same decade of the 1930's, Paul Schilder began to work psychotherapeutically with groups. From every point of view, Schilder was an extraordinary person. With his encyclopedic mind and his tremendous scientific drive, he was the one person who might have become the Freud of group psychotherapy, had he given it his whole attention. He also possessed the flexibility of the genuine scientist, in that he was not bound by any dogmatic adherence to rules. Not only was he a first-class theoretician, but he was well-grounded in the theories of others. He was not only interested in individual patients but deeply interested in their various conglomerates in society; he was interested not only in adults but also in children. His range of interests was extremely wide. As a psychiatrist, a psychoanalyst, and a phenomenologist, he could draw on physiology, neurology, and general psychiatry to serve his purpose as an investigator. His influence on Rapaport and through Rapaport on psychoanalysis was appreciable. Rapaport referred to him as an unsystematic genius who sowed scientific seeds without any thought of the harvest that others might be able to reap.

Schilder, like Burrow, began his group interest with the body, more specifically with the body image. It was Schilder's conviction that the system of ideologies a patient develops around his body and the self associated with his body plays a major part in his psychopathology. Any injury to the body, no matter how slight, has an effect on the patient's body image, on the ideology that goes with it, and on his way of life. The exploration of ideologies is especially attuned to the group situation. The patient shares with others the basic tenets that govern his life and faces the criticism that they provoke. The group discussion often starts on an intellectual level but gradually becomes more personal and emotional. When others are able to identify with the particular ideology, the patient professing it is better able to work through it.

One rather surprising fact regarding Schilder as a group psychotherapist is his willingness to reveal his own ideology and to justify it before the group. He was, therefore, very much a member of the group in a way that therapists before him were not.

In response to a direct question, Freud once remarked that he was not a good psychoanalyst because he was too interested in finding out original facts about the patient and tying these facts to his developing theories. The same is probably true of Schilder. His encyclopedic mind ranged over so many interests in such depth that he may have experienced some difficulty in dealing with the everyday problems of everyday patients in a way that was immediately meaningful to them. He was, perhaps, a little too cognitive to be therapeutic and too theoretical to be practical.

The technique of analyzing ideologies has not really caught on in group psychotherapy, although most group psychotherapists from time to time have to deal with the ideologies put forward by their patients. But therapists are more inclined to treat these ideologies as resistances than as illuminating psychological material to be investigated in their own right.

World War II Efforts

The major impact of emigrating psychoanalysts from Germany and Austria on American psychiatry and psychotherapy has only recently begun to subside. In Britain, the effect was less marked, chiefly because psychoanalysis never managed to get a strong foothold into academic medical circles.

In Britain as in America, psychoanalysts were drafted into the Army, and they eventually congregated at centers for the treatment of psychiatric casualties. The main center in Britain was at Northfield, and Northfield's main claim to fame was that it provided a setting for the application of analytic ideas to groups and communities.

The Northfield experiment gathered together a group of analysts or analysts in the making—Freudian, Kleinian, and Adlerian. The roll call included Anthony, Bierer, Bion, Bridger, Foulkes, Main, and Rickman—all of whom later made contributions to group psychotherapy. The first phase of the Northfield experiment was sparked by Bion and Rickman. In a revolutionary way, they attempted to cut Army red tape and treat a whole ward of soldiers almost as if they were civilian patients with rights and responsibilities of their own. Ward discipline was maintained through free discussion with the soldier patients. Not surprisingly, this revolution was brought to a sudden end, but the two venturesome analysts, so far away from their private offices and couches, had made their point and had facilitated the development of the second phase at Northfield.

During this second phase, Foulkes, who at the start of the war in civilian practice had been undertaking analytic group psychotherapy, introduced his method into Northfield. In so doing, he established a milieu that was highly propitious to group psychotherapy. At the time, Foulkes looked beyond the group to the community as a whole, regarding the group instrument as a crucial one for dealing with the individual patient's network of relationships within the community.

The Northfield experiment was the training ground for group theorists, group activists, and group practitioners. There, both group psychotherapy and community psychotherapy received the vital stimulus and momentum that carried them through the unsettled postwar years. The author has described Northfield's significance this way:

To some, it presented an unrivaled opportunity to apply their analytic knowledge to a challenging new field, while for others, it carried the hope that this new method of exploring the human mind might add significant chapters to psychopathology. In many respects, it had something about it of the Vienna of early psychoanalysis, when almost everyone was a contributor of some sort because almost everything was so new. We talked, then as now, about field theory, leaderless groups, group dynamics, group tensions, the analytic approach, etc., but already group styles were beginning to separate out, and one could detect growing differences between the group-analytic groups, the Bion-type groups, Adlerian groups and Tavistock-type groups. With the dissolution of Northfield after the war, each went his own way and more or less lost contact with the others. The war had been the great harmonizer and integrator; with peace came rivalry, dissension and disruption. I do think, however, even though some of us may be reluctant to admit it, that we learned a great deal from one another in those early, encapsulated days and that, perhaps, more cross-fertilization took place than subsequent published acknowledgments admit.

Something of the same quality was noted by Main:

It was a time of freshness, activity and high morale but it would be wrong to suppose that there were no strains at Northfield. We were, after all, like any other group. There was quarreling and dissension on theory, and, as well as friendship, personal malice and rivalry, not less than in any other fiercely active organization .... The first Northfield Experiment fathered by Rickman and carried out by Bion produced some ideas about groups which have had their own developmental life ever since. Foulkes' work with groups had precedence, but it was of a different order and went in a different direction. The two developments were each legitimate, novel, brilliant; but because they concerned the newly entered area of group work the excitement and vehemence of argument tended to set them up as rival systems and for dissensions to take on personal forms.

What is apparent from these comments is that engagement in group work carries with it no immunity from group dissension and strife. In fact, at times group therapists seem to bring their group skills strategically into the polemical battle with them.

It is also apparent that the dialectics of controversy had a marked creative influence on British group psychotherapy. One seems to need the impact of thesis and antithesis to spark off new levels of theory and practice.

A third conclusion is that theorists who are loved and admired within their immediate circle but are treated outside with criticism and even hostility often appear to thrive on such a situation. Freud was a striking example, and so today is Moreno.

Foulkes and the Group Analytic Approach

Foulkes has always been an innovator, and at no time during his long career has he ceased to make original observations and contributions. As Main remarked of him:

Anyone can be a pioneer for a short time by accident, but it takes the patience and doggedness of a Foulkes to make the most of a chance setting and to become an innovator: to study, criticize, check, correct, gain colleagues, undertake experiments, erect, criticize and refine theory and grow bodies of ideas for further examination.

Foulkes was, as Main remarked, at the center of all the group treatment at Northfield,

interested, puzzled, inspiring, enjoying his work and infectiously formulating ideas about the nature of group process.

The author, as a close collaborator of Foulkes, feels that the puzzlement was the most creative thing about Foulkes. Many leading group theorists present a clear, concise, positivistic, and optimistic statement of their theoretical ideas, almost as if the ideas were all cut and dried and ready to be served out, shaped forever. With Foulkes, on the other hand, one always felt a groping toward some profound insight that was never immediately manifest but always several fathoms below in the depths. This habit of groping was sometimes mystifying, often nebulous, and almost always exasperatingly slow for those in search of immediate answers, however glib these might be. One soon learned, however, either in a dyadic or group relationship with him, that behind chiaroscuro was a subtle and steady mind at work. A personal comment from a group member, Abercrombie, is perhaps the nearest one can get to this style, which is so hard to describe, so difficult to imitate, and so effective, not only in theory but also in therapy.

It is extraordinarily difficult to communicate to one who has never been there the subtle, rich and profound experiences of being in a group conducted by Dr. Foulkes. Superficially, the group has no obvious structure or palpable texture; it may seem formless, embedded in an intangible, floating vagueness. At Dr. Foulkes' treatment of the group, or rather, one should say, his participation in it, he is in fact highly disciplined, dictated by a sure perception of strong and rigorous, but changing, patterns of relationships. What may seem to the other group participants a serene, withdrawn passivity is one manifestation of his intense involvement and of his sensitive and steely mastery of technique.

With Foulkes, more than anyone else in the field, one can say that the style is the man, and the man is his theory, so that there is a completeness about him that comes through when one is sitting with him in a therapeutic group.

His contribution on the group matrix and its ambient social network furnish the practitioner with a triple perspective on the individual patient, on the group, and on the interpersonal environment from which the group members come. The intrapsychic, the intragroup, and the intranetwork provide a comprehensive frame of reference to bolster the confidence of any beginning group psychotherapist. Technically, the advantages for the therapist are considerable. The approach enables him, as Foulkes says, to apply a figure-ground orientation to events, to locate the configuration of disturbances in all their variety within the group, and to envisage each member in a more intensive and extensive way.

The group analytic psychotherapist sees the group analytic situation rather the way the psychoanalyst perceives the psychoanalytic situation. The therapist establishes and maintains the arrangements, the setting, the fees, and the total culture in a dynamic way as essential elements for the initiation of the therapeutic process. The therapist is passive in the sense that he puts himself at the service of the group and follows it wherever it goes; but on the other side, he actively analyzes defenses and resistances. His accepting attitude embraces all communication, from both the here-and-now and the there-and-then. The atmosphere generated is one of perpetual attentiveness, tolerance, and patience. With Foulkes, as a co-therapist in the group, one gets the feeling that he is always waiting for something to happen but is in no way discomforted when nothing happens. There is no pressure on the patients to perform for his benefit, as there sometimes is with other group therapists. Occasionally, reading the protocols given by certain authors, one is left with the impression that the members are putting on a show to keep the therapist happy and interested and totally absorbed with them.

As a psychoanalyst, he inevitably focused on the transference situation—between the members and the therapist, between the members themselves, and between the members and the group as a whole. This array of reference has excited many group psychoanalysts, but the group analytic psychotherapist observes it as one aspect of the total phenomena occurring in a group. He often works through it and with it but not in the genetic sense of the psychoanalyst.

The influence of Kurt Lewin and his group dynamics is also obvious in the conduct of analytic group psychotherapy, although Foulkes himself has concentrated on the interpersonal rather than on the group as a whole. The field and its boundaries are well-delineated, and the incidents at the interface between group and outside are easy to detect. Within the field, the temporal perspective is very much on what is happening now in the field and within the individual life space of each member. The network is an important extension of the concept of life space. The current life situation and the current life network remind the therapist that the patient is only the top of the iceberg and that, to know him fully, one has to know him, as Freud once said, both from the inside and from the outside.

The intrapsychic life of the patient takes

second place to his life as a group member. In this permissive, neutral, nondirective situation, it is not surprising that a fully formed transference neurosis can often be clearly recognized in the group and, to some extent, analyzed. But the group analytic psychotherapist realizes that the transference does not develop in pure form and cannot be worked through in quite the same detail as in psychoanalysis. Some group analysts, such as Durkin, feel that the fundamental character of the transference neurosis is not affected by the group context and that it can be effectively analyzed for the purpose of achieving structural change in the personality of the patient. Durkin is fairly convinced that a systematic analysis of the resistance inherent in the defensive transferences can be carried out, that infantile conflicts can be resolved, and that working through does occur in group therapy.

The group analytic approach also takes note of the patient's development in his early family setting as it reappears in the transference.

Very little work has been done on the development of the ego's capacity to create and to maintain a group relationship. A conceptual model that is also developmental could be very useful in group psychotherapy. There is an implicit assumption in psychosexual development that a person passes from a one-body to a two-body to a three-body and finally to a multibody situation, using Rickman's terminology. In the theoretical development proposed by Talcott Parsons, these external groups are internalized in terms of the role played by the individual members. Susan Isaacs also described early group developments in nursery school children, pointing out that group relationships at this stage of life are evanescent and vivid and that hostility is often the factor that draws the children together, either in attacking or in defending their rights and areas.

Foulkes and Anthony have described in detail the construction of the group situation, the material arrangements for conducting a group, the natural history of group development, and the phenomenology associated with the group situation, such as resonance, mirroring, chain phenomena—all indicating the reactivity of the members to one another.

Bion and the Leaderless Group

Bion is tentative about describing himself as a group psychotherapist, as are many analysts on both sides of the Atlantic. Perhaps such work is beneath their dignity, or they do not wish to be labeled unorthodox, but one is left with the conclusion that there is something peculiar about working therapeutically with more than one patient at a time. Bion admits to little more than that he had an experience of trying to persuade a number of patients to make the study of their tensions a group task. It is, perhaps, permissible for a psychoanalyst to be interested in group psychology, since Freud had that interest, but group psychotherapy is not for analysts, and it is true that Freud never attempted to practice it.

The best way to describe what Bion does in a therapeutic group is to use his own words:

At the appointed time members of the group begin to arrive; individuals engage each other in conversation for a short time, and then when a certain number has collected, a silence falls on the group. After a while desultory conversation breaks out again, and then another silence falls. It becomes clear to me that I am, in some sense, the focus of attention in the group. Furthermore, I am aware of feeling uneasily that I am expected to do something. At this point I confide my anxieties to the group, remarking that, however mistaken my attitude might be, I feel just this. I soon find that my confidence is not very well received. Indeed, there is some indignation that I should express such feelings without seeming to appreciate that the group is entitled to expect something from me. I do not dispute this but content myself with pointing out that clearly the group cannot be getting from me what they feel they are entitled to expect. I wonder what these expectations are and what has aroused them.

The effect of this type of group management is almost predictable. The group comes with the high expectation that they will be treated, and the therapist does nothing about it at all. He simply wants to discuss their expectations. The group does not like what he does with them, and they see his behavior as provocative and deliberately disappointing. They feel that he is perverse, that he could behave differently if he wanted to, that he has chosen to behave in this peculiar way out of spite.

Bion then points out that it must be hard for the group to admit that this could be his way of taking groups, that perhaps he should be allowed to take them in his own way, and that there is no reason why he should take groups in the way expected by the patients.

The group members, of course, know that he is a very clever and well-known clinician, so that he cannot be doing what he does for want of knowledge or technique. They are inclined to interpret his attitude as artificially naive and egotistical.

It becomes clear after a while that—because of Bion's tentative, evasive, and noncommittal attitude and behavior—the group cannot stop themselves from being preoccupied with him. Eventually, they can stand it no longer, and one of the members begins to take over and repair the iatrogenic damage. This deputy leader wonders why Bion cannot give a straightforward explanation of his behavior. Bion can only apologize and state that he, too, feels that his explanation that he is in the group to study group tensions is really inadequate, but he confesses that he is unable to throw any light on the matter. The group seems determined to find out what *his* motives are for coming to the group, not what their own motives are. The group situation seems about to break down because of the inability of the group to tolerate the therapist's behavior, and a movement gets under way to exclude the therapist from the group or, if exclusion is not possible, to ignore his presence.

Eventually, a member speaks up on behalf of the therapist, only to state that the therapist must have some good reason for taking the line he does. This statement relaxes the tension in the group immediately, and a more friendly attitude toward the therapist becomes apparent.

A lesson is slowly emerging in the group, and this lesson is pointed out to them—namely, that it is difficult for an individual member to convey meanings to the group that are different from the meanings the group wishes to entertain. This lesson annoys the group, but they are then informed that they have every right to be annoyed. Nobody ever explained to them what it means to be in a group in which Bion is present, and nobody ever explained to Bion what it is like to be in a group in which all these individual members are present.

The only disagreeable member of the group at this point is the therapist, and he points out that he thinks his interpretations are disturbing the group. A crisis is now reached. Certain members may well have discovered that membership in a group run by Bion happens to be an experience that they do not wish to have. The group has to face the fact that some of the members may want to leave.

Bion then tells the group that he considers the emotional forces underlying this situation to be very powerful. He is, he says, merely one member of a group possessing some degree of specialized knowledge. Although he is no different from any other member of the group, they are quite unable to face the emotional tensions in the group without believing that the therapist is some sort of god who is fully responsible for all that takes place. When the group turns resentfully and somewhat anxiously to another member, Bion sees them as looking to this other member to be leader but without any real conviction that he could be the leader.

The conversation dies down. For most members the experience is becoming painful and boring, so a fresh thought occurs to Bion, and he passes it on to the group. He tells them that they seem determined to have a leader and, moreover, a leader with certain characteristics that are not easy to describe. Why should they have any leader at all?

Both Foulkes and Bion seem on superficial inspection to be like corks floating on the sea of group turmoil, never sinking under the fury, and apparently drifting aimlessly at the mercy of the group. As the Bion and Abercrombie accounts illustrate, this impression is highly illusional. Both Foulkes and Bion, while seeming to follow the group, are subtly leading it to a resolution of its tensions and other problems.

Slavson and Analytic Group Psychotherapy

Slavson, although not a qualified psychoanalyst, stays close to the psychoanalytic model. He refers to his method as analytic group psychotherapy, which contrasts in more than name with the title used by Foulkes of group analytic psychotherapy. With Slavson, the prime emphasis is on the analytic; with Foulkes, the emphasis is on the group. This is not to say that Slavson is not aware of the group process, but he has battled constantly and vigorously for the autonomy of the individual patient in the group. Each patient, he insists, must remain a detached entity in whom intrapsychic changes must occur.

In the therapeutic group, according to Slavson, it is each patient for himself, and the therapist should, therefore, concentrate on the individual rather than on the group as a whole. Slavson recognizes that the individual members affect one another in a variety of ways, including sibling and identification transferences and mutual empathies that make for a collective experience based on the integration of the individual member into the group. The group tends to catalyze the dynamics of the individual patient, accelerating regression, weakening defenses, and at least transiently impairing individuation.

Slavson differentiates between transference and what he calls the basic solidity of the therapeutic relation—what psychoanalysts refer to as the therapeutic alliance. He recognizes that the transference is modified both quantitatively and qualitatively in the group, where he perceives levels of transference.

Slavson has been prolific in his group writing, and his influence on American group psychotherapy has been enormous. He has instigated its development as a profession, its recognition as a therapeutic discipline, and its acceptance as an area of worthwhile research by behavioral scientists. He has also appointed himself as a watchdog who can be depended on to bark at strangers and bite the wild men who haunt the fringes of group psychotherapy. Because of him, group psychotherapy in the United States operated for many years as a branch of applied psychoanalysis, which had two effects: This arrangement was a powerful impetus to the development of group psychotherapy; at the same time, the arrangement set limitations to the further growth of group therapy as a form of treatment in its own right. Slavson has introduced a number of terms and phrases, some of which have become incorporated into general use. Because of his didactic skills, this tentative branch of therapeutics can now be codified into textbooks. As a theoretician, he is more categorical than creative, and there is a positiveness about his position that the state of the art hardly merits.

Perhaps his greatest contribution has been the development of group therapy with children—in its play form with preschoolers and in its activity form with those in the latency phase. The psychological treatment of children in any form poses a number of technical problems, largely because children at different stages of development are almost different species. They think differently, feel differently, and act differently. These differences necessitate treating them differently, which is what Slavson set out to do. Perhaps because he was not a developmental psychologist, his conclusions about what children could or could not do and could or could not understand were essentially faulty. As a consequence, his group work with children, although novel and interesting, is lacking in a rich developmental background. Nevertheless, his expectation that children prefer to act out rather than speak out is confirmed by his protocols. His patients do abreact physically in groups. The group analytic approach to children makes no such assumption. As a result, the patients undergo conversational catharsis, which goes to show that children in therapy have a habit of living up or living down to the expectations of the therapist. What the analytic group and group analytic approaches have both established beyond question is that group psychotherapy can be applied naturally to children. As Slavson says:

Group experience holds limitless growth possibilities for children.

This is true not because children are limited in their understanding but because children, like adults, can learn to make use of people according to their therapeutic needs.

Today, the activity-interview method sounds a little old-fashioned in the light of modern ego psychology. For Slavson, the child is a function-mechanism whose psychological development results not from thought but from action, not from knowledge and ideas but pragmatically through experience and association. Because the child is immature and cognitively deficient, he must be treated through action and by action, using controls and affectionate guidance rather than interpretations. To child psychoanalysts, this type of release and ego-strengthening therapy rings a familiar bell. For a long time the child was considered unanalyzable because he was allegedly unable to free-associate, develop transference, handle deep-going tensions, or work through resistances. Today, an interpretative form of psychoanalysis can be carried out with quite young children. Likewise, today interpretative forms of group analytic psychotherapy can be carried out with quite young children, and acting out is treated as a defense in children, as it is in adults. In fact, what Socrates described as the remedy of sweet words is effective with all human beings at all stages of life, since words specifically separate them absolutely from the dumb brutes.

There is much argument in the literature as to who began group psychotherapy and where. Various claims have been made involving different therapists and different countries. But the group idea was really part of a *Zeitgeist*, as a result of which there was a gradual convergence of ideas that characteristically led to the plethora of approaches that usually antedate the evolution of any unified theory. Slavson felt that, unlike many other techniques in psychiatry that had their beginnings in Europe, group psychotherapy originated in the United States—and quite understandably so, since American culture is essentially a free group culture. It is probably truer to say that the United States is a place where things catch on because there is more freedom for them to develop. And this is as true for an individual therapy such as psychoanalysis as it is for group psychotherapy.

Wolf and Psychoanalytic Group Psychotherapy

In the two decades of the 1930's and 1940's, several psychoanalysts began to carry out therapeutic work with groups based on the psychoanalytic model. They followed the free-associative technique and attempted some degree of psychoanalysis with each patient. Schilder and Wender were two of these psychoanalysts, and Weininger was another. Weininger's method was essentially different in that he confined the entire treatment session to one patient, with the others in the group playing the part of spectators. The psychoanalytic approach came to fruition in the hands of Alexander Wolf, who began to develop psychoanalysis in groups in the first place to offset the burden imposed on many patients by the cost of individual psychoanalysis.

For Wolf, the group situation is not essentially unfavorable to the type of psychic work carried out in ordinary psychoanalysis, such as the uncovering of infantile amnesia, the interpretation of transference, the analysis of dreams, and genetic reconstruction. He assumes that the patient's unconscious is as accessible in the group situation as it is in the individual psychoanalytic one and is explorable by identical techniques. The group situation is thus conceived of as a set of interlocking psychoanalytic situations.

Whereas Slavson has continued to believe that transference cannot be as intense in groups as in individual treatment and that interpretations in groups cannot penetrate into areas of personality as deeply as in psychoanalysis, Wolf believes that the group situation often allows for deeper analytic exploration than is possible in individual psychoanalysis. The reason he gives is that the group ego, with which each member gradually comes to identify himself, offers the necessary support for more radical probing. The tolerance for anxiety, which is the limiting factor in all psychological analysis, is upgraded by the group. Not only is each member a source of support for other members, but he is also an ancillary therapist in his own right—capable, after a certain amount of group experience, of a well-high professional analysis of the material.

One of the most debatable practices inculcated by Wolf has been his attempt to direct the course of treatment in a series of preconceived stages. Since Freud's early suggestion that the period of treatment be portioned off, like a game of chess, into an opening gambit, a middle phase, and an end game, various therapists have attempted to distinguish a natural historical development in the course of therapy. Group therapists have also succumbed to this evolutionary exercise, and some have built up elaborate stratified models of therapeutic development. A few, like Wolf, have gone even further and have tried to impose a dynamically logical sequence leading to a programming of therapeutic tasks for the group.

In view of these psychoanalytic and quasianalytic approaches to group psychotherapy, one can only wonder what course Freud himself would have taken had he followed through from group psychology to group psychotherapy. No doubt, his preoccupation with group leadership would have led him to concentrate particularly on the functions of the group therapist and on the relationship between the therapist and the group membership. Although well-aware of the individual mechanisms of identification operating within the group, his closely argued discussion of Le Bon and McDougall would have led him eventually to the concept of the group functioning as a whole.

Whether Freud would have created a group dynamics out of the workings of the nuclear Oedipus complex seems less easy to conceive. However, Foulkes has pointed out that the Sophoclean tragedy could without distortion be considered in group terms, as the hero and the chorus interact in the working out of the plot. The same inescapable emotional tie unites all the people on the stage; at any one time, some are active, and some are passive, and at moments of high tension the conflicting tendencies in the group also find their spokesmen, who voice feelings common to all. The group's defensive mechanisms, operating to preserve an ignorance of its own wishes and projecting them instead onto some individual scapegoat, are very much like the driving demand of the chorus that the hero fulfill its group expectations. The scapegoat is frequently the conductor, who is called on to know the things that the group does not as yet dare to know. The re-enactment of the drama of a conflict under the guidance of the conductor can lead to a re-evaluation and re-integration of feelings, which finally make the presence of the conductor unnecessary.

Freud might have accepted this transposition. He would most certainly have reached the conclusion that any event in a group must be regarded as something that potentially involves the group as a whole and that, like the Oedipus complex in the individual patient, can express itself in a wide variety of configurations. The therapist's task is to examine this matrix and locate—to use the language of Foulkes—the crucial disturbance. It is hardly likely that Freud would have been content to make a simple extrapolation from the psychoanalysis of the individual patient to the psychoanalysis of the group without considering the nature of the transformation involved. He was too aware that something fairly radical took place when what he termed the group of two was extended to encompass a much larger number of persons. He was a group psychologist on his way to becoming a group psychotherapist but was deflected by pressing intrapsychic considerations.

It was left to others to follow his lead, and group psychotherapy has undoubtedly profited from the fact that a number of dedicated people have made it their life work to carry on where Freud left off and to pursue the path to its logical conclusion. Every discipline must be explored to its very edge of non-sense and beyond, so that practitioners can learn from recountable experience where the impossible lies. It is fairly certain that Freud himself would have soon recognized that the group is not the most suitable place to analyze a transference neurosis, and he would then have focused on group formations as the nub of therapy in the group situation. (It is one of the historian's prerogatives to speak for the dead, who can no longer speak for themselves!)

Powdermaker and Frank and the Eclectic Approach

By 1953, the literature on group psychotherapy was already voluminous, although the body of established knowledge was still small. There was a wide range of group practice from simple exhortation to profound psychoanalysis. The gamut, according to Slavson, ran from

the authoritarian approach of Low, the confessional-inspirational method of Pratt and his followers, the didactic technique of Klapman, the aesthetic activation of Altschuler, the drama forms of Moreno, the social-educational method of Bierer, and the quasi-analytical approach of Wender and Foulkes, to the psychoanalytic method of Schilder.

Therefore, Powdermaker and Frank thought it necessary to carry out some studies on how group psychotherapy works. To observe and study the therapeutic process, however, they had to decide on some form of group psychotherapy. Their choice fell on the analytic for two reasons: They thought that it would be of greater help to their patients, and they thought that the analytic approach offered considerable promise of adding to the understanding of group dynamics in relation to therapy. The next question was: What choice of analytic? Here they decided on an eclectic compromise that tries to draw from the best of everyone while eschewing their faults.

Their eclectic treatment is of importance in the history of group psychotherapy because it induced a large number of therapists to practice it. Even today, many American group psychotherapists continue to use the method without being aware of its origins. This composite technique is best summarized by Powdermaker and Frank themselves:

Our approach to group therapy with neurotic patients had points in common with that of Foulkes, Ackerman, Slavson, and Wolf, and we were influenced in our thinking by Schilder's analytic concept and Trigant Burrow's emphasis on the study of group interaction. We were stimulated by Bion's descriptions of the group process but avoided his exclusive attention to it. Although our groups were not social groups as were Bierer's, the leadership was completely informal. We differed from Schilder in not using questionnaires and set tasks, and from Wender, Klapman, and Lazell in that in no case did the psychiatrist in charge give case histories or systematic presentation of psychiatric concepts. We encouraged interaction among the patients. We helped them to examine their attitudes and behavior toward one another (*process*) as well as the personal material which they presented (*content*).

The striking and unique thing about this venture is that it was simultaneously engaged in treating the patient and studying the process. This dual approach is, unfortunately, unusual in the history of group psychotherapy. The attitude toward research, nevertheless, was essentially clinical, and the patient's needs were always put before the investigation. Both the individual patient and the group were brought under scrutiny, although the examination of process was organismic rather than elementaristic. Their method was to single out and describe patterns of change involving individual patients, the group, and the therapist, and these descriptions were termed situation analyses based on running accounts.

An illustration of a situation analysis will help to clarify the way in which significant developments within a session can be delineated and stored for later examination in relation to previous and subsequent sessions. The example given is abstracted from a first meeting and demonstrates the rallying of the group after a typical sticky beginning.

Doctor	Nonsupportive, passive, silent.
Group	Patients seemed to know they should be discussing personal matters; afraid to reveal themselves to others; talked on impersonal subjects. Tension rose.
Central patient	X, dominating member; repeatedly tried to get focus of attention.
Situation preceding rally	Group talked on impersonal subjects.
Precipitating event	Doctor intervened: "Have you any idea of the trend of the discussion?" Tension rose sharply. X after trying in vain to question others, introduced rallying topic.

Event   Rally round topic: feelings about psychoanalysis and resistance to therapy.

Effects   Intimate discussion of illness. Relief of tension.

On several occasions over the next seven sessions, the crucial role of the therapist in precipitating a rally was nicely brought out. He precipitated a rally mainly by indicating to the group, in an uncritical way, that he was aware of their difficulty and that he was not at all anxious or uncomfortable about it.

If more such careful investigations had been carried out over the last two decades, the history of group psychotherapy as a branch of scientific medicine would be completely different, and therapists would be less confused by the confusions and the wild uncertainties that pervade the field today. Of even greater interest: The follow-up evaluation was included in the study and underscored the advantage of constantly monitoring work in this way. It cannot be emphasized too strongly that the lack of such basic procedures is a serious handicap. True, evaluation of therapy is a major methodological problem, but even tentative efforts in this direction are better than none and would certainly help to maintain a vigilant self-critical posture, without which therapists are at the mercy of every passing therapeutic whimsy.

If good or even acceptable evaluative techniques had been available, the Powdermaker and Frank investigation would have been a great and epoch-making one instead of simply an interesting and unusual attempt. For example, changes were assessed somewhat loosely in terms of symptoms, social adjustments, and characteristic responses to such stimuli as the Rorschach test. Such assessments were good enough for the time but would demand more rigorous application today.

From a conceptual point of view, the study was curiously barren, as if the authors were frozen in their methodology and unable to go beyond the observed facts. In their defense, however, it should be emphasized that, at the present time, group psychotherapy stands more in need of facts than of concepts, and there is much need for another such detailed study.

New Developments

The term "new" has a serious limitation when it is applied to a rapidly growing field in which anything new soon changes into something old. However, the beginnings of group psychotherapy are still near enough to have the term "new" simply denote something not there from the start. There are new developments by the pioneers Moreno, Slavson, Foulkes, Bion, Bierer, Dreikurs, and others who are still with us and still actively developing; and there are new developments by those who have invaded the field within the last two decades.

Moreno, although practicing a particular form of group treatment that is different from classical group psychotherapy in the way it is set up and structured, has generated a number of important theoretical concepts that have become part of group psychotherapy and are acknowledged by both analytic and nonanalytic schools. He has claimed, with some justification, to have fathered many of the new movements, such as encounter groups, training groups, and existential approaches. His warming up procedures have been incorporated into laboratory exercises used by most of the new methods, and his sociometric tests have been widely employed, not only by sociologists and social psychologists but also by group therapists desirous of sampling group characteristics during the on-going life of the group.

Within recent times, a cascade of experimental approaches has inundated the group arena, so that the more conventional procedures have been transiently swamped by fresh waves of novel and largely untried techniques to which the public has oriented itself because of the novelty, the implicit seductiveness, and the promise of quick change. Often there is a pursuit of the unusual for its own sake on the part of the therapist and a craving for new experiences in human relatedness on the part of the patients. It is difficult to say whether the bewildering situation today in the field of group psychotherapy reflects the primitive phase of its development or the disturbing nature of the world. Perhaps both.

If anxiety was the menace to our patients 20 years and more ago, alienation has emerged as the imperative concern now. The multiple and miasmic urgencies of life today have brought about an impatience with slower historical procedures, and immediate existence in all its calamitous ramifications has become the focus of therapeutic concern. Anything outside the here-and-now is poorly tolerated by the driven inhibitants of this nuclear age. The situation—first postulated by Trigant Burrow many years ago, when he saw therapists and patients in the same predicament—has been incorporated into the existential group movement.

The group therapist is no longer the most psychologically knowledgeable member of the group, the recognized and revered expert in theory and practice; instead, he stands out only by virtue of being the most honest, the most sincere, the most authentic, and the most accepting, both in his commitment to life and to the group. In fulfilling this role, he is obliged to be as open and as honest about himself as he expects the group members to be about themselves. He is offered no special privileges, no diplomatic immunity, no special status. He is a human being among other human beings, a patient among other patients—but perhaps a little more aware of what is implied than are the others in the group.

The development has been a fascinating one. Although it was Freud who first talked of the leaderless group and the deep anxieties that this situation aroused, it was Bion who put these theoretical ideas to the clinical test and examined the panic that ensued at the deepest levels. The group analytic approach, on the other hand, keeps the therapist in the background but sees him as indispensable to the therapeutic life of the group; he does not have to prove his indispensability by defaulting. Today, in some circles, the therapist has become the model of the good patient. He lays on the table not only all his countertransference cards but also his self-recognized human failings, so that he can no longer claim differentiation from his fellow members because of his mental health or superior clinical insights. He is no longer an alarming model of conventional normality. As a consequence, the group can get closer to one another without guilt or shame, since there is apparently no conscience figure to watch over them like the eye of God.

This godlessness has been much exploited by encounter groups. Under the highly emotional impact deliberately fostered by such settings, an exhilarating sense of freedom from prohibitions and inhibitions is rapidly generated. To the uncritical and naive observer, the internal censors seem to have been eradicated or at least put to sleep. Unfortunately, the vacation from conscience is more apparent than real and more short-lasting than claimed. The return to conventional circumstances soon reactivates the dormant conscience and may even intensify its more punitive and primitive qualities. Fenichel wrote that the superego is soluble in alcohol; it is also soluble—as Le Bon, McDougall, and Freud pointed out—in the ecstasies occasioned by close group interaction, but there is always a hang-over when reality once again asserts itself. This is, in fact, the oldest lesson in psychotherapy: The internal structures of the mind were not built in a day and cannot be reconstituted over a weekend.

American vs. European Group Psychotherapy

Psychotherapy, like other social institutions, is extraordinarily sensitive to cultural influences. The organizational competence of American group psychotherapists has fast brought about a professionalization of group psychotherapy in the United States. What is gained by annual and regional meetings, with their opportunity for scientific interchange, is to some extent lost by the conforming influences of the Establishment. It is here that the experimentalists have a necessary role to play. Every movement is both embarrassed and vivified by its lunatic fringe; heresy, as St. Augustine once pointed out, can be both a threat and a stimulus to progress. The recent rash of experimental approaches has led to some understandable alarm in established circles but also to a surprising willingness to consider these approaches as potential contributions awaiting the test of time and experience. Although American group psychotherapy at times gives the impression of originating from committee work, there are enough un-psychotic and unpsychopathic experimentalists in the field to ensure a measure of vitality to the group movement. What is not acceptable and what can be incorporated into the body of knowledge must engage in a running battle if the field is to advance.

The criterion for acceptance has been laid down in somewhat categorical fashion by Slavson. According to him, all sound psychotherapies have five elements in common: relation or transference, catharsis, insight or ego-strengthening or both, reality-testing, and sublimation. In an acceptable technique, at least the first three of these five criteria should be present. These canons are too much in some respects and insufficient in others. The criteria refer to group psychotherapy solely as a treatment and not as a scientific practice, so that blatantly nonscientific techniques could find acceptance. Many of these nonscientific techniques, especially the cathartic variety, are put forward in Messianic fashion, advertised with Madison Avenue skills, and practiced with a complete absence of discrimination. Their proponents seem singularly blind to all shortcomings and tend to respond to the enthusiasm of their patients rather than to the considered criticisms of their colleagues.

The situation in Europe, especially in Britain, is somewhat different, with the disequilibrium on the other side. There is a striking absence of professional government. The field is small, the practitioners are few, and the handful of theoreticians wend their own lonely ways far from the clamor of conventions. They behave, in all respects, like gifted amateurs, seeking an internal consistency in their systems and failing to respond to outside comment. By American standards, the approach in Britain is less dramatic, less positive, more ambiguous, and given to understatement. There is something peculiarly reticent about the procedures employed, reflective of the culture as a whole. Here, for example, is a comment by Foulkes and Anthony:

The group-analytic approach is complex but not spectacular. It lays stress on under-emphasis and sees merit in the minimum. It recognizes the importance of the conductor's role, but it prevails on him to function as much as possible behind the scenes in the background.

The absence of affirmation sometimes verges on the negative side, so that the technique may seem, to Americans at least, eccentrically unforthcoming. There is a defaulting tendency on the part of British group therapists that can mislead not only their colleagues but also their patients.

CONCLUSIONS

For a scientific purpose, a system of group psychotherapy should demonstrate certain characteristics: It should be impartable to students by the ordinary routines of training, including training therapy, and impartable to colleagues who do not wish to join an esoteric cult to complete their understanding; it should provide a therapeutic model that helps to explain the process of therapy and the process of change; it should carry out periodic research evaluations on the efficacy of its treatment; it should be flexible enough to develop and alter under the impetus of further knowledge and practice; its proponents should remain eternally vigilant with respect to the tightening grip of dogma and fully aware of the limitations as well as the assets of their particular treatment model; and, finally, the system should provide an economic, elegant, and powerfully explanatory theoretical framework linking together group psychology and group psychotherapy in an indivisible whole. There should be special regard paid not only to the individual patient's status and behavior in the current group but also to him as a member of many human groups from infancy on. Group psychology must become developmental if group psychotherapy is to develop further.

These unseasonable reflections may not be altogether in keeping with the contemporary mood, and the bias is often unashamedly blatant. But they do try, in Nietzsche's terms, to bring the past into a living contact with the present for the ultimate good of both. The past looks much better viewed in the context of the present, and the present gains enormously in the logic of its position when it is placed in the perspective of time. From such beginnings, each practitioner must improvise a serviceable history for himself.

REFERENCES

Abercrombie, M. L. J. Group Analysis International Panel and Correspondence, *2:* 145, 1970.

Ackerman, N. W. Some general principles in the use of group psychotherapy. In *Current Therapies in Personality Disorders*, p. 279, B. Glueck, editor. Grune & Stratton, New York, 1946.

Anthony, E. J. Reflections on twenty-five years of group psychotherapy. Int. J. Group Psychother., *18:* 277, 1968.

Bierer, J. *Therapeutic Social Clubs*. H. K. Lewis, London, 1948.

Bion, W. R. *Experiences in Groups*. Tavistock Publications, London, 1961.

Burrow, T. *The Social Basis of Consciousness*. Harcourt, Brace & World, New York, 1927.

Ezriel, H. A psycho-analytic approach to group treatment. Brit. J. Med. Psychol., *23:* 59,. 1950.

Foulkes, S. H. *Introduction to Group-Analytic Psychotherapy*. William Heinemann, London, 1948.

Foulkes, S. H. *Therapeutic Group Analysis*. International Universities Press, New York, 1965.

Foulkes, S. H., and Anthony, E. J. *Group Psychotherapy, the Psychoanalytic Approach*. Penguin Books, London, 1957.

Freud, S. *Group Psychology and the Analysis of the Ego*. Hogarth Press, London, 1953.

Klapman, J. W. *Group Psychotherapy: Theory and Practice*. Grune & Stratton, New York, 1946.

Lazell, E. W. The group treatment of dementia praecox. Psychoanal. Rev., *8:* 168, 1921.

Le Bon. *The Crowd*. E. Benn, London, 1952.

Lewin, K. *Field Theory in Social Science*. Harper & Brothers, New York, 1951.

Main, T. F. GAIPAC Meeting, London, August 1969. Group Analysis International Panel and Correspondence, *2:* 133, 1970.

Moreno, J. L. *Who Shall Survive?* Beacon House, New York, 1953.

Mullan, H., and Rosenbaum, M. *Group Psychotherapy*. Free Press of Glencoe, New York, 1962.

Powdermaker, F., and Frank, J. D. *Group Psychotherapy*. Harvard University Press, Cambridge, 1953.

Pratt, J. H. The principles of class treatment and their application to various chronic diseases. Hosp. Soc. Serv., *6:* 401, 1922.

Schilder, P. The analysis of ideologies as a psychotherapeutic method, especially in group treatment. Amer. J. Psychiat., *93:* 601, 1936.

Slavson, S. R. *Analytic Group Psychotherapy*. Columbia University Press, New York, 1950.

Slavson, S. R. *A Textbook in Analytic Group Psychotherapy*. International Universities Press, New York, 1964.

Wender, L. Group psychotherapy: a study of its application. Psychiat. Quart., *14:* 708, 1940.

Whitaker, D. S., and Lieberman, M. A. *Psychotherapy through the Group Process*. Atherton Press, New York, 1964.

Wolf, A., and Schwartz, E. K. *Psychoanalysis in Groups*. Grune & Stratton, New York, 1962.

2

Freud: The First Psychoanalytic Group Leader

Mark Kanzer, M.D.

FORMATION OF THE GROUP

The belated appearance of the *Minutes of the Vienna Psychoanalytic Society* provides an opportunity to survey the first recorded instance of analytic group therapy. To be sure, therapy for themselves was not the conscious purpose of the members, but it was a significant instigator and concomitant of their scientific proceedings. This unintended aspect is among the more interesting features, especially as it left a distinct imprint on the development of psychoanalysis itself.

The intimate relationship between the organization of the group and the therapeutic process began when Wilhelm Stekel, who had recently undergone therapy with Freud, proposed regular meetings at which other followers could discuss analysis with the founder of the movement. Thus the Wednesday Evening Society came into being. The exact date of Stekel's treatment is uncertain, but it presumably began in 1901 and may well have continued after the meetings were initiated. In any event, the fantasies now so common among patients—to engage in work with the analyst and ultimately to become an analyst oneself—thus achieved their first gratification.

These fantasies, oedipally motivated, usually extend to the wish to eliminate the

Presented in part as the seventh Nunberg Lecture, 1970: "Sigmund Freud: Group Leader and Educator."

analyst and take his place. Such a wish may well have entered into Stekel's constant rebelliousness and ultimate break with the Freudian school. The same constellation was even more marked in the case of Alfred Adler. He also underwent treatment with Freud, a significant fact little noted in the commentaries on their relationship. This information seems to have been divulged only in later years, when it came to light among the posthumous papers of Freud, which were not published until 1960.

In the early days, the analytic procedure was rudimentary as compared with later standards. Indeed, until 1918 it was not considered necessary for an analyst to have undergone a preliminary phase of treatment himself. In January 1907, for example, Max Eitingon, the first analytic candidate, arrived for a two-week visit and was "analyzed" by Freud as they strolled through the streets together. In the evening, Eitingon attended meetings of the society, where he questioned Freud critically about his doctrines and elicited clarifications that are still important.

Psychoanalytic education and treatment thus went hand in hand, as had been the case since Freud's own clinical insights and self-analysis had reinforced each other to create a new dimension in psychology. This mutual interaction did not come to an end at any precise time; indeed, it continued throughout Freud's life. Until 1901, he intuitively used Wilhelm Fliess as his "analyst," sending him letters that were actually sessions combining explorations of personal and scientific problems. After a break with Fliess, these activities were carried over to the meetings with the group and into transferences toward the individual members.

The nature of transference was still obscure, however, and was especially difficult to recognize beneath the facade of educational, scientific, and organizational enterprises that engaged the growing society. Moreover, Freud's own status, actual and psychological, underwent rapid change after the group was formed, complicating the task of self-analysis. Where previously he had been predominantly a disciple and "son" learning from such older men as Bruecke, Meynert, Charcot, and Breuer and had even placed himself in a filial position toward the somewhat younger Fliess, he was now a prominent figure and an older man sought out by pupils and "sons" of his own. He was distinctly the oldest in the group, and Otto Rank and Fritz Wittels were actually young enough to be sons. His external position also changed markedly as he emerged from the isolation, hostility, and derision that had surrounded him as the first analyst and as he gained recognition from an increasing number of followers.

The first group was very different from a modern psychoanalytic society. For several decades now, members of psychoanalytic societies have been required to prove their eligibility by completing their own analyses, demonstrating an ability to analyze others, and providing certification as to the soundness of their education. None of these preconditions was possible in the beginning. The early followers were drawn largely from nonmedical circles, few possessed therapeutic experience, and none except Freud himself had been subjected to more than a modicum of personal analysis. There could be little debate about the principles of the young science. They might be accepted or rejected, but Freud alone had used the necessary investigative tools and was the only authority in the field.

Indeed, analytic knowledge itself was in its infancy. Even by 1906, when the membership had risen to 19 and the first formal minutes were being recorded by Rank, the indispensable background for the discussions was to be obtained from a few works, whose essence might easily have been limited to *Studies on Hysteria, The Interpretation of Dreams*, and the consolidation of the libido theory in *Three Essays on the Theory of Sexuality*.

EDUCATIONAL AND SCIENTIFIC ASPECTS

Freud, searching in 1914 for the causes of the many withdrawals and painful schisms in the previous few years, wondered whether matters might have turned out more favorably had he organized his following along the lines of an educational institution rather than as a society of ostensible equals. The fact is, however, that inevitably the group had functioned as an educational enterprise from the beginning, although the therapeutic and personal aspects were never far from the surface.

The early followers, representing varied professional backgrounds, had in common a devotion to intellectual and cultural advancement. It was a period of rapid change, but progress in the physical and industrial sciences was not matched by corresponding achievements in the mental sphere. Laborious attempts by neurologists to explain psychological activity in terms of brain functions were doomed to failure and had been abandoned by Freud himself in 1895. More was to be learned about human motivation and behavior from contemporary writers like Ibsen, Strindberg, and Gide than from the neurologists. Freud was able to place the writer's insights within the framework of a scientific psychology.

His own vision of psychoanalysis extended beyond the boundaries of the clinical. He recognized that the abnormal could be encompassed and treated only within a total perspective of human behavior. *The Interpretation of Dreams* had already sought to eschew the neuroses as source material and to fashion the outlines of a normal mental apparatus from a study of thought processes during sleep. Freud's research thereafter produced in rapid succession insights into behavior in everyday life, wit, religion, literature, and the normal maturation of sex life.

In the selection of prospective members for the group, Freud deliberately sent invitations to representatives of nonmedical specialties—musicologists, teachers, a publisher, etc. When Max Graf, a music critic, was invited to join the circle, he expressed his astonishment and was told that Freud wished to include experts in other fields who could discuss his theories from their own viewpoints. Later, Graf was assigned the task of investigating the psychology of great musicians and the process of musical composition. An important study of Wagner's *The Flying Dutchman* resulted. Freud definitely intended to use his group not only for the members' own education but beyond that to propagate psychoanalysis among the most diverse elements and thus spread the psychoanalytic movement. He was a crusader, and this group was the first of his legions of educators.

Within the group of physicians in the society, few had psychiatric training—the specialty at that time was virtually unknown—and Freud drew from each what he had to contribute to psychoanalytic insight. The pediatrician was especially welcome, for child observation was already recognized as particularly crucial for the confirmation and future development of Freud's postulates. Thus it may be said that the membership of the society was calculated, so far as possible, to be an assembly of the widest range of cultural representatives available and to lend social reality-testing to Freud's clinical perspectives.

Although dissensions within the group have received great stress, the fact is that the conflict-free area of growth was far more significant than the dissensions. The experiment launched in 1901 was, despite Freud's misgivings after the painful schisms of 1911 to 1913, a tremendous success. These pioneers were participating, and may well have sensed it, not only in a struggle for a new key to themselves and all humanity but in one of the greatest intellectual and therapeutic experiments of all times—the realignment of man's vision to include areas of his mental processes hitherto excluded from consciousness. In this sense, they were actually speeding the progress of biological evolution, which has allied the specifically human with the dominance of conscious control over the forces that make for individual as well as group survival and enjoyment in life.

THERAPEUTIC ASPECTS

The therapeutic aspects of the learning process were inherent in Freud's teachings. His clinical experience provided the inner core of his data and insights, which inevitably extended to the deepest motivational levels within his followers. The recognition of one's own neurosis, at least in projected form, lies latent even in the unenlightened or normal person, and Freud's adherents tended to belong to neither category. Many of them, Jews like himself in a world that was destroying even their traditions, were also rejected by or alienated from the institutions that lend the individual a sense of relatedness to his culture. Their search for an acceptable identity was individual and social, therapeutic and adaptive.

His followers often made their acquaintance with him through his books, and their reports display an intermingling of intellectual enlightenment with hopes of cure and even the sense of a religious experience. The contemplation of Freud's work on dreams was, according to Hanns Sachs, like "a moment of destiny for me."

A. A. Brill made his adherence to Freudianism conditional upon a scientific trial that may be more justly compared to an ordeal of faith. Unable to recall the name of a patient, Brill invoked the method of free association, about which he had recently read, to pry the secret from the unconscious. It was in vain. Later he wrote:

I became discouraged and thought to myself, "If that is the way to find a thing through the Freudian method, I shall never be a Freudian."

Awaking toward morning the next day, he wrestled with the problem for another hour and was rewarded with the recollection he sought.

If I had not been able to find it, I probably would never have continued to take the slightest interest in Freud.

Freud would doubtless have concluded that the outcome of this self-devised act of faith was determined neither by chance nor by divine intervention but was an inner decision, already made, that was gradually, like a hypnotic command, given access to consciousness.

The 20-year-old Rank also sought out Freud after he felt a sense of revelation while reading *The Interpretation of Dreams*. He was impelled to present himself to the inspired author and consult with him about a manuscript on art that he was writing. Rank's true purpose—to be accepted as a disciple—was accomplished. Freud was so impressed that he undertook to advise Rank about his studies and finally in 1906 brought him into the society both as a potential contributor to the nonmedical side of psychoanalysis and as the paid secretary of the organization. This latter position not only helped support the youth but resulted in the valuable minutes that he kept for nearly ten years.

The traditional myth of Ulysses and Telemachus suggests itself in this connection, the search of the father for the son and the son for the father. Rank, who at 16 had repudiated his own alcoholic father, did so passively by refusing to speak to him and by retiring into a troubled schizoid world of diaries, art, and contemplated suicide. The new vision that he sensed as Freud explained the meaning of dreams made possible an outward turning to an object world where he found actual contact with a more encouraging father. Later both men collaborated in scientifically evolving the concepts of the family romance, birth anxiety, and the myth of the birth of the hero.

The aura of the legendary adhered also to Freud's recruitment of other young men, such as Tausk and Sachs. Their recruitment into the society followed along similar lines and made the group a vehicle for the establishment of father-son relationships. To study and crusade with Freud was no mere educational exercise. It meant friends, financial aid, a cause, and a career. There would be patients, aid in writing papers, and positions as teachers, editors, and officers in organizations as Freud's spell conquered the outer world as remarkably as it established dominance over the unconscious. "I am a conquistadore!" Freud exclaimed in a triumphal moment. Even the dissenters made their way

by breaking with him and lending themselves as spokesmen and witnesses for the opposition.

The therapeutic aspects of the society's sessions were further heightened by the fact that the meetings were held in his office. Wittels reminisced in 1924:

> The couch and the armchair behind it were the arena of Freud's Nibelungen labors. For us, each article was laden with symbolism.

Some had literally stretched out on the couch and would never be entirely freed from the symbolism.

Wittels' natural recourse to the epic and the myth to describe the atmosphere of the sessions was shared by other members of the group. On Freud's fiftieth birthday, May 6, 1906, they presented him with a medallion which bore his portrait on one side and on the other a line from Sophocles hailing Oedipus as one "who divined the famous riddle and was a man most mighty." Jones tells of the emotion with which Freud confessed his own youthful daydream of seeing his bust among similar tributes to famous professors and engraved with just that line. The transferences and countertransferences operating within the group could scarcely be better epitomized than through this episode.

Conduct of the Meetings

Certain parallels between the conduct of the meetings, as devised by Freud, and the investigative techniques of psychoanalysis also intensified the therapeutic aspects of the proceedings. Probably Freud's own personality was a common factor in both situations —the educational and the therapeutic.

The Neutral Educator. Freud always presided, so distance was established between himself and his followers. His position as chairman, reinforced by his authority as the foremost analyst, ensured that all remarks were ultimately addressed to him. Correspondingly, he is said to have preferred addressing a particular person, real or fancied, so that, as in analysis, a one-to-one relationship was established, despite the group setting.

Free Association. An aspect of free association adhered to the peculiar system in force for the regulation of the discussions. After a presentation, each member of the group was called on in turn and obliged to speak when his name was drawn from a Greek urn, which stood in their midst like the embodiment of psychic determinism if not of fate. The resistance of patients to verbalization under such circumstances found its counterpart in the anxiety experienced by members who were prone to escape on one pretext or another before the drawings began. The imperatives of the urn were to become the targets of more open rebellion as group resistances to Freud mounted.

Topics of Discussion. The themes of the unconscious and of sexuality were always in the foreground and in themselves provided natural bridges between the educational and the underlying therapeutic aspects of the discussions. Nunberg describes the tendency of the meetings to drift from the analysis of patients to self-analysis of the members themselves, of their sexual difficulties, memories, fantasies, and personal lives. The conditions for modern group therapy had been created and were to be partly resolved empirically and with scientific insight by Freud and the other participants. Large areas proved insurmountable through self-analysis, so they required other measures of control.

Interpretations. In the discussions that followed the presentation of a paper, Freud alone had the privilege of intervening at will. The lucidity of his expositions, as impressive in spontaneous utterances as in his writings, lent to a summing-up of the impact of an interpretation. Graf, Wittels, and Reik remember him as always speaking last. Actually, this was by no means the case, and Wittels is probably correct in surmising that, after Freud had spoken, a subject was closed for them.

Working Through. Submissive acceptance, the product of awe and relative ignorance, was, of course, countered by ambivalence, negativism, and increasingly informed and independent judgments. The working-through processes, after the interpretations, were diffused through channels of education, therapy, scientific achievement, acting out, dropping out, neurosis, and—in some instances—suicide. Freud naturally became the focal point and mediator among the various strivings that sought expression. When his mediations were successful, he promoted the differentiation of aims and the transformation of instinctual into neutral energy; when they were unsuccessful, the opposite was the outcome. His own personality was at the center of the entire system.

Freud's Personality

Freud's actual personality was revealed to his followers only gradually as it crystallized out from the aura of genius, first encounters, and structured settings for scientific debate. This crystallization was never complete, no matter how long they knew him and no matter how close they came to his inner circle. There is much agreement that nuclear to this inaccessibility was a certain aloofness. Andreas-Salome wrote:

He enters the class with the appearance of moving to the side. There is in this gesture a will to solitude, a concealment of himself within his own purposes, which by his preference would be no concern of his school or his public.

Similarly, his published self-analyses tell us more of his life than any autobiography has ever revealed, yet one does not really discover in them the inner self of Sigmund Freud.

Only Stekel, according to Ernest Jones, who was not quite accurate, ever dared to address him more familiarly than as "Herr Professor." It is notable that, even after many years, followers were apt to refer to themselves as his pupils or, with a note of deeper reverence, to call him "the Master." Letters addressed to and from his oldest associates were scarcely less formal. Graf spoke of the meetings in terms that compare Freud with a Moses presiding over a religious sect that was sometimes provoking in its insubordination, and Tausk alluded earnestly to psychoanalysis as a "scientific religion."

Yet Freud does seem to have unbent, as far as he was capable, with the group. He appreciated their enrichment of his intellectual and social life after his years of isolation as the first psychoanalyst. He played the part of host, serving coffee and cigars and bringing back gifts from abroad for the "Wednesday gentlemen." The minutes show him engaging in jokes, such as that all cooks were paranoid, especially his own, or crying out unguardedly that a certain patient was an "absolute swine." In contrast to earlier statements, in letters to Fliess, which have been construed as indicating a premature end to his potency, he remarked on November 18, 1908, at the age of 52, that he would write on love when his sex life was extinguished. The human side of Freud and his personal opinions were also revealed when he chided a young colleague, Wittels, for views derogatory to female physicians. Nevertheless, he himself was rather dubious that medicine was a proper field for women, although he joined in welcoming them to the society in 1910.

Still, a deep chasm remained between Freud and his followers. Here one must take cognizance of Freud's unique intellectual qualities and of an orientation that has been called rigid but that was probably another manifestation of the same firmness of commitment and adherence to scientific reality-testing that had led to the discovery of psychoanalysis and was continued into its development and defense. Graf recalls Freud as a brilliant speaker to whom words came readily.

On the most difficult subjects he spoke as he wrote, with the imagination of an artist, using comparisons from the most varied field of knowledge. His lectures were enlivened with quotations from the classics, especially from Goethe's *Faust*.

In the minutes, illustrations from case histories and dreams follow in unending and fascinating succesion as new ideas are constantly adumbrated. A stream of publications bore out the promise of these ideas. Views that his students had laboriously acquired were swept away by the latest bursts of insight. Such a man, as Nunberg pointed out, was an impossible ideal, beyond emulation or identification, and a source of constant frustration to such ambitious followers as Adler and Tausk.

Many felt that he was overly critical in his judgments and intolerant of opposition, yet the minutes rarely bear out this impression. His efforts to teach the correct analytic approach to the inexperienced were, it is true, unremitting, and the contributions that others made did not always seem to him as important or as valid as they were to their exponents. Yet he was mild and scientific in most interchanges, accepted with little challenge and even with admiration the consistent opposition of Adler, and seems to have gained his reputation for severity more because of his role as a superego figure than because of his actual conduct. He was no doubt sincere in his statement in later years that he was disposed to tolerate the shortcomings of his followers in view of their courage in accepting psychoanalysis. Yet these followers seem to have understood and resented this tolerance as well as the conscientious and unremitting efforts to educate them.

Freud's reminiscences, his letters to friends, his fantasies, and his behavior indicate that the tolerance often wore thin and merged into resentment at the unending forms of resistance he encountered. Educational ambition as well as therapeutic ambition can be self-defeating to all concerned. Freud's self-image seems to have been that of a patriarch conveying visions of the truth to bickering and unworthy followers, a man for the ages lost among Lilliputians who sought to usurp his accomplishments rather than benefit from them. He inquired of Andreas-Salome why they could not all be like Rank, the dutiful son, although he already sensed the delayed rebellion that would assail him from even that quarter. He was indeed a tormented titan. However, Freud's greatest opponent came from within himself—from the beleaguered ego that sought to be freed from the same patriarchal superego and, still incompletely analyzed, had to be projected through unconscious sympathy into a counteridentification with his own critics in the society.

THE GROUP'S PROCEEDINGS

The ferments taking place within the group during the educational process may be followed with almost autosymbolic accuracy in the first volume of the *Minutes of the Vienna Psychoanalytic Society*, covering the period from October 1906 to June 1908. This volume opens with a presentation in which Rank dutifully applies the teachings of Freud to a new field, mythology, and closes with a full-fledged challenge to Freudian theories and personal leadership by Adler and his paper on aggression.

Rank's Presentation

Rank's study, "The Incest Drama and Its Complications," was the forerunner of his classical work, *The Incest Motif in Poetry and Saga*, which Freud himself considered the foremost contribution of his students during this period. Freud's own commentaries could not have been more painstaking, systematic, impartial, or helpfully intended. However, the young man, appearing for the first presentation before the group and the awe-inspiring father figure, may well have felt rejected. In any event, although Rank had anticipated an early publication of this work, its appearance was delayed for five years, as he noted in the introduction, because of inner inhibitions rather than external difficulties.

Freud first took up the manner of Rank's presentation, finding it loose, as did other discussants, and offering concrete suggestions for a more coherent organization of the material. Then he carefully reviewed the contents, citing clinical studies that would have bearing on inferences derived from literary themes and their assumed connections with the personal lives of authors. Such measures, aimed at limiting speculation, were further buttressed by Freud's insistence on a multidisciplinary approach that did not claim for psychoanalysis a disproportionately important share in the total constellation of events. Thus, where Rank wished to approach the madness of Orestes as a psychological reaction to the murder of his mother, Freud reminded him of the need to trace in the legend the ascendancy of a patriarchal over a matriarchal form of society.

Similarly, Freud took exception to the inclusion of the Titans Uranus and Cronus among the examples of beings with incestuous dispositions. After all, he pointed out dryly, there was no one outside their family with whom they could have had sex. In the course of his discussion, Freud casually introduced the concepts of the family romance and the antithetical meaning of primal words, concepts that were not to appear in his published works for several years.

The distance in grasp and style of exposition that separated Freud from his followers at this point indicates the vast scope of the educational task that lay ahead. Some withdrew from the group, especially under the pressure of the remorseless urn, which did not permit temporizing. Among the early drop-outs was Phillip Frey, a schoolteacher who had written on analytic subjects but who on this occasion felt it appropriate to complain that Rank had interpreted everything "according to the Freudian method." Frey could see no reason for regarding the poetic image of a shackled hero as the psychic projection of an inner inhibition. He also took exception to interpreting as a castration the removal by Oedipus of a sword and belt from his father's body. After all, Frey pointed out, the hero did not even know that the victim was his own father.

For the most part, the comments of other participants were similarly naive or unrestrained, evoking from Freud only patient explanation. Adolf Deutsch, a physiotherapist, simply made the point that the previous speaker, in some brief remarks, had already anticipated what he himself had to say. Eduard Hitschmann, who was to become a great analytic biographer, considered Rank's work on mythology a superfluous extension of Freud's discoveries about the Oedipus complex and predicted that such one-sided incest-hunting would bring the speaker to a sad end. This all-too-prophetic remark was fulfilled only after Rank had given up the Oedipus complex for an equally one-sided devotion to the birth trauma.

Paul Federn was already sufficiently advanced to take a more favorable attitude toward Rank's research, but he was surprised at the ubiquity of incestuous tendencies. Adler went even further in supporting Rank, citing clinical experiences to confirm several of his interpretations of sexual imagery. Nevertheless, he gave a hint of future divergences with the remark that attempts to explain criminal acts by tracing them to their sexual roots explained nothing—a contention that, put in less drastic form, would have coincided with Freud's treatment of Orestes. Stekel, as was to be the case regularly, couched his criticisms on a personal level and found Rank's paper schoolboyish. At the same time, with a slap at "the Master" himself, Stekel, like Frey, complained that the myth had been "seen through spectacles colored by Freudian teachings" but without going beyond Freud. Certainly this attempt to go beyond Freud was Stekel's own consistent aim.

The minutes do not confirm the notion that Freud was surrounded by yes men or showed resentment of their criticisms. The interchanges after Rank's presentation were typical of later meetings, with Freud offering brilliant and thorough appraisals of the material and seeking to find his way constructively to differences between himself and other members of the group. Stekel and later Sadger and Wittels made it difficult to keep the exchanges on a purely educational level. Sometimes personalities presented problems; at other times persistent intellectual disagreements cloaked negative transferences or approaches that were genuinely incompatible with psychoanalysis.

Developing Hostilities

From 1906 to 1908, the group showed impressive progress in understanding by the members and in the level of the discussions. On the other hand, emotional attacks on each other increased in frequency and intensity, and a particular charge—plagiarism—became rampant. In the plagiarism charges, there is the appearance of a resistance that has crystallized. Hostilities, displaced from Freud to one another, found intellectualization in the idea that these others sought to deprive them of their claims to originality. These recurrent charges revealed an inner resentment of their own need to borrow from Freud and their wish to identify with his envied originality. In time, the hostility and the accusations of stealing their ideas were turned against Freud himself.

Stekel and Adler lend themselves especially well as examplars, respectively, of the frankly emotional displays of transference difficulties and of the more subtle manifestations hidden behind intellectual exchanges.

Stekel. The note of sibling rivalry that prompted Stekel to greet new members with a notable lack of charity, already apparent

in relation to Rank, was duplicated a few months later when Wittels made his first presentation, on the psychology of female assassins. Wittels concluded with the injudicious remark that he did not like hysterics, and Stekel, opening the discussion, retorted that this remark was a projection of the hysterical tendencies Wittels shrank from recognizing in himself. The charge was probably true. Wittels, like Stekel himself, had a gift for promoting the appearance of regressive trends within the group.

Charges of plagiarism were especially apt to emanate from Stekel, as when he played an important part in driving Alfred Meisl out of the society after Meisl's presentation of "Hunger and Love" on January 23, 1907. Although Meisl's differentiation between sexual and nonsexual instincts was approved by Freud himself on this occasion and the speaker was bringing to the fore the need of the analyst to give more heed to the self-preservative tendencies, ultimately the ego, Stekel rejected Meisl's claim to priority with the sneer that

no one else would want to use Meisl's few novel ideas.

As he had done with Wittels, Stekel proceeded to turn from the substance of the presentation to an analysis of the speaker himself, interpreting the argument that nonsexual instincts required consideration as a sign that Meisl was sexually repressed. Freud took the occasion to support Meisl's contentions and made the important observation that both sexual and nonsexual instincts join in guiding the infant to its first love object— a formulation that anticipates the later concept of narcissism and even Hartmann's descriptions of the undifferentiated phase and the inborn apparatus of the ego.

Stekel was the most vocal in his personal criticisms of others and the most sensitive to criticism directed against him or his ideas. Freud was fond of Stekel as a good companion but objected not only to his ill-considered attacks on others and his intuitive and superficial approach to analytic problems but also to his lack of scientific conscience—that is, to Stekel's disregard for the truth, as Jones sets forth. Stekel and Freud's ultimate break, expectably enough, came during a tilt that mixed personal, scientific, and administrative motives. After Freud made Stekel an editor of the *Zentralblatt fuer Psychoanalyse*, he requested him to permit Tausk to write reviews for the journal. Enraged at this sign of favor to a sibling rival, Stekel refused and was unmoved by the argument that his own appointment involved responsibility to a psychoanalytic organization and should not be used for personal motives detrimental to science. Freud had to withdraw his support, and their break followed.

Stekel's special qualities provided assets as well as liabilities for the development of psychoanalysis. His free use of intuitive judgments without consideration of methodology and theory placed him in a position to recognize—though with typical overgeneralizations and distortions—the elements of bisexuality, fears of death, and symbolism in dreams. Insights—and dangerous overgeneralizations—also appeared in his early recognition of characteristics of the aggressive drives at a time when Freud found himself unable to regard them as other than particular manifestations of the libido. As one of three members who opened a discussion on suicide (all three—Tausk and Federn were the others—would one day become suicides themselves), Stekel could deliver himself of the striking statement that

the suicide is tormented by a deep sense of guilt; no one kills himself who has not wanted to kill someone else.

Moving away from his pansexual position as he became more aware of the death drive—a term he introduced but did not use in quite the same sense as Freud—he proclaimed that hate was older than love, aggression deeper than sex. The jumble of half-baked and ill-considered propositions that poured from his pen moved Freud and others members of the society to plead in vain that he restrict his output and not bring psychoanalysis into disrepute. Stekel retorted that he was accustomed to finding that his contributions met with little understanding but were ultimately taken up into the writings of others, not least of all by the Herr Professor.

Group Rebellion. With a rising tide of discontent discernible among the disciples

toward the end of 1907 and the beginning of 1908—a collective adolescence, one might say, that reflected emergence from antecedent dependency but with a continuing need for Freud's guidance, which was now galling—Freud himself began to show dismay and a longing to pass on the leadership to someone else. Roazen reports that Freud wrote in a self-analytic mood:

What personal pleasure is to be derived from analysis I obtained during the time when I was alone . . . an incurable breach must have come into existence at that time between me and other men.

The growth of a psychoanalytic group in Zurich and the proposal that a first international meeting be held in Salzburg in April 1908 made Freud turn hopefully to Jung on February 18 with the suggestion that Bleuler preside. "My Viennese colleagues would behave better," he predicted.

Two stormy meetings of the Vienna society on February 5 and 12 supply background to Freud's complaints against his own group. At the first of these meetings Adler brought forward a recommendation that a change be made in the usual methods of conducting the sessions. The urn and its coercive authority came particularly under attack in a transparent displacement from the leader himself. Next, Federn suggested that measures be taken to curb "intellectual communism"—that is, plagiarism. Isidor Sadger, so often the victim, wished the chairman to take more definitive steps to suppress personal invectives and attacks.

With these proposals, the long-standing discontents were finally brought to the surface of group consciousness for discussion. It remained for Graf to go more deeply into the subject and indicate that the proposals "stem from a feeling of uneasiness." Tactfully, he related this feeling to the fact that the group was on the way to becoming a full-fledged organization rather than simply the invited guests of the Herr Professor. Graf suggested that the meetings be transferred from Freud's office to a different site.

Freud responded that he was opposed to using his powers as chairman to suppress any utterances except those conversations that might disturb the speaker. For himself, he waived the right to protect his remarks from plagiarism—a deeply ironic statement. Then, confronting the underlying issues more directly, he expressed the opinion that, if the members could not stand each other or freely express scientific opinions, perhaps the entire enterprise ought to be abandoned. However, he had hopes that deeper psychological understanding might yet appear and assist in overcoming the difficulties. Clearly, he was referring to some advance in self-analytic insight.

Freud's stand, expressed with restraint and dignity, seems entirely correct from both the educational and the therapeutic viewpoints. He took as his baseline an educational situation in which chairman and participants were expected to maintain an alliance directed to promoting the scientific and educational aims that constituted the purpose of the meetings. Self-analysis, promoted by these meetings, should be used to correct divergences from the announced aims.

That Freud would transmute the experiences of this session into scientific and self-analytic terms was to be expected, and the echoes of those experiences are heard in references of later years to

the uncanny and coercive characteristics of group formation. . . . The group wishes to be governed by unrestricted force; it has an extreme passion for authority. . . . The primal father is the group ideal, which governs the ego in the place of the ego ideal.

The destiny of the primal father to be overthrown and replaced by one of the sons was further elaborated in *Totem and Taboo* and was reasserted, despite better scientific knowledge, in *Moses and Monotheism.* Freud seems to have perpetuated, in his appraisal of group dynamics, unanalyzed fragments of his own family romance.

On February 12, a committee headed by Adler and appointed to consider the proposals put forward at the last meeting, recommended the abolition of the urn and a widening of the educational process by including book reviews on a more regular basis and brief case presentations by individual members and by giving more notice about longer papers to be presented so that

all concerned could be better prepared. The sense of these changes was to formalize the meetings, give the members a greater share of the responsibility, and reduce the overshadowing personal influence of Freud. There was no real solution to the problem of the "ill humor in the empire," as members put it euphemistically, and even the proposal to abolish the urn was blocked, probably out of deference to Freud. However, like the leader, this fetish was stripped of some of its authority. It could still be used to summon members to speak, but they were within their rights if they decided to ignore its call.

Certainly the meeting at Salzburg in April was not conducive to greater harmony. Freud unmistakably favored Jung and the Zurich group. When he went to America the next year, he took none of the Viennese in his retinue. With his increasing inner and outer withdrawal from the Vienna society, a gap had to be closed.

Adler. A counter claimant for the leadership of the Vienna group, Alfred Adler, had long been on hand, pursuing a relationship to Freud that was governed by a curious dialectic process. Adler brought to the fore precisely the areas of the personality that had found representation in the Freudian system with the greatest difficulty—aggression, the ego, and social adaptation. Freud, aware of these short-comings, found in Adler a constant reminder and stimulus to consider these problems, so he welcomed Adler's contributions and treated him with marked respect. The antipathy with which he could react to Stekel and Sadger was almost never in evidence with Adler—but neither was there any warmth. The same might be said of Adler's own behavior toward Freud.

The evolution of the Adlerian system of psychology may be followed in considerable detail in the minutes of the group. His interests were centered successively on organic inferiority, aggression, and the masculine protest. With less self-consciousness than Freud's scrutiny of his own dynamics, Adler was doubtlessly reflecting his personality structure as it unfolded under the impact of transference and analytic teachings. Adler was 14 years younger than his archrival, and the key to his personality may be found in early rickets, which prevented him from walking until the age of four. Thereafter, he repeatedly fell and was involved in street accidents because of the unsteadiness of his legs. Inhibited in his motor activity, he read a great deal and was well versed in many cultural topics, like Freud himself. His interest in becoming a physician was also an outgrowth of his ailments during childhood. Lifelong jealousy of an older brother paved the way for the ambivalence he showed toward Freud.

On November 7, 1906, Adler presented a paper, "On the Organic Bases of Neuroses," in which both his potential contributions to analysis and his inevitable future divergences from Freud were apparent. The prime motivating power of the mind, he held, was to be found in inherently defective organs, which influence the psychic superstructure so that it becomes a medium for cultural adaptation to the defect. Certain points of correspondence to Freud's instinct theory may be discerned. If the Adlerian and Freudian systems were to be reconciled, however, a bridge was needed to the concepts of infantile sexuality and repression. This bridge was not created on this or later occasions.

Freud's responses were at first cautiously favorable. But when, on March 5, 1907, Adler implemented his theoretical outline with a case presentation, a minor but distinct cleavage between the two men became observable. Where Adler assumed that a patient had developed talent as a speaker in order to overcompensate for initial stuttering, Freud held that the stuttering was an inhibition of earlier powers of speech. It became increasingly apparent, as Freud repeatedly pointed out, that Adler's use of analytic tools and inferences was very limited and that he took the leap from biological assumptions to social adjustments through a rarefied psychological atmosphere.

The implication of the organic in all behavior, as construed by Adler, began to approach mysticism and yielded dogmatic obsessions rather than empirically derived conclusions. Adler looked for speech defects in singers, visual defects in dramatists, abnormal palatal reflexes in cooks, etc. He saw in symbols the representation of inferior organs striving for a certain degree of perfection. Few of the members responded favorably to these constructions, and complaints were common that Adler was dragging organic inferiority into every situation to the detriment of a truly analytic grasp and to the boredom and irritation of the group.

Next, Adler's interest was obsessively displaced to the instinct of aggression, which became the instrument for his most useful contributions to psychoanalysis. He made the valid point that rage was the emotion corresponding to aggression, just as love corresponded to the sex instinct. Many useful clinical observations and theoretical formulations were later added. The concepts of turning against the self and of reaction formations to aggression proved permanent additions to instinct and ego psychology and a nucleus for formulations about the superego. Adler saw in the fear of death a self-reproach for wishing the death of another person, in altruism a defense against sadism (as in the choice of medicine for a vocation), and in the Marxist concept of the class struggle (Adler was an active social democrat) an opportunity to sublimate aggression constructively and make history consciously. When he sought to combine Marxism and Freudianism in a single framework, Freud repudiated the effort, perhaps a little too peremptorily. Adler saw culture as expanding the self, Freud as limiting the self.

Freud did not so much reject the contentions of Adler on the subject of aggression as insist that aggression was merely an aspect of the libido. Nevertheless, under the prodding of his opponent, Freud accepted Adler's ideas of a "confluence" of sex and aggression, but applied it to a fusion of sex and ego instincts. Significantly, many of Freud's early comments on the ego came about under the impetus of discussions with his adversary.

In general, Freud's appraisal of Adler's system was correct and even admiring. The rival framework, he repeated over and over again, represented an excellent contribution to insight into the surface of the personality—the ego, consciousness, social adaptation. But it did not reach down into the unconscious, it avoided the sex instinct, and its concepts of the neuroses and therapy drifted further and further from the Oedipus complex and the indispensable doctrine of repression. This appraisal of Adlerian psychology was equally correct.

There was little acrimony or even impoliteness in these exchanges over the years, and it is difficult to reconcile the even tone of the exchanges with the traditions of Freud as a despot embattled in defense of his analytic principles. His sharp words are usually to be found directed toward coarse and provocative personal behavior or toward slipshod presentations of analytic thought, like Stekel's, rather than toward the honest and consistent exposition of a different viewpoint. Freud's likes and dislikes of his followers were often apparent and had little to do with their analytic orthodoxy. Rank, the good son and loyal disciple, seems to have been neither more nor less favored than Wittels, a perennial naughty boy whom Freud found amusing. Sadger, who made quite important contributions to classical analysis, was distinctly disliked because of his personality by Freud—and by most other members of the group.

Transformation of the Group

The personal side of the relationship between Freud and Adler was at first obscured behind their polite intellectual discussions, but it figured increasingly in the rifts that grew between them and accompanied a crisis within Freud himself. Adler's boldness in reaching out for intellectual and political dominance of the group was complementary to Freud's increasing withdrawal from the Vienna group and his preference for the Zurich contingency. Freud reasoned that the academic status and Aryan backgrounds of the Swiss offered a greater guarantee for the future of psychoanalysis than did his Viennese colleagues, although it is to be doubted that such rationalizations provided the true motives. As the second International Psycho-Analytical Congress, to be held in Nuremburg on March 30 and 31, 1910, drew nearer, Freud pushed plans to transfer the leadership of the psychoanalytic movement to Jung and its headquarters to Zurich.

Sandor Ferenczi, who had been chosen to convey this message to the Viennese in Nuremberg, succeeded only in uniting the the angry delegation behind Adler and Stekel. Freud then decided to resign from the presidency of the Viennese group and to recommend that Adler succeed him. That he should select the man who was the greatest threat to analysis as his successor, even if he regarded him as the most able member of the society, seems to require explanations that have not been forthcoming. Perhaps, as Adler indicated, the choice was not Freud's alone to make. A hint of deeper psychological motives appears in a letter to Ferenczi on April 3, in which Freud refers to himself as a "dissatisfied and unwanted old man." An inner bond with the rebel against the father and the paternalistic aspects of psychoanalysis seems to have been present.

The stage was set for a remarkable group confrontation on April 6, 1910, after the return to Vienna. With the contemplated transition in power from one leader to the other on the agenda, the group meeting was a veritable occasion for a totem meal involving Freud and his "primal horde." Before the assembled group, Freud undertook to carry through his intentions of politely ceding the leadership to Adler, who would have none of this evasion. He criticized Freud for his behavior at Nuremburg and spoke—almost in the language of *Totem and Taboo*, published two years later—of the banding together of the group against the founding father of psychoanalysis. Adler then offered a program that clearly promised to replace Freud's administrative and intellectual leadership with his own. The membership was to be widened, as it soon was to admit more of Adler's friends; the society would remove from Freud's office; it would publish a journal, which in time Adler and Stekel edited; and Freud himself, while retaining leadership, would be relieved of administrative duties. Later, Adler used publications of the society and introduced courses to make psychoanalysis a cover for his own views.

Stekel, as first commentator, could not imagine how the group would exist without

Freud, whom he nevertheless accused of harboring a deep hatred against Vienna. He suggested that Freud remain as president, Adler be made vice-president with administrative duties, and the forthcoming publication be used to prove, despite the leader's apparent doubts, that Vienna and not Zurich held the key to the future of psychoanalysis. Others joined in the discussion in much the same vein. A note of sadness dominated, not the bitterness and readiness to sweep aside Freud that Adler alone had sounded. Local patriotism emerged repeatedly in the feeling that Freud had mistakenly prized the Zurich analysts as offering a better soil than the Viennese for the future. Wittels commented that his countrymen possessed, as the Swiss did not,

a neurosis which is necessary for entry into Freud's teachings.

Sadger added—in graceful enough fashion for once—that, although Freud had been fed up with the Viennese for two years, they were still ahead of the Zurich group because of his "steady leadership, instruction and advice." A solution was found when, in response to vigorous demands that he at least accept an honorary presidency, Freud agreed to retain a scientific chairmanship while the presidency went to Adler.

At the next meeting, April 13, the transition was sealed symbolically with the total abolition of the urn and the agreement to move the meeting place from Freud's office. The transformation of the Wednesday Evening Society of guests invited to discuss psychoanalysis with the professor into the Viennese Psychoanalytic Society was complete.

Although the occasion had its melancholy aspects for both Freud and the group, it actually marked the successful completion of a phase in which their mutual purposes had been achieved. Psychoanalysis was no longer a one-man discipline, and, although Freud would remain the intellectual leader throughout his life, the society had become a congregation of scientists with varying views and degrees of competence; it was no longer an assemblage of students who sat at the feet of a master. His faults could now be

discerned, tolerated, and understood, just like their own. The children had grown up. The former students, like former analysands, had become sufficiently detached to form new object relationships that still left Freud realistically a teacher and prophet.

What lay ahead for Freud himself at this point was a relapse into temporary isolation and inner scrutiny, from which he emerged strengthened, the guilt for primal parricide shifted from himself to his successor, and free to rid himself and the movement of a truly incompatible element. It is scarcely a coincidence that the topic chosen for his own presentation at the Nuremburg congress dealt with the problem of countertransference. Throughout 1910, this subject was on his mind. In October, after some months of rest and a period of travel with Ferenczi, he wrote this latest favored disciple and former analysand (whose future revolt was already discernible), conveying some of the thoughts that had been distilled from the experiences and temporary setback with the group:

I am not the psychoanalytical superman that you construed in your imagination, nor have I overcome the countertransference

Ferenczi had evidently been engaged in reversing the analytic procedure and exploring the psychology of Freud himself. The master confessed to difficulty in revealing his secrets and acknowledged that his disciple was correct in attributing this difficulty to a permanent incapacity to reach out to others, which was a residue of the traumatic termination of his relationship with Fliess. Freud's disposition to terminate close relationships traumatically went back much further, however. He diagnosed himself, in this letter to Ferenczi, as having regressed to healthy narcissism rather than to paranoia.

As for Adler, once the reins of power were in his hands, he abandoned caution and quickly gave scope to views that carried him increasingly away from the Freudian school. The members of the society, educated by Freud and chastened by their guilt toward the rightful leader, found this departure intolerable, and Adler was forced to resign after a few months in office. This act, too, was part of the group's progress in becoming an educational organization, confident of its own purposes and judgment. When Freud turned toward the group again after a period of self-scrutiny, it received him gladly.

On the personal side, Freud, like Adler, had an ambivalent relationship with an older "brother"—his nephew John, who was a year older than Freud—and guilty memories of a younger brother, Julius, for whose death he felt responsible. With John, he liked to take turns in playing Julius Caesar and Brutus, thus alternating in the murder and revival of a "brother." Adler himself emphasized in his clinical studies the importance of birth order in a family, and his ambivalence with respect to his own brother may well have complemented Freud's. In accepting the opportunity to be Caesar, Adler seems to have opened the way to Freud's long pent-up desire to enact Brutus.

The educational aspects of these meetings promoted an ultimate dominance over the therapeutic, but they also seem to have fostered the emergence of repressed transferences long hidden beneath the cool intellectual exchanges between Freud and Adler. Observers like Graf and Wittels supply pictures of Freud and Adler sitting side by side at the meetings, puffing furiously at cigars. In 1911, the year of the break between them, Freud described, in an addendum to the Schreber case, which helped to precipitate their estrangement, a commentary on the myth that the eagle (Adler) establishes its lineage by looking into the sun without blinking. If it does not, the father casts it out of the eyrie. One eagle apparently failed the test. Adler found a similar image and told Freud that he did not propose to stand in his shadow forever. But Bottome relates that Adler confessed, toward the end of his life, that he had not, after all, caught up with his older brother.

CONCLUSION

The group that gathered about Freud for instruction in psychoanalysis had multiple functions to perform. It provided a means for continuing his self-analysis and initiating him into group dynamics. It also seems to have provided an impenetrable haven for some resistances. The ostensible educational aims of the other members were all but swallowed up at times by therapeutic needs, aspirations for a career, and a climate that made them into propagandists or antagonists of a revolutionary new concept of the human mind. The triumphs and failures of the group found dramatic expression in the intertwined and opposing personalities and ideas of Sigmund Freud and Alfred Adler.

REFERENCES

Andreas-Salome, L. *The Freud Journal*. Basic Books, New York, 1964.

Bottome, P. *Alfred Adler*. Vanguard Press, New York, 1957.

Brill, A. A. *The Basic Writings of Sigmund Freud*. Random House, New York, 1938.

Freud, E. *Letters of Sigmund Freud*. Basic Books, New York, 1960.

Freud, S. *The Origins of Psychoanalysis*. Basic Books, New York, 1954.

Freud, S. On the history of the psychoanalytic movement. In *Standard Edition of the Complete Psychological Works of Sigmund Freud*, vol. 14, pp. 7–66. Hogarth Press, London, 1957.

Freud, S. Group psychology and the analysis of the ego. In *Standard Edition of the Complete Psychological Works of Sigmund Freud*, vol. 18, p. 57. Hogarth Press, London, 1957.

Graf, M. Reminiscences of Professor Sigmund Freud. Psychoanal. Quart., *11*: 465, 1942.

Jones, E. *The Life and Work of Sigmund Freud*, 3 vols. Basic Books, New York, 1953–1957.

Nunberg, H., and Federn, E. *Minutes of the Vienna Psychoanalytic Society*, 2 vols. Basic Books, New York, 1962 and 1967.

Reik, T. *From Thirty Years with Freud*. Hogarth Press, London, 1942.

Roazen, P. *Freud: Political and Social Thought*. Alfred A. Knopf, New York, 1968.

Sachs, H. *Freud, Master and Friend*. Imago, London, 1945.

Wittels, F. *Sigmund Freud*. Dodd, Mead, New York, 1924.

3

Psychoanalysis in Groups

Alexander Wolf, M.D. and Emanuel K. Schwartz, Ph.D., D.S.Sc.

INTRODUCTION

In 1937 one of the authors (Wolf) began reading the available literature on psychoanalytic group therapy—namely, the work of Trigant Burrow, Paul Schilder, and Louis Wender—and then approached J. L. Moreno for some training in psychodrama. Moreno received him warmly and conducted him into the audience of a theatre. Shortly afterward, Moreno appeared on stage to tell of a young schizophrenic woman who was waiting backstage. He said she had a recurrent problem: a succession of emotional involvements with one clergyman after another. Her present attachment was to a cleric who took her for automobile drives in Central Park. Moreno placed two chairs on the stage, facing the audience, and announced that these were the front seats of an auto. He called the patient out and then said, "Dr. Wolf, would you mind coming up here?"

With considerable anxiety Wolf climbed onto the stage and was introduced to the patient as the clergyman with whom she was presently involved. Moreno directed Wolf to take the driver's seat and the patient to sit beside him, and they were off in Central Park. Wolf and the patient were advised to interact spontaneously.

Wolf has only a hazy recollection of what transpired. He recalls mainly his anxiety at being placed in this position, his vagueness about his role and responsibility to the patient, and his final relief when he walked off the stage to a round of applause—for

what, he still does not know, unless it was compassion for his obvious distress. The impact on him of this experience was such that it took him years to acknowledge the value of psychodrama, and he has never made it a part of his therapeutic armamentarium.

But stimulated by the group therapists he was reading, Wolf proposed to a number of his adult patients that they consider continuing their analytic treatment in a group setting. Without exception they expressed an interest, even eagerness, to participate in such a program. In 1938 the first group had its first meeting. The participants were excited and stirred by the experience. As a result of the patients' and the group leader's enthusiasm, word got around of the availability of this form of therapy. By 1940 five groups of patients were in treatment, one of the groups made up of five married couples.

Why in the 1930's did there exist such readiness to join a therapeutic group, when ordinarily there is resistance to the exposure of subjective disability? First, the economic depression had led to considerable collective activity to cope with the poverty and emotional distress of the time. Second, most patients could not afford the expense of individual analysis. The opportunity to undergo analysis at less cost in a group setting met three needs: (1) treatment in depth, (2) therapy at a fee realistic for those financially deprived times, and (3) a supportive and cooperative community for the concerted struggle against a common outside enemy, impoverishment, and a common inside enemy, neurosis.

Psychoanalytic Methods

From the outset the attempt was made to introduce psychoanalytic methods. Patients were confronted with their resistances. Dreams were asked for, presented, and interpreted. Patients were encouraged to free-associate to dreams and fantasies. Transferences to one another and to the therapist became apparent. Working through of resistances and transferences became a major commitment.

It quickly became clear that the encouragement to express associations, thoughts, and feelings freely led to much interaction of a highly charged quality. These interpersonal responses were both appropriate and inappropriate. Patients became increasingly familiar with the characteristic distortions each made and traced these distortions in time to specific familial antecedents. In the course of working through, the patients were encouraged to choose more reasonable alternatives in reality.

Going Around

There seemed to develop in every group three or four patients who were the most active participants, a second circle of three or four who were moderately expressive, and a third circle who were least contributive. Among the last might be one or more silent members. A device was used to try to engage such patients in interaction. They were asked to go around—that is, to say whatever entered their minds about each member in turn and without deliberation, a kind of free association about the others. As this was done, the target patient was asked to respond with his uncensored thoughts and feelings about the member who was going around. In the early years this practice was used more extensively than it is now. Today, interpersonal engagement generally takes place spontaneously. The introduction of going around is now limited largely to trying to involve a silent, withdrawn, or detached patient.

Starting

The first group meeting in 1938 was approached with considerable anxiety by the therapist. He was uncertain about what to expect. He projected the possibility that group members would refuse to talk, no matter what prodding was done. In his concern over such an eventuality, he lectured quite inappropriately on what he thought would be fruitful procedure. It was with some relief to all that the patients demanded to be heard, and the therapist relaxed and listened. In subsequent first sessions of newly formed groups, the therapist gave up these anxiety-provoked lectures. He simply announced the importance of saying freely what was thought and felt, mentioned the usefulness of dreams and free association, and requested that whatever was said in the group not be divulged outside the group.

Over the years it was learned that it hardly mattered how one started the first session. No matter what procedure was proposed, group members were propelled into participation and interaction by their own needs. Beginning group therapists often expressed an initial anxiety "Suppose they don't talk?" was a major concern. One therapist would start by asking each member to tell what brought him to treatment. Another would ask each patient to state his chief complaint. Still another would ask for dreams. A fourth would ask the members to talk about the kinds of parents they had. It was felt that this last method relieved patients of the anxiety of exposing themselves and at the same time fostered group cohesion based on their being victims of parental mishandling.

One therapist could not be induced to start a first meeting, no matter what proposals were made about initiating participation. He had asked some of his patients if they would be interested in entering a therapeutic group. Most of them expressed a wish to join one another in treatment. The therapist in his anxiety kept postponing the starting date. But as pressure from the prospective members became greater, he felt obliged finally to set a date for a first meeting. At that first session the analyst simply announced how he had been approaching the meeting with anxiety and asked the members about their anticipatory feelings. Each confessed to his own anxiety about meeting with a group of disturbed strangers, not knowing what to expect. Some reported sleeplessness and disturbed dreams. A certain community feeling, a cohesion stemming from the shared affect, developed, and the patients and the therapist left the first session with a sense of identification. This approach seemed a good one and was repeated with new groups in succeeding years. But the analyst eliminated his initial statement that he himself was anxious at the outset.

Alternate Meetings

Another development occurred very early—in fact, right after the first meeting. Some group members hesitated to disband. They retired to a restaurant, coffee shop, or cafeteria and continued their talking for a half-hour or an hour. Later, reactions to what went on at these postsessions were explored with the therapist at the regular meetings in his office. One patient was indignant that another had spoken too loudly about him in the presence of a waitress and was, therefore, exposing him and his problem to an outsider. Another patient was noticeably reticent at these postsessions, in fear of being heard by strangers at a nearby table. Most of the members, however, reported in time a sense of feeling different, of behaving more freely away from the analyst. Members who had not attended these postsessions gradually managed to join them. In the search for greater privacy from strangers, patients offered the security of one another's homes. Thus was born the alternate meeting, the session without the immediate presence of the analyst. These meetings proved to be so productive that, in the formation of new groups, the analyst proposed that alternate sessions become an integral part of the therapeutic regimen.

Originally, meetings with the analyst took place three times a week for an hour and a half at a time—on Mondays, Wednesdays, and Fridays—with alternate meetings on Tuesday and Thursday evenings, starting at about 8 o'clock. The latter sessions lasted about two or three hours. Before long, patients began to complain of the amount of time they were giving to meetings. Accordingly, regular sessions were cut to two a week with two alternate meetings a week.

PSYCHOANALYSIS IN GROUPS VS. OTHER GROUP THERAPIES

All group therapies share three fundamental ingredients: (1) a group therapist and at least two patients, (2) multiple interaction among the group members, and (3) limits on what takes place. Psychoanalysis in groups, one form of group therapy, shares these three parameters. There is, however, an additional ingredient basic to psychoanalysis in groups: the exploration and working through of intrapsychic unconscious processes.

The Therapeutic Group

In order to practice group psychotherapy, the therapist must have a group. One therapist and one patient do not make a group. A therapeutic group demands at least three persons, two of them patients and the third a therapist. There is no psychotherapy without a therapist. And there is no therapeutic group if two of the members are therapists and the third is a patient; this is a group setting, but the treatment is individual. Two patients and one therapist or a number of patients and one or two therapists provide structurally for the simultaneous presence of hierarchical and peer vectors. The therapist fills the need for a responsible authority figure. Two or more patients afford an opportunity for peer relatedness.

The presence of authority in the person of the therapist and of peers in the persons of patient group members provides for an interplay of vertical and horizontal interactions that elicits parental and sibling transferences. The distortions projected onto the peers are generally diluted versions of more intense projections onto the therapist. The claim is sometimes made that these dilutions interfere with the emergence of intense transferences to the therapist and, therefore, promote resistance. But the authors have found that, where transferences to peers as parental figures are worked through, the patient sooner or later is confronted with his projections onto the therapist. Having worked through, if only in part, the less threatening aspects of parental transference onto his peers, the patient is able to face more easily the authority of the parent invested in the therapist. There are occasions when a peer, because of his particular character structure, will elicit a more threatening transference than the therapist. But this kind of distortion is diluted by reality. The peer is, in fact, only a peer and, therefore, more devoid of parental authority than he seemed at first.

In the individual treatment setting it is not easy for the patient to affirm himself. The presence of peers often enables a person to seek and usually get support in the horizontal vector, even in the face of the authority of the therapist. The therapist alone with a patient may impose more control over him than when a number of patient-peers are present.

Sometimes the presence of a number of patient-peers may lead a therapist to deny his status. He may renounce his role in the face of group pressure or doubt the appropriateness of his activity and his authority in the face of group criticism. He can become somewhat intimidated in the presence of his projected family in the group, a transference problem. Just as the therapist can have difficulties with the group and need the support of a co-therapist, the patient may need the support of co-patients in order to ventilate deep-seated attitudes toward the therapist.

In the therapeutic group the focus of attention moves from one patient to another. This is the principle of shifting attention. No one patient has the exclusive attention of the therapist. The more patients there are, the greater is the diffusion of attention from the therapist as well as from patients. For many, this shifting of attention gives them time to assimilate and work through whatever insights they have obtained. For others, it represents some freedom from continuous scrutiny, which in individual treatment can be experienced as immobilizing. For still others, it becomes a form of resistance, of avoiding examination of their intrapsychic distortions.

Shifting attention can be a means of working through the demand that one be the only child in the family, a problem that is sometimes not adequately challenged in the dyadic therapeutic relationship. Group therapy, with its insistence that there are others besides the self, provides a medium for working through the irrational transferential demand that no one else be heard.

Another consequence of group structure is the phenomenon of alternating roles. Each patient is required by the presence of others to listen, to try to understand them. New kinds of activity, of feelings, or responsiveness are induced. A patient would not necessarily experience these reactions if he were the therapist's only patient. In the group, each person listens, gives counsel, tries to understand, reacts, feels empathic, becomes annoyed, and elicits reasonable and irrational responses. He seeks help and offers help. He experiences interaction on a peer level, an experience that is not available to him alone with a therapist. In individual treatment, the difference in status and activity between patient and therapist is so marked and the roles of helper and helped are so clearly defined that a patient has less chance to alter his role and his activity. As soon as other patients enter the treatment structure, the role-limits and dimensions are enlarged by new kinds of activities.

Multiple Interaction

Here again, the structural situation encourages group members to respond to one another. Patients become involved with each other as well as with the therapist. In nonanalytic group therapy the interaction is largely phenomenological and deals with manifest content. There is much acting and some acting out of a verbal nature. Here-and-now responses take precedence over an examination of historical determinants. There is preoccupation with group dynamics: cohesion, what the group is feeling or doing, group themes and climate. Special topics may be discussed, and patients protest if a member tries to divert the group from a prevailing subject. Group roles, group rituals, group traditions, and a group history emerge in the course of interaction. To some extent these phenomena determine the ways in which patients and therapists behave over a period of time.

Multiple reactivities encourage forced interaction, thereby engaging the more reticent and reserved patient. For the withdrawn, cautious, or silent member, pressure for engagement is difficult to resist. The anxiety of the beginning group therapist that the members will be silent is often relieved by the discovery of patients' pressure for participation.

Early in the development of group therapy, when it appeared that one or more members resisted engagement, the practice of going around was introduced. It consisted of a patient giving his impressions and reactions to the other patients, who would then respond to him. In recent years such formal procedures have been used less frequently. Reliance on spontaneous interaction demonstrates that patients demand participation of one another. As a result of such forced interaction, there is little necessity to ask for a formal going around.

There are always some patients who are actively participant and others who are passive. The latter are responded to for their nonverbal communication until they are able to speak. The emphasis in group psychotherapy is on interpersonal communication and social integration.

In the multiple interaction that prevails in group therapy, a homogeneity tends to develop in which group members join or submit to whatever theme, climate, or tone is set by a dominant member. On the other hand, attention may suddenly shift from one theme or member to another without an examination in depth of how or why this phenomenon occurred. Patients counsel or advise one another and suggest alternative solutions to each other's current dilemmas. There is more emphasis on what the group is or is not doing than on the individual. When the therapist encourages the group to function in this way it remains homogene-

ous and nonanalytic. Group members under such influence identify with one another rather than differentiate themselves. The result is that the group becomes more cohesive as treatment emphasizes the likenesses among patients. Group conventions take precedence over individual differences, and patients conform to group rules. Personal exception is rejected and unrewarded.

Homogeneity vs. Heterogeneity. All therapeutic groups have relative degrees of homogeneity and heterogeneity. Nonanalytic group therapies tend to sponsor homogeneity. A group therapist may select patients with similarities: a shared psychovisceral symptom, a common diagnostic category, a similar chief complaint. The psychoanalyst in groups tries to provide more diversity in organizing his groups. Although he acknowledges certain similarities among patients, he is alert to each patient's uniqueness and is sensitive to each member's right to be different. For there is psychopathology in the formation and cohesion of a homogeneous group that too often rejects the stranger as deviant. The psychoanalyst in groups sees a positive value in the complementarity of differences, in man and woman relating constructively to one another just because they are different, of parents and children breaking the generation gap. He sees homogeneity as insular, isolated, snobbish, and antisocial.

If there are several homosexuals in the group, for example, the analyst is not only aware of their manifest similarities but alert to the differences in historical development that led to the underlying psychopathology. Given a group of alcoholics or obese patients, the analyst is cautious about making an interpretation that assumes his observation is equally insightful for all members. Rather, he sees the end product of homosexuality, alcoholism, or obesity as having divergent origins and different bases for its persistence, despite similarities in operational forms.

When group members and the analyst, even in the most homogeneous group, examine each other deeply, they find that each person is different from his neighbor in his history, his development, and his psychodynamics. A working out and working through takes place that makes each patient more interesting to the next. A regard for one another in difference becomes more appealing than the superficial pseudocollusion of similarity and identification. Divergence in healthy resources for gratifying and realistic involvement—not just differences in pathology—can be the basis for mutual interest and acceptance. The novelty that stirs the membership to try to understand and accept their differences represents a reciprocity based on contrast. While the members study one another in depth, they nevertheless discover and grant each other areas of commonality.

The analyst in groups is not concerned so much with the collective effort as he is with the emerging wholesome individual ego. He is not preoccupied with how the mystique of the group feels, an irrational projection, but with how the individual in the group thinks, feels, fantasies, dreams, and behaves.

In nonanalytic group therapy as well as in psychoanalysis. in groups there are, of course, similarities and differences among patients, no matter how homogeneously or heterogeneously the groups are organized. It is of considerable importance, however, whether the therapist emphasizes similarities in order to achieve a superficial homogeneity or whether he emphasizes differences. The more the emphasis is on similarities, on homogeneity, the more the leader is limiting himself to the manifest and is practicing nonanalytic group therapy.

In nonanalytic group therapy, the patient may be encouraged to repeat his submission to earlier familial demands to conform. The therapeutic group, by resisting differentiation, simply reinforces the original traumatic experience. In psychoanalysis in groups, the exploration of intrapsychic processes enables the patient to understand in greater detail the nature of his submission to members of the nuclear family and members of his current group. He is encouraged to find his way out, to recover his repressed ego. The psychoanalytic group sponsors his individuation, his nonconformity, the recovery of his lost self.

It is impossible to organize an absolutely heterogeneous group. All people share certain characteristics and submit to certain characteristics, certain demands for homogeneity. A therapist does not place children or adolescents with adults in analytic groups. He places these three different age groups with their peers. He does not place mental retardates with the intelligent or the psychopathic with the nonpsychopathic. Even the analyst in groups organizes his groups along specific lines and selects patients for certain characteristics. Nevertheless, unless he demands increasing homogeneity, the likelihood is that the group will become more diversified as analytic treatment goes on.

The members of a unisexual group in analysis tend to become more diverse. If the group consists exclusively of men, there comes a time when they ask that women be introduced into the group. If the group is made up exclusively of women, they ask for men. If the the therapist insists on promoting homogeneity, he limits the extent to which analytic exploration may be done. It is the experience of the authors that patients who make progress in treatment ask that the other, the different, be invited to join the group. This is usually an indicator that the therapist is doing analytic therapy.

Limits

The question of limits has always been a problem in psychotherapy was well as in society at large. The Ten Commandments, state and national laws—these are examples of society's attempts to set up controls. The use of the couch, the limits set against action and acting out, the promotion of free association, fantasy, and dreams—these are examples of the analyst's attempts to control inappropriate activity.

In this time of increasing national and international violence, there is a growing cult of physical activity in group psychotherapy. Some of this activity surely has its constructive side. But parts of the activity are just as certainly acting out. Violence has entered the sanctum of group psychotherapy, promoted perhaps by the encouragement to aggression in society at large: the threat of nuclear war, bombings in civilian life, murder, the drug traffic, political and racial fanaticism. Disregard for justice and the law is increasing, with a corresponding loss of orientation toward the reasonable need for limits and the moral and human consideration of the rights of others. There is in this dilemma a diminution of human feeling, a rejection of humanity—of oneself as well as of others.

Without limits there is no order in therapy or in life. Yet when controls are demanded, there must be room for protest, for innovation, for initiative, for the divergent point of view, for variety and change. Unless the therapist assures ample opportunity for such self-expression, he does not promote healthy disinhibition, self-discovery, mutual exchange, and mental growth. The therapist must, therefore, deny limitlessness and at the same time sponsor the assertion of fancy, thought, and feeling. He needs to exercise some control yet support the privilege of free speech. He needs to decide what and when to limit and what and when to promote. And he needs to be able to explain why he denies in one situation with one patient what he promotes in another.

Both therapist and patient need to develop the attitude that there is a need for limits before treatment can be effective. Limits do not imply rigidity or inflexibility. Rather, they create the opportunity to change. They provide for re-examination and reconstruction based on the emergence of new experiences and new understanding.

One of the characteristics of emotional disorder is the pursuit of limitlessness. The patient often tries to overcome his anxiety in an inappropriate way. The search for absolutes or for immortality is such an irrational aim. It is related to the irrational hope for omnipotence. Treatment needs to be limited in duration, in number of sessions in a week, in the length of each session, in activity, in participation. The therapist's and the patient's agreement to limit themselves is a commitment to reality. The ingredient of limits is essential to all forms of psychotherapy.

Number of Patients. It is not easy to define limits. One therapist may be unable to treat more than six or seven patients in a group. Another may find it congenial to work with numbers up to 10, 12, or 15. It seems doubtful that one can practice psychoanalysis in a group made up of more than 12 or 15. As already pointed out, a definite lower limit for the size of a group does exist: three, one therapist and two patients. The authors' view that the upper limit ought to be eight or ten is not a rigid one. They have themselves worked with groups of 12 to 15. But they are not aware of analytic groups larger than 15 and question whether it would be possible for an analyst to follow adequately what was going on in such a large group.

Time. Ought the duration of group meetings be limited? A recent development in group therapy has been the appearance of marathon sessions lasting two or three days with one therapist or with alternating therapists. Some marathons have been reported to last a full week. The authors do not believe it is in the patients' or the therapists' interests to attend unconscious processes for such extended periods. Such induction has in some instances led to psychotic reactions. It is impossible to do analytic therapy without resistance, and the prolongation of sessions to entire days represents the pursuit of nonresistive limitlessness.

The authors limit their group meetings to one and a half hours, but the time might be extended to two or two and a half hours. Just as the regular session should be limited in time, so should the alternate meeting. Although a group may have an alternate session that lasts longer than usual, the members inevitably resist unduly prolonged sessions.

Moreover, it makes sense to limit the length of time a patient remains in any given group. If he does not appear to make some progress in six to 12 months, continuing in that same group seems of doubtful value. A time limit should be placed also on his remaining in his particular group for more than four years. Beyond this time some patients seem to deteriorate in their capacity for cooperative endeavor with the same group of participants. Such members might well be referred elsewhere for treatment.

Activity. Sometimes the analyst in groups is too permissive of patient activity. He needs to take a stand against sexual relations and physical aggression among group members. A monopolist may, for example, dominate a group, with insistent demands that he always be heard at the expense of the others. Or a masochist, by assuming the position of scapegoat, may repeatedly invite group members' aggression.

Families. Psychoanalysis in groups, the authors believe, should be limited to patients initially unknown to each other. Such a view excludes family members as well as married couples from analytic groups. It is not appropriate to make parents and children or husbands and wives aware of one another's unconscious processes. There are too many potentials for mutual destructiveness in such exposures. It is, however, possible to do group therapy with families and married couples when the therapist plays some interpretive, supportive, guiding, and mediating role.

Most married couples get along without full awareness of the details of their prior history or of one another's unconscious processes. The exposure of these details might threaten the stability of a marriage. For most couples, the less they know about the significance of one another's dreams, the better the marriage. It is a rare couple, but there are a few, who, the more they know about one another in terms of unconscious processes, the better they get along. These unusual married couples may do well in psychoanalysis together.

Kinds of Patients. Limits need to be imposed on the introduction of certain kinds of patients to psychoanalytic groups. Not everyone is suitable for such therapy. Severe alcoholics who cannot come to meetings sober need to be excluded, as do drug addicts who come to sessions under the influence of drugs, seriously handicapped stutterers, the mentally retarded, epileptics, hallucinating psychotics, the actively deluded, suicidal and homocidal patients, the psychopathic, cardiac patients who develop pain under emotional stress, patients more than 50 or 60 years old, adolescents less than 18, the very seriously depressed, and the manic. Such patients can be better treated in nonanalytic group therapy. If they improve,

they may become suitable for psychoanalysis in groups.

The Therapist. The analyst must also impose limits on himself. He should be available to patients for the whole of their appointed time. He should neither keep them waiting to start a session nor see them beyond the time of the regular meeting. He needs to deny himself sexual and aggressive acting out with patients. At the sessions the analyst may not himself be disturbed, unable to concentrate, intoxicated, drugged, hallucinating, delusional, very depressed, or suicidal. He must not be homosexual. He must have undergone psychoanalytic training and have been an analysand in individual and in group analysis.

Whether he admits it or not, every therapist has a point of view, a philosophy, a personality. Regardless of any assumed manner determined by theory or technique, his underlying commitment and his behavior are revealed to the patient. His position with regard to the human condition shows itself in the appearance of his consulting room, the clutter or neatness of his desktop, the kind of wardrobe he has, the paintings on his walls, the color and light in his office, the quality and volume of his speech, how and whether he responds to phone calls during sessions. The patient experiences him in what he selects to analyze and in what he seems to neglect, in whether he engages vital or trivial issues, in whether his attitude is welcoming or rejecting at first meeting, in whether his greeting is warm or distant. The therapist indicates his approach to life by his hopefulness or cynicism, by whether he attends the patient's associations or pursues his own fantasies. His preferences are demonstrated in whether he asks the patient to use the couch or the chair, whether he prefers to see the patient alone or in a group, whether he asks to see members of the patient's family or not. Every therapist betrays to his patient his sense of what he believes is relevant and irrelevant. He exposes himself and his values to the patient not only by the content of what he says but also by how he says it, by the way he behaves.

Although the analyst ought to prompt the

patient to become interactive and involved in his group, he must make sure that the patient evolves his own way of life, just as long as it is not based on unreality. The analyst does not try to govern or dominate the patient. He would rather help the patient find his way for himself in the enrichment and revival of his own ego. The therapist does not think there is only one way—his own—to maintain a gratifying human existence. He enjoys and endorses the wholesome, original, and inventive differences among his patients and advocates their creative and realistic dissimilarities. In this regard he encourages each patient's distinct and personal emancipation. An analyst helps to liberate his patient as long as he analyzes resistance, transference, and the repetition-compulsion.

Patience. An important requisite of every therapist is patience. He must listen patiently. Yet he cannot wait forever. His tolerance must have some limits. Everlasting, gentle forbearance is not possible to maintain, nor is it in the patient's interest. Endless patience leads to interminable analysis. Therefore, the analyst can persevere only within limits. This position is not a justification for impatience. Rather, if a patient, despite an analyst's tolerance for his plight, makes no move to change, the therapist must press him at opportune times to make some effort in a healthier direction. It is inappropriately patient for the therapist to sit tolerantly by while the patient remains endlessly uncommunicative or apathetic. If under these circumstances the therapist consistently indulges this passivity, he is very likely annoyed with, disinterested in, or antagonistic toward the patient.

Fallibility. There is another important communication from the therapist to the patient: the therapist's acting as though he had all the answers. The reality the therapist must acknowledge is that no one has absolute knowledge or absolute certainty. The patient may wish to find in his therapist the helper who knows all and may become disturbed that his confidant has human fallibility, but he ultimately accepts the reality of their mutual uncertainty, their partial comprehension. In this way he

becomes able to give up his pursuit of absolutes, of omnipotence or impotence. He becomes able to accept and choose partial powers as more relevant and realistic. If the analyst can acknowledge his limitations, the patient is freer to give up his own obsessive pursuit of infallibility, his enforced belief in his own perfectibility. If the analyst does not have to be flawless, always the ideal, infinitely powerful, the patient is freer to give up his dream of almightiness.

Affirmativeness. The therapist ought not be engaged exclusively in pointing out the patient's psychopathology. If a group member sees only what is sick in the others, the analyst points out what is healthy. He acknowledges the positive resources in each patient and makes them obvious to him. He emphasizes the inquiring, searching edge of the patient. He is alert to the patient's longing for sexual gratification. He stresses these resources in patients so that they may see themselves more positively. He looks for what he can affirm, for the capacity to resolve an enigma, a conflict presented in the fantasy, in the dream, in the encounter he is having with another patient. It is this kind of engagement that is very likely the most significant part of the analyst's participation—his devotion to the germinating ego in the patient. What may be the growing edge in one patient may not be the same in another. The analyst's awareness of these differences helps patients also to appreciate each other in unlikeness, helps men and women, young and old in the group to like one another just because they are different. This acceptance of variety leads the members to experience the reality that the cause and resolution for one patient may not be the key to health for another.

Flexibility. The therapist is not rigid; he is flexible. For him, people have the capacity to change. They are in no final state of being. This does not mean that there is no limit to the duration of treatment. When treatment comes to an end, the patient's life goes on, his development continues, he goes on changing, even in the absence of the analyst.

In his flexibility the analyst bends and yields. He does not thoughtlessly hold to outworn doctrine. He tries to see the other's point of view. As the patient presents new facets of himself, the analyst feels free to change his mind and his previous assumptions about him. While he respects and follows various customs tested by analytic practice, he is watchful for a refreshing and receptive idea and new clinical experience. He is interested in innovation rather than in doctrine, but he is vigilant about seeing that freshness does not deteriorate into gospel. In his awareness that professions of faith lead to suppression and discouragement, he is life-affirming rather than life-denying. He is hopeful about himself, about life, and about his patient's chances of getting well. He is optimistic. He believes in human beings' capacity to change, in their ability to renew themselves. He is in love with life, with people, with experience. At times he is anxious and afraid. Still he enjoys his family, his friends, his patients, his colleagues, his students, and his life experiences. He enjoys work and play, whether his own or that of others.

The therapist is dedicated to helping the patient work out his destiny with other people, to social intercourse, to good fellowship, to the individual's living and working with others. At the same time, the therapist is equally committed to the value of the patient's own evolution and his capacity to think and feel and act in his own behalf. For every patient his own growth and development are primary.

Exploration of Latent Material

Group therapy that introduces psychoanalytic means is concerned not only with the manifest but with understanding the latent in patient interaction and function. The analyst takes the lead in the search for unconscious processes by promoting free association, the analysis of dreams, resistance, and transference. The search for unconscious motivation and processes leads patients away from the here-and-now and into the there-and-then, into historical determinants. Group therapy is converted into psychoanalysis in groups only when this element—the investigation of intrapsychic material—is introduced.

Under such circumstances the other parameters take on new depth and meaning. Hierarchical and horizontal vectors cease to be merely current experiences with authority and peers but acquire parental and sibling transferential qualities that are re-experienced, and conscious plans are introduced to work through these distortions.

The intercommunication characteristic of multiple reactivities is no longer promoted simply for cohesive socialization, which admittedly has its psychotherapeutic benefits. Interaction is also used to proceed from the interpersonal to the intrapsychic, from the manifest to the latent. The pursuit of the intrapsychic in the interpersonal stresses self-knowledge that leads to personal integration. And personal integration leads to more wholesome social integration. Nonanalytic group therapy frequently imposes a more superficial social integration that disregards the personal psychodynamics of the individual.

In nonanalytic group treatment, there is reliance on the principle of forced interaction in order to engage the resistant member. In psychoanalysis in groups there is no serious objection to such means, but engagement is based more on freedom of choice for the individual, on understanding and respect for the patient who is not yet ready to participate, on the hope that he will see fit to join the group members, on trying to understand his resistance and helping him to work it through.

In nonanalytic group therapy the patient may be either well-served or victimized by the principle of shifting attention. The patient overly concentrated on may welcome a respite from group examination. Still another member may find himself too frequently bypassed. Little if any time is spent in a study of each member's psychodynamics in provoking the response he gets and the latent nature of these reactions. The contrast when psychoanalytic means are introduced is striking. The patient who is focused on may be masochistically provoking whatever latent sadism exists in other members. Manifestly he is a monopolist, but on a deeper level he may be trying to exclude his younger siblings from getting parental attention. He may be demanding attention in an oral-incorporative way. Or, he could be receiving much attention because of his narcissism, his exhibitionism, or his phallic overbearance. There are multiple possibilities. The bypassed member may be latently the good child quietly waiting his turn—hurt, disappointed, enraged at being neglected. He may be frightening to the other patients, who vaguely sense in his silence an enormous hostility they are afraid of tapping. Here, too, the bypassed patient, like the monopolistic one, may have any one of a series of unconscious determinants that require exploration in depth.

In group psychotherapy, with the principle of alternating roles, members are sometimes asking for help, sometimes giving it. In psychoanalysis in groups some members use the role of helper as a way of resisting treatment. The same is true of those who are always helplessly demanding. The analytic group searches for the historical determinants that have imposed this particular repetition-compulsion in order to work it through.

The analyst in groups introduces an activity not generally available in other group therapies: He interprets the nature of unconscious processes in the interaction among the patients and between them and the therapist. The patients learn in time how to understand the latent meaning of their contributions and make significant interpretations as well. Their impressions are sometimes appropriate, sometimes not. Unconscious material is worked out and worked through. The patient develops insight, which helps him understand his disability. He is thereby able, with the support of the analyst and the other patients, to struggle to resolve his difficulties.

The nonanalytic group psychotherapist may use many of the means of the analyst. But unless he emphasizes an exploration of latent content, he is not practicing psychoanalysis in groups. The analyst in groups does not limit himself exclusively to the search for unconscious manifestations. If he entirely neglects manifest behavior, he is practicing individual analysis in a group setting. Analysis in a group requires attention to horizontal and peer vectors, to multiple reactivities, and to unconscious processes, with special emphasis on the last. But individual similarities, manifest behavior, and group dynamics are neither neglected nor denied.

PSYCHOANALYSIS IN GROUPS VS. INDIVIDUAL ANALYSIS

Good analysis may be done in either a one-to-one or a group setting. But the dyadic relationship and the relationships in a group provide for behavioral differences in the therapist and in the patient that are both quantitative and qualitative. Patient and analyst will have problems whether they work in the one-to-one or in the group setting, but certain disturbances become more evident or more acute in one or the other situation.

The Analyst's Motivation

In individual analysis the analyst believes that the intensity of the transference relationship is a motivating and ultimately therapeutic influence. He adheres to the need for concentration on the analyst as the means by which unconscious processes can be exposed most expertly. He is dedicated to the necessity to work out and work through parental transferences directed toward him as the central difficulty.

The analyst in groups values interaction among peers as well. He believes in the necessity to work through sibling as well as parental transferences invested in the peers rather than in isolated reliance on the authority of the analyst.

Group therapy seems to attract authoritarian as well as self-devaluating kinds of therapists, among others. Dominating leaders appear to look on individual treatment as deeper than is possible in the group, even though they practice group therapy. Self-devaluating leaders prefer to work in the group because they have little regard for their competence as individual analysts, and they esteem patients as more able cotherapists. The therapist's preference for the dyadic or group field in which to work may have both healthy and unhealthy determinants.

Privacy and Exposure

The dyadic relationship offers the patient more security in terms of privacy. The group is more threatening at first because it poses the possibility of exposure. Once in a group, the patient discovers before long that he becomes increasingly secure with his fellow patients. He finds, too, that revelations beyond the confines of the group are unusual, are told anonymously, and are no serious limitation to treatment. The compulsive gossip is analyzed rather than excluded or extracted until he has overcome this pathological necessity. Patients fearful at first about joining a group are generally more anxious about exposing themselves to strangers than afraid that their confidences will be revealed outside the group. Their concern often is that they will be rejected for having shortcomings.

Many patients feel they are pretenders to honesty, that underneath their facades of respectability and good citizenship they are wicked, deceitful, and inadequate. The need to maintain the appearance of health keeps some from ever consulting a psychotherapist. For others, this dynamic forces them to seek out the individual analyst, who alone will guard their secrets. For some, the analyst's tolerance is not enough. They remain with the conviction that he is quite singular in his forbearance and that, if others knew of their deceit, they would be pariahs. For these patients, psychoanalysis in a group offers more realistic protection and security because there they can test the reality of compassion in a more heterogeneous community. For patients who overestimate the attitudes of others, who fear being accused of unnaturalness or wrongdoing, the group is reassuring. Once introduced to a group and there convinced of their own virtuousness, these superego-ridden patients may become the pharisaical custodians of propriety in the group. They may arrogantly denounce as transgressors in the group the visionaries, dreamers, and poets, as if these were now the apostates from decency. By taking on the mask of offended virtue before unscrupulousness, they can more easily hide their own deviation.

Tolerance

How tolerant are patients of one another compared with the forbearance of the analyst? And what is the effect of permissiveness on the course of treatment? Should limits be set to indulgence? Why is it that patients humor so much in one another?

Some therapists expect group members to be so intolerant of one another, so unaccepting of difference, that they try to constitute the group as homogeneously as possible rather than work through to the enjoyment of variety. The characteristics in patients that enable them to accept one another are empathy, healthy identification, pathological identification, bilateral acting out, complementation, and equality in difference. Group members can at times be more intolerant of repeated pathology than the therapist. His interest in psychopathology, its origins and ramifications, may make him too lenient about its persistence. Patients may act out, but they also become frustrated by it and make vigorous demands for more reasonable alternatives. Some patients tolerate conflicts and differences of opinion better than the analyst does.

Relatedness

Patients in a group generally feel closer to one another than to the analyst. If a patient had no siblings, had a remote father, and was attached to his mother, who discouraged relations apart from her, he may prefer to be in individual treatment in order to maintain his close tie to the mother figure in the person of the analyst. Although this may be his transferential preference—a current representation of his wish to reestablish his relatedness to his mother—he would do far better to join a therapeutic group, where his pathological symbiosis could more readily be worked through. Relatedness in a group is partly transferential, but there is a larger component of realistic, friendly intercommunication than in the hierarchical contact with the analyst.

The relatedness of the patient and the analyst in the dyadic setting is not frequently pseudoclose when the patient is in a deep transference neurosis, with the analysand in a symbiotic tie to the mother surrogate in the analyst. The patient in his transferential need of the therapist-as-mother may express his love and need for love but suppress his hostility in fear of losing the emotional support of the analyst. In the group the deeply ambivalent character of this relatedness is more readily revealed and expressed with the support of the patient's peers. So his reaction to the therapist is in this sense deeper in the group, even though the relatedness between patient and analyst may not seem, at first, to be as close as it was in individual treatment. Yet this is a working through with the support of sibling peers and father surrogates, effecting a necessary separation from the mother, with strengthening of the ego as a result.

Relatedness needs to be explored in terms of its reality-oriented or bilateral transferential content. Analysis, whether individual or group, should lead to a multiplicity of discriminating relationships. In treatment, dyads and triads need to be investigated to see whether they are disturbed, transferential, obsessive-compulsive, or realistic and appropriate. In individual treatment, patient and analyst are closer and more related than they are when the patient is in a group. In the individual setting the two are more deeply involved in the detailed nature of the relationship, in greater exploration of the intrapsychic life of the patient. But the individual setting is more isolating and limiting in fulfillment. It remains more characteristically a fantasy relationship. Its illusory quality makes it more frustrating than the patient's relations with members of his group. If the group analyst provides a large number of individual sessions, the relationship to him may acquire the closeness characteristic of individual treatment.

Because group members offer one another some fulfillment of mutual needs, whether in acting out or in meeting nonarchaic expectations, they feel closer to one another than to the therapist. They experience one another more in reality than they do the analyst, who maintains his anonymity. The closeness of all relationships in the group needs to be estimated in terms of reality and illusion.

Whether in individual or in group analysis, the relationship with the therapist tends to be symbolic. The relationship with group members is more realistic. The dyadic relationship offers only one other person with whom to relate, whereas in the group there is the opportunity for simultaneously experienced multiple contacts. The authors believe it to be a limited relatedness if a person is able to relate to only one person at a time. The promotion of exclusive one-to-one relations as a way of life is too binding and isolating.

Mutual understanding is a factor in determining relatedness. Patients are not obliged to know and have insight into one another in the same way as the analyst. In part, patients are able to accept one another because of their limited comprehension. They are, in part, wary of the therapist because they believe he can see through them. Some patients cautiously or eagerly look to him for insight or greater understanding, depending on their resistances and on how the therapist offers his insights.

Reality

Reality and illusion determine relatedness. An examination of reality elements in the dyad and in the group, therefore, becomes relevant. The analyst ought to be more reality-oriented than the patient. If the group is heterogeneous, the reality that each patient is confronted with is various. This diversified reality puts pressure on each patient to make a flexible and appropriate change in character. He discovers, too, that reasonable alternatives do not emanate only from the therapist. The fact that he is witness to other members' making all sorts of realistic changes in adaptation lessens his neurotic need to comply and submit to any prevailing will or authority. He sees that he may rely on his own choices and be supported in this pursuit by the good will of his peers rather than yield to another's demands. In this way his ego is strengthened, and his view of reality is enlarged.

Multiple Transferences. Critics of psychoanalysis in groups have remarked that the multiple transferences elicited in the group interfere with the patients' capacity to apprehend reality. In dyadic analysis, transference tends to be more fixed and lasting, and the analyst can more readily detect what is real from what is inconsistent with reason. In a group, although many transferences may prevail for a time undiscerned and unexamined, sooner or later they are seen and analyzed. Each patient in the group invests other members with a variety of transferences determined by the specific stimuli of their different personalities. This kind of manifold responsivity is not evident in the dyadic relationship because of the relatively uniform behavior of the analyst, but surely the patient responds in as many ways as do group members once he is in a group situation or with persons other than the analyst. The vividness, diversity, and volatility of these more shadowy transferences are often not seen and are, therefore, nonexistent for the dyadic analyst. The more numerous transferences one sees in a group may elicit for a time a greater unreality, but the task of working through provides substantial elements for a more comprehensive resolution of broader aspects of the patient's disorder.

The Analyst. Another aspect of reality concerns the degree to which the analyst unmasks himself in the individual or the group setting. In the group, the analyst tends to let himself be seen more readily. Stimulated by the numbers of patients and their many needs and obliged to face them all in a circle, he responds verbally and nonverbally in ways he ordinarily does not exhibit behind the couch. Some analysts, on the other hand, show less of themselves in the group, where they keep themselves apart, only to become more involved in the one-to-one relationship.

A group may provoke a therapist to expose more of his wholesome and neurotic reactions but will block his acting out sexually. One psychiatrist reported in the course of his own treatment that he was masturbating his female patients. Attempts to analyze his acting out failed. His analyst placed him in a therapeutic group. The psychiatrist became enthusiastic about the experience, and his therapist encouraged him to practice group therapy. Before long, the psychiatrist had placed all his patients

in groups and was unable to continue his acting out. Only then was it possible to work through his difficulty successfully.

When the analyst shows more of his real self, as he does in a group, various patients use this exposure differently. It may elicit healthy reactions in some. Others, however, may misuse the therapist's disclosures to exercise their own pathological compulsions. The emergence of the actual character of the therapist is neither desirable nor undesirable as such. The important issue is how the patient reacts to it and how the therapist analyzes the patient's response.

In a group, there is both more distortion and more objectivity than in individual psychoanalysis. If, however, the therapist in a dyad becomes distortive, he can be more hurtful because there are no other patients present to control him with their critical attention. It is possible in a group to examine the therapist realistically with the contrasting and comparative views of different members. A traditional analyst may maintain that the therapist ought to remain unknown, an enigma, a fantasy. The authors are more inclined to believe that he should be active, responsive, and interactive but flexible enough to be a passive listener as patient needs require.

The Intrapsychic and the Interpersonal

Interaction in psychoanalysis in groups demands more reality-boundness than in the dyadic relationship. In the group, there is a social expectation that, even though the patient expresses his own thoughts and feelings, he also needs to consider the ideas and feelings of the other members. This important therapeutic emphasis is frequently neglected in individual treatment. This social demand prevents hazardous retreats into morbid loss of contact with reality. It helps the patient to recognize and later to understand his own provocative role. It gives him the opportunity to examine the intrapsychic as well as the extrapsychic effects of his expressed associations and behavior while affording him the encouragement to go on to further free associations.

In the analytic dyad, the analyst does not

usually react with his own distorted intra-psychic thoughts and feelings to the patient's productions. In this respect the analysand has very few occasions to evolve a perceptivity to the requirements of the other. For some years a psychologist has been giving projective tests to the authors' patients. By the patients' awareness of the other during these tests, the psychologist has been able to detect with fine discrimination which of them have been in group analysis and often for how long. One of the results of effective analytic therapy ought to be not only self-understanding but also conscious-ness of and consideration for others.

The dyadic analyst often rejects the patient's reactions to him as distorted, projective, and transferential. He tends to interpret the patient's impressions of him as genetically predetermined and, therefore, irrelevant to the present, to the analyst as provocateur. Too often, this assumption is misleading. The impact of imposing such unreality is that the patient becomes too insulated and uninvolved with the other.

Consider the patient on the couch who protested to his analyst that he was not listening, that he was unresponsive. The therapist, in turn, accused the patient of being overly suspicious and distrustful, of demanding excessive attention like a spoiled child. At this point, the patient sat up on the couch and faced the analyst, who was dis-covered answering his mail. This example shows how a therapist can misuse his role. The patient was, in fact, aware of reality, and the analyst was telling the patient that his real perceptions were a distortion. No group therapist could succeed with such a misrepresentation of reality.

Forced interaction in the group is fol-lowed by analysis of the intrapsychic ma-terial. This process is not available in dyadic analysis, where the therapist cannot engage the analysand with the affective intensity of co-patients. If a patient in one-to-one treatment is encouraged to free-associate too extensively, his intrapsychic preoccupation may produce an excess of self-involvement and withdrawal. Dyadic analysis is a protracted self-examination that can become too self-solicitous, self-inaugura-tive, and self-echoing if the therapist is largely scrutinizing and rarely interactive. One-to-one analysis is often an experience in relative isolation with little responsive ac-knowledgment.

Some group leaders focus now on one patient, now on another, conducting in-dividual treatment in the group. But this is not the way the authors practice psycho-analysis in groups. They prefer to explore the patient in his interaction with fellow group members, his nuclear and current families, his analyst, and his colleagues and friends beyond the confines of the group. Furthermore, analysis in a group is not a version of social psychology or group psycho-dynamics. In dyadic analysis, whatever interaction takes place during treatment sessions occurs between patient and thera-pist, and the patient's relationship to the analyst tends to be the primary focus. More useful one-to-one analysis is also concerned with the patient's involvement with mem-bers of his family and with his friends. The individual analyst's view of the patient is limited by the fact that he sees only the interaction between the patient and himself. Group members provide each other with multiple possibilities for interrelatedness, which enables the analyst to see the pa-tient's larger, faceted self. Also, the thera-pist is removed from the interaction, free-ing him to an extent from the subjective distortions to which he is liable when he is more directly involved.

Forced Interaction

The patient in individual analysis may easily preserve his tendency to noninvolve-ment because the analyst maintains a scrutinizing function without the charac-teristic give-and-take of group members. It is a formidable task to stand apart in the analytic group, where patients induce and encourage one another into mutual response. The leader is commonly less active and less vigorous in enjoining change, for the patient may misperceive such pointedness as disap-proval or as a decree to which he is required to submit. The analyst may hesitate to be aggressive, out of concern that his precon-ceived, organized design for treatment may become confused.

The analysand, in a dependent relationship to the analyst, sees no anxiety-free alternative to his symbiosis. In the evolution of his neurotic adaptation, he has acquired a series of complementary neurotics who mesh, interlock, and feed his archaic needs. The proposal that he give up his maladaptive ways to persons with whom he has always maintained these patterns is very alarming to him. His complementary neurotics may resist his attempts at a different adaptation because his disturbed behavior better meets their own antiquated needs. They may not accept a change in the character of their relationship. They advise against and try to prevent a healthier way of behaving.

In the analytic group, members are quite forceful in pressing for choices and activity other than the old and outmoded. They assert strongly and repeatedly in favor of a search for new ways and new enterprises. They present the patient with samples of success in new ventures. They stimulate novel points of view and new feelings that are not kindled by the analyst. In the heterogeneous group, multiple appropriate and inappropriate suggestions are made for different alternatives to the pathology. Patients tender and advocate diverse and workable possibilities. They urge on each other more mutuality and less childlike affective attachment to the analyst. As a result, greater persuasion and influence are brought to bear on the patient to take positive action.

The alternate meeting also promotes novel opportunities for interrelation because the observing parent surrogate is not present. Here, too, there is a working through of the symbiotic tie to the therapist as new adaptations are attempted without his continuous support. His absence leaves room for patients to compete for leadership. At regular meetings, patients tend to be less interactive than at alternate meetings, and they may pursue a relationship with the analyst. The presence of co-patients forces them to be competitive for his recognition and analysis.

In dyadic treatment the patient may live comfortably in the mistaken belief that he and he alone has the therapist's total regard, unless the reality strikes him that the analyst also attends other patients. Because of the presence of multiple peers in the group, the occasion and expedience for developing a deep transference neurosis to the therapist are more circumscribed. The co-patients, by direct action in undertaking new alternatives, demonstrate to the less venturesome patient more wholesome choices than regression. Their manifest example is often more stimulating than the therapist's suggestion that the patient has the right to choose rather than compulsively repeat. Forced interaction induces the group analysand into a multiplicity of roles. To the extent the analyst is reasonably flexible and to the extent patients play a variety of roles, more wholesome and more morbid responses become manifest. The patient learns to assume different roles and to accept multiple differences in others and in himself. This development expands his personality. Forced interaction, alternation in roles, the acceptance of differences, and heterogeneity are interconnected.

Multiple Reactivities

Multiple reactivity, a characteristic of group therapy, is given fuller play in a heterogeneous than in a homogeneous group. It is not present in the dyad except to the extent the therapist is able to evoke diversified reactions. It is available indirectly in the dyad when the patient talks of his responses to persons outside the treatment milieu. But then the therapist is required to see through the analysand's subjective distortions in his accounts of events outside the consulting room. In the group the analyst is a direct observer of how the patient reacts to others in a multiplicity of situations. Through the variety of their provocations, the group members evoke a larger picture of the patient's disorder. At the same time, they call for a more inclusive reconstruction in the face of a greater variety of appropriate and inappropriate expectations.

The patient in a group has an opportunity to take part in an invaluable exercise not available in the dyad. He becomes aware that all people do not necessarily react as he does to the same provocation. He finds that, when he feels one way, others feel differently; when he wants to share a feeling, another person wants to retire in self-examination; when he is feeling warm, the object of his empathy is about to castigate him for his offensiveness during a previous encounter. But he does not learn that there is never any complementarity of interaction. He learns, in fact, that there are as many mutually responsive interactions as antagonistic ones.

Multiple Transferences

The analytic group speedily and successively furnishes the patient with a number of evocative stand-ins who excite multiple transferences more readily than the analyst alone. Each group member invests every other member with a variety of transferences in the course of every group session. In dyadic treatment such a variety of misperceptions of the analyst does not occur in a given therapeutic hour. The fluctuating distortions in the group follow from the multiple interaction in which the relationships among members change from time to time. Transference is more inflexible in dyadic analysis. Similar shifting of transferences to the analyst may be seen in one-to-one treatment only if the patient is very unstable.

Some patients homogenize the whole group into a single transferential figure. This coalescence is a phenomenon that, of course, does not occur in individual treatment, at least not in the treatment setting. When it occurs in the group, the members are misperceived as one parent and the analyst as the other. Very likely, similar distortions are made in social situations, but the individual analysand is generally not aware of them. The distortions can be dealt with in the group, since the difficulty becomes manifest. The patients must be urged to react to the other members as individuals, to distinguish one patient from the other, to look for differences in them, to see them in reality.

Sibling Transferences. In dyadic analysis, parental transference is usually the prevailing distortion. Transferences to siblings tend to be disregarded or casually discussed as being less noxious because they do not as a rule manifest themselves in the same deeply felt way. In the analytic group the presence of peers provides the stimulation for the evocation of sibling transferences, and they can be readily seen, examined, and resolved. The availability of peers provides the opportunity to work out and work through problems with members of the family beyond the parents. Group members are not always perceived as familial surrogates, but, because this distortion is a generally recurrent finding, it needs to be looked for.

Parental Transferences to Peers. Transferences to peers may have a parental as well as a sibling quality. The investment of co-patients with mother and father distortions is usually experienced as less formidable than when the therapist is perceived as a symbolic parent. Because the peers are also perceived in reality as less authority-laden than the analyst, the parental transferences to them are less intense and more easily resolved. Some patients who assume aggressive or dominating roles may elicit strong parental transferences, but even here the awareness of their relative equality in reality as peers reduces the distortive predisposition. The preliminary experiencing and working through of mother and father distortions invested in peers makes it easier to resolve the same distortion when patients begin to undertake, as a later experience, the resolution of the more difficult parental transference to the analyst seen in the hierarchical vector.

Transferences to the Therapist. In the group setting, the transferences to the therapist are more fixed than those made to co-patients. Transferences are more stable with relation to the analyst because his role is more consistent than that of the patient, who plays multiple roles and elicits, therefore, a multiplicity of transferences. In dyadic analysis, transferences to persons other than the therapist are only approximately or inaccurately understood because the analyst is dependent on the patient's filtered reports of interpersonal exchanges. In the group, these same transferences are present within the treatment setup. Transference to the therapist is less attended at first because patients find it easier to work whatever distortions they make with peers seen in the hierarchical vector than with the reinforced authority of the analyst. In dyadic treatment as well, if the analyst first works out and resolves transferences toward persons in the patient's life outside the consulting room, it then becomes less difficult to work through transference to the therapist. If the strategy is transposed, if the analyst tries to work out and work through transference to him as an introductory procedure, he usually encounters greater resistance.

Countertransference. No analyst is totally free of transference or countertransference involvement. To the degree it is present, the therapist experiences trials and crises in his struggle to understand the patient and to see him objectively. In the group, the analyst's inappropriate behavior is more quickly seen by patients, who demand more germane responses from him. As a result, there is protection against the misperceptions of the analyst. A patient alone with such a therapist has no co-patient allies to support him in confirming his belief that the analyst is distorting reality.

Occasionally, the therapist's countertransferential difficulty takes the form of compulsively trying to induce a transference neurosis in the patient. By so binding the patient to him in a symbiotic tie, he may in some instances remove the patient from productive and invigorating relations with his peers. The analytic group tends to counteract such exploitation.

Analysis of Transference. Transference is dealt with somewhat differently in individual analysis and in group analysis. In dyadic treatment, the analysis of transference tends to be one of the major functions of the therapist. The patient often plays a lesser part in this activity. In the group, however, patients call attention to each other's misperceptions and make proposals for more realistic alternative ways of functioning.

If a patient suggests to his individual analyst that he, the therapist, is in transference or countertransference, the analyst may become defensive and irritated. He may then accuse the patient of trying to reverse roles or otherwise suggest that the analysand is distorting the facts. A member of a group may also reject the suggestion that he is in transference, but he is more likely to accept the interpretation, especially when the transferences are seen as bilateral or trilateral, as they almost always are among interactive patients. This willingness among group members to consider and admit to their multilateral distortions refines and enriches the insight into the multilateral nature of transference. The provocative nature of each member in eliciting the transference of each patient is observed more clearly in the group than in dyadic analysis, where the therapist is more reluctant to admit to his inciting role. This denial cannot be so readily maintained in the group in the face of a number of patients concertedly pointing out how his behavior provoked a particular patient response.

In the group, transferences are generally interpreted as bilateral or trilateral. In individual analysis they are generally analyzed as emanating only from the patient. The therapist is supposed not to transfer or countertransfer, which is an illusion.

In dyadic analysis, the rigidity of transference generally exceeds its duration in the group. Its persistence in individual treatment is promoted by the one-to-one situation and the separation from peers, inducing thereby a sometimes persistent and prolonged transference neurosis or psychosis. In the group, patients are invested with mother-surrogate and father-surrogate distortions, but, because they are also seen in reality in the horizontal vector and because they can move so freely in reacting subjectively from one patient to another, their transferential misperceptions are less virulent, more moderate, more yielding, more readily relinquished for reasonable alternatives. Quantitatively and qualitatively, patient-to-patient transference is different from that of patient-to-analyst.

Displacement

Group members frequently displace affect onto one another as a means of evading their responses to the analyst. This displacement is both expedient and resistive. An individual analysand may describe his attitude toward a person outside the treatment room, when, in fact, he is reporting how he feels about the analyst. In the group, a member may in the same way be responding to a fellow patient or to all his co-patients as stand-ins for the therapist. There is greater likelihood of secreting displacement in dyadic analysis because the inciting cause that leads to such proxy formation is often not discernible.

Support

A patient experiences a greater sense of security in a group because there is a probability there of finding co-patients who encourage his healthy or disturbed aspirations. The analysand in a dyad is usually less sure of getting support for his strivings when he is dependent on only one other person.

Relief and assistance are necessary requirements in all treatment. They are means by which the faltering resources of a patient may be promoted. By having his positive potentials encouraged, the analysand is stirred to show his disorder, his pathology, his gradually recalled history, and his suppressed feeling. The analyst's support is circumscribed because it is derived from the hierarchical position and because it is offered in kind, in degree, in quality and quantity that he believes to be relevant and required. He may deny offering this relief in the concern that it may deepen the patients' symbiosis.

In the group, sustenance is derived from other patients as well as from the analyst. The helpful function of co-patients is particularly apparent at the alternate meeting. Members often reveal problems there for the first time. Then only through the support of fellow patients is the exposed material presented at the regular session with the analyst. Some members need to be encouraged by the analyst in the dyad before they are able to reveal certain difficult history or problems in the group. There are more chances of finding greater and various kinds of support in the dyad or the group in multiple therapeutic settings. The patients and the analyst offer different kinds of help. Co-patients' support is more spontaneous, more impulsive, more compulsive. The analyst's is more purposeful, more useful, more discriminatingly applied.

Human beings are, in general, ready to extend themselves to someone in need. The patient in a group is an observer of a co-patient's unhappiness. The open or guarded emotional display of a problem usually evokes an affective reaction. The patient in anxiety who looks to his fellows for support, who verbally or nonverbally appeals to them for help, is generally not resisted but analyzed. Group members generally try to alleviate one another's distress with a sincerity that is as artless as a cry of suffering.

A sense of well-being achieved by a patient in the mutually supportive struggle to get well makes the members feel closer to one another. The distressed patient needs more than compassion for his suffering; besides understanding and insight, he needs reassurance. There is, however, the hazard that in a readiness to offer support, one may promote in a member the tendency to appear in pain in order to get consideration.

Such a maneuver may lead co-patients to reject the claims of the victim, particularly if he agonizes obsessively. One encounters members who respond to all expressions of disturbed feeling as simulated and dishonest. They seem not to be able to tolerate vexation, sadness, or tears. At the other extreme are patients who are compulsively supportive and serving. Their obsessive need always to come to the assistance of others in distress requires analysis.

A patient seldom stands alone in a therapeutic group. If he is in need of emotional support, usually one or more members stand by him. If he is masochistic, he may manage to arouse a good deal of aggression in other patients. If a patient is generally criticized by the group and has no ally, the therapist may have to support him.

A schizophrenic young woman entered a group but remained silent for four months. Invitations to participate were useless. All efforts to engage her failed. At about the start of her fifth month in the group, one of the more vocal and aggressive patients said:

I've had enough of your silence. If you won't participate for yourself, I want you to speak and react to me. You're of no use to us or yourself as you are; you're deadwood in the group. You're either going to talk tonight or I'm going to drive you out of the group. We've treated you gently up to now—like a baby lamb. Tonight it's different. Talk or get out!

Gradually, one after another, the group members joined him in the demand that she speak. These demands went on for half an hour.

The analyst noted that the patient was flushed, perspiring, tremulous about the mouth. He was the only one who knew the seriousness of her diagnosis, and he felt a mounting concern that her ego might not be sufficiently strong to withstand such concerted verbal assault. Accordingly, he suggested that perhaps the others postpone their pressure until another meeting, since the patient seemed unable to respond. The group reacted angrily by telling him the devil could take him and turned on the patient once more. The analyst was startled to hear the patient shout at him:

Yes, drop dead! This is the first time they've shown so much interest in me—and you try to stop them!

Then she burst into tears. Shortly afterward, she began to talk and became a verbally active member of the group. The analyst was relieved that she was able to participate.

Although the analyst at first thought the patient needed an ally against the group, he was only too glad to discover that the patient did not need his support in this situation. There are, however, other instances when it is advisable to put out feelers to see whether a particular patient is able to handle himself in the face of group aggression.

The most moving experience in the group is not the comfort offered to the ailing but the attainment of fulfillment in reality, the triumph over the neurotic adaptation, the conscious alternative choice over the obsessive one. It is a moment that comes when the previously estranged group members accept and enjoy one another, when they treat each other like human beings instead of brutes.

Some members try to hide or suppress their feelings, fearful that the emergence of affect may be regarded as a sign of pretense or inadequacy. In reality, at bottom most patients seem to wish one another well. But too often patients are reluctant to admit this because the expression of warmth is sometimes looked on as sentimental. Such feeling leaves the patient in a vulnerable position. This secreted but sooner or later manifest wish for mutual gratification and success in reality is an influence in the group that makes patients in part restorative for each other.

Aware that basically there exists in all his patients a hope for mutual growth, good will, and maturation, the analyst plumbs for this response whenever it is appropriate to do so. He tries not to allow a meeting to conclude in generalized sadness over the dejection of a member near the end of a session. The leader does not simply attempt to cover the depression among the patients with a rallying and inspirational buoyancy that would be out of place. He may, however, agree that the immediate bleakness is indeed saddening but not without some hope of resolution. If his intervention is effective, the session ends on a more promising than painful note. Rather than obsessively trying to end each meeting in optimism, the analyst needs to promote the feeling that he and his patients are not caught in everlasting failure simply because of the present discouragement, that there is opportunity ahead for more work together, that they shall before long find their way out of their current trouble and disquiet.

The analyst may point out, when necessary, the basic existence in each patient of a persistent longing for a richer life that enables him to endure the present adversity. In this way, the end of a session holds some hope for a return to the beginning of the following meeting. Just as the analyst cannot assure a member of absolute satisfaction at the end of therapy, he cannot terminate every meeting in gladness. What he can do is assure his constancy of effort and skill. He can persuade the patients of the value of struggle that will make his efforts more fulfilling at the end. In part, he can support the analysand by demonstrating how the patient's past history, repeated in the here-and-now, inevitably leads to frustration. By choosing a more reasonable alternative, the patient can escape his repetition-compulsion. The therapist need not emphasize only the past or present; he can point to a more positive future, with less disability and failure. He can underscore the temporary nature of current disillusionment, which need not prevail in time to come. In this struggle there are usually co-patients whose reassurance can be depended on for support.

Interpretation

The analyst guides the group members from multiple interaction to the search for unconscious motivation, from the manifest to the latent. By this means the historical bases for the activity is brought into consciousness. Patients who object to the movement from manifest behavior to the investigation of unconscious motivation and persist merely in catharsis or verbal acting out of affective interaction are in resistance. When they accept the idea of the relevance of the latent material, they begin to offer interpretations of their own. Some of these interpretations are most valuable. In the main, however, they are not systematically timed. An analyst may carefully consider when to introduce an interpretation, but a patient reacting spontaneously is liable to be wild, and a poorly timed interpretation is only partially heard or not heard at all.

Accountability

The patient in individual analysis is generally not held accountable for his wildest fantasies of love or hate, of sexuality or homicide. The analyst fosters this illusion to enable the patient to speak freely and regress with the assurance of support and without fear of retaliation. No such security in illusion is available in the group. Expressed fantasies, dreams, thoughts, and feelings are met with all sorts of emotional reactions: fear, anger, rivalry, hostility, rage, anxiety, sensuality, etc. This responsiveness makes each member aware that, although he is always free to say what comes to mind and heart, he is accountable for what he says and does.

There is, therefore, more at stake in speaking up in the group. It becomes more hazardous, for there are always consequences. The wonder is that patients nevertheless do speak up. They always have allies, frequently the very members to whom they are being reactive. This setup is much more reality-oriented than is the individual setting, where the benignity of the analyst sponsors the illusion of nonaccountability.

In a way, it is dangerously irresponsible for the therapist to permit this kind of illusion to go on for too long without limiting

it, without showing the patient the consequences of his thoughts and feelings, especially if he tends to express them or act them out beyond the consulting room. The analyst's leniency, permissiveness, and forbearance cannot be limitless. Group members quite appropriately hold each other responsible. This is salutary, for it seems to be more realistic to do so. At the same time, group members are enormously tolerant in the recognition of the value of regression as long as it is in the service of the ego. The nonisolatedness of the interaction in a group, when compared with the dyadic setting, supports the need to be aware of the other, the necessity to maintain communication. If treatment deprives a patient of awareness of the consequences of his expressions, it denies him orientation, a place among his fellows, an ego. Whatever he says becomes a whisper lost in the wind, and he becomes equally uncertain of his place.

The emotional storms of individual analysis in the security of the therapist's tolerance do not produce the impact often seen in the group. One result of this difference in the two settings is that group patients become readier to take their chances to say what needs to be said, with awareness of the risk.

The demand that members in groups be accountable to one another is a humanizing value. Although patients are encouraged to speak up, they should also be responsible for what they say. The investment of transference in one another tends to make one misperceive the other, in some instances as the authoritarian parent who must be aggressively dethroned. The patient is asked to see in his parent-surrogate group member a person with an internalized, abused childself. The therapist asks his patients to find in one another not only the destructive authoritarian parental figure but some realistic, legitimate authority who is entitled to rights and privileges.

Group analysis cultivates a sense of social responsibility among patients. This is one of its values. The conditions that the dyadic therapist demands of the analysand relate mostly to paying a fee, not physically hurting the analyst, and not damaging his furniture and books. The largely tolerant stance of the analyst occasionally institutes or maintains in the analysand a frustrating inclination to take favor as his due and to complain if it is not always as immediately available as a pacifier. If the analyst does not frustrate and analyze this inappropriate anticipation, the exploitative patient's abrasive and inordinate claims for support are intensified. In the group no member can maintain such exemption from obligation without protest from the others. This protest is wholesome. The demanding, dependent patient is required to react with increasing resourcefulness, autonomy, and responsibility if he hopes to develop better relations with others. This pressure to relinquish the dependent tie to a parent surrogate is a valuable influence in resolving a persistent transference neurosis.

Control

Psychoanalysis in a group would become untenable and dissolve if every member were emboldened to act impulsively on every flash of feeling or thought. The group limits acting out that endangers the mutual effort to resist the gratification of archaic longings. And it is necessary to limit certain activities to meet the needs for some social order in the group.

Impulsivity and compulsivity require a study of just how, when, and where this insufficiency or excess of inhibition developed. If few controls were imposed on a patient by his nuclear family, he may choose an individual analyst in the hope that the surrogate parent may likewise exercise little discipline. If the inducement to acting out took place with nonfamilial figures outside the home, he may choose group therapy. Or the opposite may turn out to be the case. The patient may choose an individual analyst in the wish to find a parental substitute who will limit his impulsivity, his pathological repetition. If the peers in the nuclear family insufficiently controlled him, he may seek in group therapy peers who will help to limit him.

Repetitive Patterns and Flexibility

Repetitive patterns may become apparent in dyadic analysis before they do in a group.

This is true in part because the analyst tends to be more experienced as a single parental surrogate. Therefore, the repetitive transferential distortion manifests itself more obviously in dyadic analysis. But transferences also emerge in the group. They appear, however, in more variety because more transference figures are available from the outset. Because of their multiplicity, it may seem, at first, more difficult to designate the various transferences in the group. As a result, the impression may be that the patient has less rigidity than was at first thought. But the fact is that in the group he is exposing a larger variety of transference reactions. As treatment goes on, the inflexibility of these transferences becomes clearer.

In dyadic analysis, the patient is not required to make many flexible adaptations to the changing expectations of persons. The individual analyst does not usually make the multiple demands for health that members of the group do. Of course, they also have irrational expectations of mutual adjustment to one another's pathology.

Dyadic analysis tends to expedite the development of transference. One-to-one treatment promotes the evocation of repetitive patterns with the idea that an unvarying relationship between patient and therapist is essential to ultimate change. Diversified responses tend to be regarded as resistive to the repetition of transference and its final resolution. The individual therapist sees the constancy, regularity, and routine of characteristic distortion as the essential basis for therapeutic intervention.

The dyadic analyst, therefore, is doubtful about the value of psychoanalysis in a group, since uniformity of response seems not to occur, group patients appear not to persevere in their reactions. The analyst may believe there is too little assurance in foreseeing how patients will respond to one provocation or another. But if he affords himself any clinical experience in a group, he encounters a real and characteristic continuity of reaction in each patient, even among the most heterogeneously stimulating membership.

The heterogeneity of a group makes room for the patients' more flexible choices. For the impulsive member there are patients whose rigidity helps him to exercise greater control. For the superego-ridden member there are patients in the group who support his right to allow himself more privilege. The mutual support of peers provides a less severe and more permissive influence than the illusory and actual authority of the analyst, whose interventions are experienced as more unequivocal.

The coexistent and synchronous presence of horizontal and vertical vectors is also a factor that promotes flexibility in response. If only one of these dimensions is available, as in dyadic analysis or in a leaderless group, there is less flexibility and greater rigidity.

Hierarchical and Peer Vectors

The phenomenon of transference in psychoanalysis in groups can be made more intelligible if one understands that the group provides for the simultaneous presence of peer and hierarchical relationships. By supplying a lateral vector as well as the vertical vector found in dyadic analysis, psychoanalysis in groups provides the patient with the freedom to relate to peers. These horizontal relationships may be facile or awkward, depending on each member's past history. One common dilemma with sibling surrogates involves rivalry.

In dyadic treatment, the vertical dimension prevails, with the analyst seen as a parent surrogate. In the power-invested one-to-one climate, it may not be easy for the analysand to convey what he would like to say. In a group, the access of peers in some measure shrinks the ominous influence of the leader, and interaction among the members is usually freer. However, the opposite may occur. The analyst may be easier to talk to than the co-patients. A patient may coalesce the members into a single parental surrogate figure so that even fellow patients are misperceived as being in the vertical vector.

If the analyst is dogmatic, the peers support each other judiciously and injudiciously in defying his predominance. For some of the patients, this support is salutary; for others, it is obsessive. In any event, it challenges the analyst, who is thereby less able to dominate the membership of the group.

Effective treatment leads to a sense of equality between patient and analyst. But actual parity cannot be achieved in dyadic analysis. It can, on the other hand, be accomplished with one's peers in a group setting. The achievement of a sense of equality in the group enlarges the hope and the feasibility of parity between analysand and analyst. In dyadic treatment, where the patient is always being assisted by the analyst, a healthy sense of equality in difference is more difficult to achieve. Fortunately, only a few dyadic therapists regard the patient as infantile and helpless and see themselves as models—dead certain and infallible. In the act of practicing psychoanalysis in groups, the therapist rejects such assumptions about his patients and himself. He sees wholesome potentials and sources of help among group members. He does not see himself as the only source of assistance, insight, innovation, and inducement to healthful change.

The dyadic therapist's all-knowing position tends to sponsor illusion. Because he is the only other person available to the patient, the latter is dependent on the analyst's views. The analysand has only the therapist's associations for testing reality. Group members, however, provide multiple others to define the nature of reality and of unreality.

Equality, Freedom, and Hostility

Whenever there is superiority and inferiority among persons, with limited independence for the inferior, enmity and hatred can be anticipated. Disaffection occurs when impartial opportunity is not available. The vertical character of dyadic treatment denies the analysand's feeling of parity. If the analyst stresses the analysand's disorder, the patient more than ever feels disparate, inadequate.

Parity, independence, and freedom are more readily experienced in the group. There, patients have more room to ventilate, less acute anger, more empathy, more compassion, and more realistically positive affect than in the dyad, where angry and warm feelings are more commonly dependent, childlike, and distorted—that is, one-sided.

On occasion, however, members of groups are inappropriately harsh and cruel with one another. The authors do not subscribe to the view that good treatment must entail trial and punishment. The adherents of such a principle, whether patients or therapists, have residual unresolved sadomasochistic difficulties. The aggressor is acting out a negative transference and his prey a compliant one. When this phenomenon takes place in a group, the therapist must analyze the bilateral distortions early to save the participants from damaging one another. Tolerance and compassion cannot develop during prolonged mutual attack. They grow only in a more wholesome atmosphere. Repetitive anger does not lead to mutual regard unless a member has never been allowed to express negative feelings. But if he is encouraged to ventilate his hostility, he will later be obliged to redeem himself, before other patients will trust his good will. Malice is usually met with resentment, open or concealed. The group analyst needs to be watchful for ways and means to deal with the disorder of hate.

Retaliation and Fulfillment

In the psychoanalytic group there is more response to both transferential and realistic expectations. It is the analyst's function to analyze the mutually hurtful character of bilaterally fulfilling archaic needs and to promote the gratification of more realistic requirements. The illusory exemption from retribution and the frustration of antiquated expectation that theoretically prevail in dyadic analysis may not always be a salutary influence. The analyst's need to overprotect a patient from his peers has something to do with his concern that they will damage each other. Patients, in fact, turn out to be not so hurtful. They demonstrate their healthy resources and their potential for growth in the decent and tolerant ways they treat each other.

There is an inclination in some quarters to regard the interaction between patients as just as significant and valuable as that between analyst and patient. Interaction among group members is generally less intense. In dyadic and group analysis, the authority of the leader is both real and illusory. To regard the leadership of the therapist in the dyad as an illusion and the authority of co-patients as genuine, or the opposite, is to misconstrue the quality of leadership in the dyadic and group settings.

Psychoanalysis in groups is effective because, in part, it does not deny the participant his freedom to examine his many-faceted affect about genuine and illusory hierarchical figures and peers. He has more of a chance in a group to retort and to gratify himself in fact and in fantasy in both the peer and hierarchical vectors. These gratifications, both wholesome and sick, in which he is supporter and supported, heard and hearing among his fellows, have an important place in group analysis.

Genetic and Current Material

Interaction among patients followed by free association often leads to the recollection of significant genetic material. Either the interaction spontaneously generates free association, or the analyst promotes it. By this means, history is made available in the group, unless the analyst or the resistive patient rejects it for an exclusively here-and-now experience. At times, the therapist may have to initiate the process of cultivating an interest in free association to early derivatives and their history, the relevance of the past to its repetition in the present. If the analyst evades this responsibility, the patients will also do so and become less resistively involved in here-and-now expressions of affect, thought, and behavior.

In dyadic analysis, preoccupation with current events in the patient's life outside of the therapeutic milieu is resistive. In the dyad, the interaction is largely in terms of transference and the emerging transference neurosis. In the group, current events in and outside of therapy play an integral part in analysis. The impromptu thought and feeling, the extemporaneous, the present occasion are subject to examination and are explored for understanding. In the dyad, even in responses to the analyst, the preoccupation is with history, partly on theoretical grounds, partly because the therapist believes he cannot or should not interact.

Data

In dyadic analysis, the material for study is provided as a sequel to the actual event—

that is, it is furnished out of recollection of the experience. The only original and verifiable data that are experienced are provided in the patient's responses to the analyst. In the group, the stuff of analysis is available not only in terms of historical recollection but also on the basis of interaction with co-patients. The accent in the group is on bilateral interaction, which is then enlisted for understanding the unconscious urges and motives that generated it. The engaged group members join in an exploration and analysis of the shared experience. In dyadic analysis, an interaction outside the treatment room can be comprehended only by hindsight. In the group, the participants can be seen in action, direct observation can be made of how the episode began, and a detailed study can be made of the motives of the provocateur as well as those of the reactor. Group members tend to object to overlong, repeated stories, whether historical or current in nature. In the therapeutic dyad, an obsessive concern with the analyst can also turn into an insulating, symbiotic, and illusory experience.

Some therapists, even group therapists, think they can get to know their patients in greater depth only in the dyad. An issue to be raised here concerns what they learn more about. Another issue is whether the material that emerges is more useful in treatment when it becomes available in the dyad. There is no question that the analyst can learn more about certain things in the one-to-one setting. But he can discover still other things in the group, things that may escape him in the dyad. It should be noted, however, that the order of data is different in the two settings.

The dyadic analyst is denied by the one-to-one relationship a full view of the patient. He does not experience the analysand in the many-faceted interactions provoked by other people. He is not an actual observer of the patient in response to his fellows. He has not available for direct examination the multiple transferences that more totally characterize a patient. Nor is he fully aware of his analysand's positive potentials in the wholesome ways he relates to others. The therapist tends to see his patient as more dependent than he is because the analyst is always in the hierarchical status of helper to a needy person. On the other hand, in the group each patient is expected at various times to come to the support of a co-patient. Being a helper is a new role for a patient in treatment, one that reveals a fresh facet, previously unknown to the analyst—a capacity to sustain, refresh, and offer understanding to another, which in some respects is reparative to the helpmate in its ego-building quality.

Resistances and Defenses

Resistance yields more readily to psychoanalysis in a group. Patients directly challenge one another's resistive maneuvers. They do not permit a member to escape in sleep. They do not for long permit a non-participant to continue silent. They vigorously demand an end to resistive operations. They push for change and new activity, demand interaction, object to anyone's retirement or dominance and to obsessive intrapsychic preoccupation or grossly fantastic ways of nonrelating. They press for coexistence, verbal intercourse, plain speaking.

By sustaining and criticizing one another, patients penetrate defenses more readily. Some therapists believe that defenses are weakened under attack in the group but that the anxiety underlying these defenses needs to be analyzed only in the dyad. The analyst in a group may on occasion be obliged to support a defense at a particular moment. But the idea that defenses may be resolved in the group but the subjacent anxiety may not seems to be a fallacious view of the nature of the group experience. In the dyad, the technical skill and timing required for dealing with defenses are the analyst's. In the group, the breaching of defenses of certain patients often promotes corresponding breaches among the more defended, who experience vicariously the understanding, progress, and working through of the need to maintain certain inappropriate defenses.

Silence

Therapists are familiar with the resistive significance of silence and are usually impatient with it. However, it has other dimensions in the group. Silence is not necessarily resistive; on occasion, it represents periods of renewal, integration, meditation, or deep feeling without the need to express, act, or respond immediately to the other. While one member is quietly examining a problem by himself, another may be unavailable in resistance. Still another may be too apprehensive of exploration for the moment, and two others may be involved in an intense interaction and invite analytic inquiry. The group analyst can turn productively from one patient to another while some are provisionally silent.

If an analysand is making himself known and requires a listening silence, it is necessary for the analyst to be quiet. His inactive attention is required by the patient as an act complementary to his own. The analyst's being quiet looks like passivity on a manifest level. It is, in fact, his chosen activity appropriate to the patient's needs.

Anxiety

Anxiety emerges when defenses or resistances are attacked or dissolved. Some patients feel little apprehension in the bipersonal situation but are obviously threatened at the idea of entering a group. Often they are symbiotically tied to a mother surrogate and fearful of the environment and persons apart from her. Other patients who were historically in dis-ease in the nuclear family or with an original parental figure and more secure in circumstances outside the family frequently find the group more reassuring than the analyst alone. They appreciate the alternate meeting more than the session when the analyst is there. The therapist may feel the same way. Depending on his original history, he may be more or less nervous in the dyadic or in the group situation. The analysand needs to be encouraged to examine the source of his anxiety and to resolve it in the setting he experiences it. If he does not do this, he is liable to avoid the circumstances in which he develops anxiety, evade confrontation, and escape resolution.

Every patient experiences anxiety. The therapist needs to know whether his apprehension is determined by realistic perception or by transference. Psychoanalysis in groups provides three means for the elucidation of transference, the anxiety associated with it, and the defensive operations used to suppress the anxiety: the consultation with the analyst alone, the regular meeting, and the alternate session. In these three settings the therapist can examine the differences in anxiety in various transferential relations.

In dyadic analysis, there is anxiety in the transferential impression of threat from the analyst as parent, generally the mother. A sense of being threatened by forces outside the analytic situation, whether in fact or in illusion, is derived from the patient's associations. In the dyad, it is hoped that the analysand will become conscious of his anxiety in the society external to the analysis and that he will be disinhibited enough with his therapist to tell him of his feelings. In the dyad, there is a greater need to become aware of anxiety stirred beyond the couch; in the group, anxiety can be revealed more easily and quickly in the course of interaction.

Some patients are more anxious in the dyad and more relaxed in the group. Alone with the analyst, they are more apprehensive about closeness to the parental surrogate, about his intensive scrutiny of their strong and ambivalent feelings about him, about the possibility of isolation with him and its attendant regressive possibilities. In the group, there is more hope of flight from exploration and, as a result, less anxiety. For other patients, the co-patient peers are more anxiety-provoking. It may be that for most patients, given a choice of milieu, they would choose the dyad over the group as less anxiety-inducing. The belief that in the group there will be less skillful intervention, less benevolence, and more eruption impels most patients to seek individual treatment. In some measure, a patient's choice of milieu is dependent on his history with parents and siblings as well as on currently popular styles of therapeutic intervention.

Shifting Attention

The experience of attention shifting from one member to another in psychoanalysis in groups diminishes anxiety by providing respites from exclusive and sometimes oppressive examination. In dyadic analysis, the patient is continuously under scrutiny. This scrutiny may produce defensiveness, resistance, a reaction to analytic pressure that can at times be incapacitating. The group, on the other hand, permits the patient periods of time for repose—to reflect on what he has just previously experienced, to consider what interpretations have been made to him, to speculate on alternatives in the process of working through—and, after being helped, he can turn to others and offer help. The shifting of attention is itself an alternative way of conducting oneself. It confronts the patient with the reality that he need not compulsively engage in a limited kind of activity.

Alternating scrutiny gives the patient an opportunity to show himself at a speed that is not too overwhelmingly anxiety-provoking for him. In the therapeutic dyad, he is under continuous scrutiny, required to expose himself. In the group, shifting attention away from him without the on-going expectation that he make himself known may provide opportunities for resistance.

Timing

One criticism of group analysis is that a member may awkwardly or discordantly offer some insight that the recipient is by no means prepared to accept at the time. The judgment is made that a precipitate or untimely offer of understanding may be too hurtful to a patient who may not be able to cope with the anxiety provoked by the confrontation. The authors' experience is that group members are, in general, able to deal with insights offered by co-patients either by resisting them or by gradually accepting them. When the therapist errs in the timing of a confrontation, the analysand becomes more disturbed because the understanding comes from a figure in authority.

The analyst in groups soon learns that it is not he alone who has the delicate touch, the exquisite empathy to know just when and how to offer insight. Surely some members are at first indifferent and unconcerned with others, but a larger number have from the start a sensitivity to their feelings. At times the analyst may be overprotective with a patient in the group, doubtful about his capacity to tolerate some newly offered interpretation. He may under such circumstances inappropriately postpone the acquisition of insight.

A co-patient does not have the expertness in timing interpretations that the skilled analyst has. But it is a common experience to find untrained members making very valuable observations about one another with an intuition and an acuity that are surprising. It is not that psychoanalytic theory and practice just come naturally to them. It is their good sense, directness, spontaneity, naturalness, enthusiasm, and artlessness, free of analytic jargon, and their obvious wish to help that give them the capacity to be reparative. The affective pitch of reaction is also a factor in their reaching one another.

In dyadic analysis, it is the therapist's exclusive jurisdiction and responsibility to determine when to offer a piece of insight. His mistakes in timing are burdened with his authority. Excitation, insight, and confrontation by group members are both more readily resisted and at times more welcomed because they come from peers. If dyadic analysts alarm patients less with their confrontations, it may simply be that they make fewer interpretations and are more guarded than necessary. If individual analysts are careful about poorly timed offers of insight, they may be just as reserved in tendering properly timed comments, thereby delaying the progress of an analysis. In the group, the therapist can more securely turn over the experience of interaction to his patients, who provoke less anxiety than he does. He need not then be fearful that their attentions will be hurtful. He is also free to step in more discreetly and discriminatively at those times when his interposition can be most beneficial. A member may at times become distributed by a poorly timed response of a co-patient, but interaction among peers usually animates, sustains, and augments the progress of group members.

Activity and Passivity of the Analyst

There is dissimilarity in the functioning of the analyst in the two settings. In the group, patients turn more to each other for affective interaction, for understanding, for confrontation and insight. In the dyad, the analysand has only the analyst to look to for such responses, but the analyst reacts in these ways only when in his clinical judgment they are indicated. As a result, the therapist in a group can generally be more of an uninvolved and reasonable onlooker as interaction goes on about him. In the dyad, where every response is turned on him, he is expected by the patient to become more engaged than he may think appropriate. Here it is more arduous for the analyst to sustain a detached, reasonable, and regardful stance. The reverse may be true for those therapists who become more insulated and detached in dyadic sessions and more affectively and inappropriately engaged at group meetings.

In dyadic treatment, the therapist may be obliged to be more animated, to cultivate the interaction that is inherent in a group. The group analyst may reduce his exertions because the group members foster the interaction.

Therapists, like their patients, choose to function in one setting or the other because they are able in one more than in the other to be more passive or active. An analyst may be more stirred, more quickened, more incited in one milieu and more immobilized, almost paralyzed, in the other. But one needs to explore the reality, the unreality, and the relationship to treatment goals of particular activity and passivity. In dyadic analysis, the analysand is generally more active and the therapist more passive. But if the patient is passive, it may be necessary for the analyst to become active. The very passive neutrality of orthodox analysis may require revision in the face of clinical experience with group analysis, in which forced interaction has shown itself to be productive. The dyadic analyst may find that, if he penetrates resistance more actively by provocation and by encouraging interaction, he will expedite treatment.

Where Analysis Takes Place

Analysis takes place largely through the interventions of the analyst. For certain patients, generally in the early phases of therapy, the most striking progress may not come in the dyadic interviews or in the group meetings the analyst attends but at the alternate sessions. This advance occurs without analytic intervention. Such improvement becomes analytic when the character of the unconscious material is explored and made conscious, when the significance of the repressed material is grasped in terms of the total experience, when the latent posture and design that produce the anxiety are analyzed.

A most significant function of the analyst is to promote the activity of the analysand in interpersonal relationships beyond the therapeutic dyad. Some analysts too nondiscriminatively prefer to limit the analysand to his one-to-one involvement with the therapist. They make the analytic relationship too exclusive of connections with others. This treatment has questionable validity because it may insulate the analysand in symbiosis. It limits the patient's choices, freedom, and growth. It circumscribes his activity within the therapeutic frame. It negates the value of transactions beyond the dyad. The same thing may take place in group analysis if the leader interferes with the patient interaction beyond the group, rejects the alternate session, and supports responses primarily to himself.

Selection of Material

In any setting, access to underlying psychodynamics and psychopathology is always incomplete, and the emphasis is chosen by the therapist. In dyadic analysis, the choices are directed by the character of the actual or subjective anxiety the patient experiences with the analyst, the analysand's capacity to trust his therapist, and his relative certainty of nonreprisal. In group analysis, the selection of material is defined by the patient's security that he will not be seriously hurt by the other members or the therapist and to the extent that he can look for assistance and relief from them. What the patient consciously and unconsciously exposes may differ from dyadic to regular to alternate meetings. His choice depends on the nature of the material, the kind of patient he is, the make-up of the group, the attitudes of his co-patients and of the leader.

In any form of psychotherapy the totality of a patient's responses is not available. It is not selective of the therapist to be occupied with catching each and every response the patient makes. It is grandiose to have to be all-knowing and aware of the slightest detail. Treatment is discriminating, selective, choosing to attend this process and phenomenon, and rejecting or analyzing another as resistive. In dyadic analysis, for example, the analyst may choose the patient's transference to him for study. Or he may scrutinize among the patient's free associations those elements that illuminate his realistic circumstances outside the treatment room. But the therapist is in a position to explore only those reactions and recollections the analysand presents. In the group situation, a wider range of material is presented. The analyst may choose to scrutinize whatever transferential response or defensive operation he believes is appropriate to work with at a certain time. He exercises his judgment in opting to examine this or that maneuver, whichever he believes is decisive, at the heart of things, one of the interconnecting elements that may explain the historically derived current behavior. He pays less regard to a multitude of other patient reactions; if he didn't, he would fail to function effectively as an analyst. If he attends everything, he is swamped and misses the core in a mass of less relevant detail. He has to be selective. He has to choose for examination the gist of things that fits each analysand, depending on his phase of evolution and growth.

Focus of Interaction

In dyadic treatment, the analyst may promote the patient's responses to him, concentrating on the analysand's disturbed reactions to him with a view to resolving them. In the group, many of these responses are directed toward co-patients, and there is intense affective interaction, both realistic and transferential. Such profoundly emotional interaction occurs rarely in dyadic treatment, where the analyst circumscribes such an eventuality by his remoteness. He

rather permits the patient's affect simply to unfold without himself becoming emotionally involved. He cannot become involved without jeopardizing the treatment relationship. He certainly cannot become inappropriately enmeshed. In the group, however, patients may be supported in response to one another and encouraged to interact without acting out. This interpersonal engagement has value. The therapist can preserve his reasonable, examining role. In the therapeutic dyad, such a posture tends to block the affective interpersonal exchange that occurs in a group setting.

Dependence on Therapy

The morbid clinging to the therapist that can develop in the course of treatment is more ominous in the dyad than in the group. It is more of a hazard, at least in its intensity and depth, in the one-to-one setting, not infrequently becoming a transference psychosis and removing the patient from reality. In a group, a member may become neurotically needful of the group, the leader, or one or another patient, but the analyst and co-patients push for interaction with others in and out of the group, which operates to resolve pathological dependency. This is valuable in exploring and working through the most serious transference neurosis.

There is a danger that some therapists may tend to develop in their groups an unhealthy association, in which patients may be encouraged merely to act out rather than work through. Here regression is extended and appreciated. Here the leader supports the patient's illness and entrenches his transference neurosis. The dyadic or group setting may be used by the analysand or the analyst to sponsor dependent ties or to resolve them. Treatment can become habituation, whether in the dyad or the group.

Working Through

The necessity for working through is often neglected in treatment, particularly by group therapists, probably because so many of them repudiate psychoanalysis or are inadequately analyzed themselves. As a result, they are confused about the analytic process and are unable to formulate a unified theory of analysis for members of a group. Their perplexity is evinced in the multiplicity of group therapies reported in the literature. The enormous volume of material made available by interpersonal reaction in group therapy may be disequilibrating to some group leaders and may make them feel that working through is not achievable.

The authors' clinical experience is that working through can be effected in a group. The profusion of material can make it easier to discover the repetitive core of psychopathology, even the transference neurosis, and can facilitate working through. Recurrence is characteristic not only of psychopathology but also of treatment. After ventilation and insight into the psychodynamics and the psychopathology, the therapist again and again suggests more reasonable, alternative choices. Only in the group is it possible to work through the bilateral and multilateral, entwined neurotic manipulations involving two or more patients. The resolution of various facets of the disorder of members at different phases in their treatment is useful in making clear the analyst's recurrent preference for reality over illusion. It is this reiteration that promotes the working through of compulsive and archaic yearnings toward the final choice of more reasonable alternatives.

A good many patients come to psychoanalysis in groups after a failure to respond to individual treatment. Frequently they have developed an increasing dependency on the therapist, with a deeply entrenched transference neurosis or psychosis. Such patients often demand concurrent individual sessions immediately after their transfer to an analyst in groups. They do so out of anxiety about breaking the symbiotic tie to the mother surrogate. The group analyst must resist these maneuvers. Instead, he must help such patients develop some independence, stronger egos, and responsibility for themselves. If group members insist that such patients function with them and the therapist resists the wish for exclusive individual support, these patients become more securely involved with their peers, more removed from the mother tie, increasingly independent of the therapist, and more

self-reliant. They become less needful of the therapist in an infantile way, more relaxed with group members and in social situations apart from the therapeutic group. A significant derivative of the group analytic experience is that each patient becomes more ego-oriented.

Termination

It is probable that successful conclusion of treatment is more easily attained in the group because it fills the therapeutic need for interaction and engagement apart from the analyst. It is the judgment of the therapist that generally determines when a patient is ready to end treatment. But, on occasion, the leader may not be fully aware of the extent to which a member has improved. Then other patients may call his attention to the fact that a progressing member has made substantial gains. A patient may feel freer to show his good resources at alternate sessions than at regular meetings, and so the leader may not be as aware as the members of the patient's considerable improvement. What requires resolution in such a case is the patient's hesitation to show his effectiveness in the presence of the group leader.

Resistance to ending treatment may be a problem not only for the patient but for the therapist as well. The observing group members help to reduce the patient's or the analyst's resistance to termination. This validation by the group does not depreciate the competence of the analyst. It simply offers him another impression on which to base his estimate and assessment. In dyadic treatment, the material is always derived from the analysand, except in the relationship to the analyst. The patient is a partial and one-sided source of enlightenment. Group members offer more evidence and reasoning for reaching a conclusion as to the propriety of ending at any given time. The patient considering termination usually seeks the opinion of the analyst. If his wish to leave is resistive, he commonly looks to his peers for allies who will support his inappropriate flight from treatment.

The recovery of one patient heartens another member with the hope that one day he, too, will be well. The release of one member is a stimulus and a promise to the others. Such an experience is not available to the patient in individual treatment. Only the member of a therapeutic group can observe another patient's getting well. The improvement of one induces the rest to try harder to attain similar well-being. The departure of a recovered patient may remotivate another at a time when he is feeling despondent. The more disconsolate are stimulated by being witness to another's restoration. They become more inquiring and searching about how this particular co-patient managed to get well in order to achieve the same for themselves. They may become more rivalrous with the departing or remaining members in the competition for return to health. This competition may have its resistive aspects. If one member is discharged as well, another may insist that he, too, has been cured when he is still quite ill. It takes little examination by the group and the analyst to expose this resistive maneuver.

CONTROVERSIAL ISSUES

Confidentiality

It is generally believed that confidentiality is essential in any form of psychotherapy. Yet the confidentiality demanded in one-to-one treatment is impossible in group therapy, where patients must share their intimate thoughts and feelings with one another. In this sense there is no confidentiality within the group itself. Some patients contend that they cannot possibly expose themselves in a group setting, but, if the therapist analyzes their anxiety and resistance, they manage to participate on increasingly deeper levels.

Patients are advised from the outset of the necessity to keep what they say to one another within the confines of the group. If a member betrays to an outsider what goes on in the group, there is a good deal of resentment, and the gossip is analyzed for his motivation. A violation of privacy is a resistive disclosure, an acting out that may intimidate the members and make them

flee the group, unless it is quickly analyzed. If the gossip cannot give up his disclosures, he may have to return to individual treatment until this problem is resolved.

Two sisters, both in psychoanalysis but in different groups, discussed with each other what transpired in their groups as a way of resisting. The result of this leakage was that they withheld from their groups and their respective analysts certain relevant associations and responses. When patients form cliques or private dyads apart from the group, they promote unauthorized disclosures that are not in their interest. It is worth noting that inevitably one or the other or both parties to this kind of acting out will report their shared secrets to still another patient or to the analyst.

The authors urge patients to unmask one another—but only in the group setting. A secret between two patients is regarded as dyadic resistance as long as their mutual confidence is kept from the other members. It is a piece of resistance, an acting out that limits the effectiveness of treatment. The authors also invite a secretive dyad to disclose the details of their clandestine relationship only within the confines of the group, try to analyze their motivation in maintaining their private pact, and try to demonstrate why its persistence is generally destructive.

Overprotection

The group is an important source of security in reality from any overprotective concern for a member on the part of the analyst or a co-patient. A single illustration of the leader's inappropriate preoccupation with the fragility of a new member may demonstrate the value of the group's response to such a distortion.

The group leader was dealing with his first group. None of the members was psychotic. A seriously schizophrenic applicant applied for admission. The therapist experienced considerable anxiety about the wisdom of introducing such a disturbed patient to a group in which the members were under no obligation to treat her with the delicacy and sensitivity he felt she required. He wondered, too, how they would respond to some of her bizarre behavior. Might not some of them flee the group at the sight of her extremity? In anticipation of their reactions and in an attempt to get them to treat her more gently than they had been responding to one another, he talked about her at a meeting prior to her joining the group. Without using words like "psychotic," "mad," and "insane," he nevertheless clearly conveyed the idea that she was much more unsettled of mind than they. He urged them to relate to her with more reserve and compassion than they showed one another.

She entered the group at the next meeting and without a word lay down on the floor on her back, staring at the ceiling. Co-patients looked at one another and the leader askance, taken aback, uncertain what to do. After some silence they disregarded her and proceeded to interact as if she were not there and had not done anything unusual. At successive meetings she did equally strange things, partly to get the group members' attention. As a result of the leader's original admonition, they continued to disregard her. After some weeks of this, she burst out in anger at the group, particularly at one man, for the inhuman neglect with which she was being treated. Again the members looked to one another and at the therapist for a guideline on how to cope with her. Nothing was forthcoming. After several sessions in which she continued to vilify the group, she began to concentrate her anger against the aforementioned man.

Finally, he could stand no more. He counterattacked her, called her "crazy," said the leader had announced before her entry into the group that she was quite mad, that the therapist had warned them to treat her delicately because she was insane, that he had had his fill of her abuse and would no longer sit idly by while she fulminated against him. He turned angrily to the group leader and blamed him—quite rightly—for forcing him to submit to such invective. The rest of the group joined him in scolding the therapist. The schizophrenic woman burst into tears but became equally critical of the therapist. Everyone was relieved that the realities were beginning to emerge, that the responsibility for this intolerable situation was the therapist's overprotective concern, which limited peer interaction as well as responses to the therapist. Equally gratifying were the schizophrenic patient's shift from anger with the group to denunciation of the leader, her final appreciation of the group's attempted kindness to her, and her apology for misplacing blame. A result of the group's rejection of the therapist's injunction against their freely interacting with her was her increasing responsiveness to all the members and her gradually becoming a more appropriately involved participant.

Closed vs. Open Groups

The authors have little experience with closed therapeutic groups. They have always introduced a new member when a patient in the group recovered and left. This procedure has the effect of maintaining the high level of productivity in the group or of revitalizing it if the same patients are together a long time without new and refreshing stimulation.

It is the authors' impression, based partly on the work of Pelz, that productive work begins to deteriorate in a group after four years together and that a closed group ought not to go on for more than one or two years. It is possible that open groups are to be preferred for certain kinds of group therapy and that closed groups might be desirable for still other kinds. For some nonanalytic types of group therapy, there may be some advantages in organizing time-limited, closed groups. But the group should be open if the therapist is practicing psychoanalysis in groups.

Depth of Therapy

The degree to which unconscious material can be exposed and worked through is usually regarded as a measure of the depth of treatment. Dyadic analysis is generally viewed as a more profound therapeutic experience than group analysis because in it the analysand attains a deeper regression to the symbiotic attachment to the mother. It is further believed that in group analysis— where transferences are evoked to figures other than the mother, such as the father and siblings—transference regression to the need for the mother can neither be worked out nor worked through. The spurious assumption is then formulated that in dyadic analysis basic conflicts and basic anxieties are resolved but that in group analysis only character and defensive mechanisms and superstructures are treated.

It is erroneously implied that in dyadic analysis the therapist deals with the more fundamental biological base and that in group analysis he works with subsequent genetic wants. Such a presumption is unsound and fictitious. It is inconceivable to work through a defense or transference without analyzing the basic conflict from which it is derived. Neither an analytic theorist nor a clinician can legitimately dissociate the analysis of conflicts and defenses from the anxiety derived from these conflicts. Neither can the analysis of transference be spuriously disjoined from the content of transference material in terms of presently existing repetitions.

Some therapists report that the transference neurosis does not develop in psychoanalysis in groups. And some clinicians believe that it does emerge in the group but cannot be worked through there. The authors believe that it does develop in the group and, like any other piece of infantile transaction, can be resolved in the group setting. Parental and sibling transferences can be made manifest, clarified, understood, and—with the conscious, voluntary participation of patients—finally replaced by appropriate, reality-oriented, discriminating, and sensible ways of relating.

A good deal depends on the cooperation of the analysand and the goals in treatment. No inadequacy idiosyncratic to the group requires that the therapist exclude certain patients or certain types of material. Depth of treatment is contingent on the particular patient, his resources, his psychopathology, and his ability to deal with his disorder. Yet the depth to which analysis can go is in some degree determined by the analyst. If he promotes the pursuit and working through of deeply repressed unconscious material, he may be said to be engaging in deep analysis—whether in the dyad or in the group.

Speed of Therapy

It is not easy to measure the comparative quickness with which successful treatment can be attained in the two settings. Most patients who leave dyadic for group analysis become less resistive. It is difficult to say whether an analysand proceeds more rapidly in one milieu or the other, just as it is hard to parallel the advance of any two analysands in dyadic treatment, because no two patients are mirror images. As a rule, an analytic group is more animating to the therapist in terms of his inventiveness, imagination, freedom of associations, productivity, and interpretive facility. The same or similar qualities emerge in the patient as a result of interaction that discloses new potentials and new horizons.

Affect vs. Cognition

Certain group therapists who are inadequately analyzed are inclined, usually overzealously, to join one or another prevailing movement, no matter how senseless or extravagant. They are usually affect-addicts given to the practice, misperceived as therapeutic, of expressing their feelings in and out of group therapy and of advocating the ventilation of emotion as a way of life for their patients as well. They are critical of reason in themselves and others because it seems to them to be too cold, detached, and unfeeling. They idealize affect as the only legitimate vehicle for communication.

What is neglected in their treatment of patients is the disclosure of the repressed history. Instead, they encourage the patient to act out the past in the present without insight. They do not enable him to re-experience his history in order to transcend it. They do not strive to work through, to search reasonably to confront him with the ways in which he misperceives the present as if it were still the past. They reject the exploration of history because they have unresolved problems with their own parents and feel compelled affectively to act out their protest against intellect. They feel they were never understood and felt for, so they obsessively rebel against reason. They subscribe to any new weird sect that gives them the reins to express their disproportionate feeling of rancor against their family antecedents.

They see themselves and are often seen by their patients as sincere, daring, and self-confident for being bold enough to show their feelings. Some of them, on occasion, scream in the course of a group session when they feel bored. For the group therapist to indulge himself this way while putting himself forward as an expert in the community's interest is like a frightened child who is afraid of his shadow offering to be a leader of men simply because he feels blindly knight-errant. This kind of rashness, which unfortunately attracts followers, is probably related to the schizoid maneuver. The schizoid maneuver (according to William Silverberg) is a characterological mental process in which anxiety is dealt with by escaping from reality, by denying reality and establishing a more satisfying illusion.

The feeling-driven group therapist responds nondiscriminatively with his own affect to the patients in his groups. Such reactions may be useful for certain patients at certain times. But a one-dimensional approach does not distinguish one patient from another. Each member needs to be treated differently because each has a differentiated, personal diagnosis, a particular psychopathology, and multiform good resources and, therefore, requires specific kinds of working out and working through. If the therapist does not differentiate one patient from the next, he is misrendering them into a uniformity incompatible with treatment. Patients are diverse and need diversified and distinctive treatment of their dissimilar needs.

Group therapists given to repetitive affective expression stir in their patients a like tendency without prompting adequate intrapsychic examination. For some withdrawn members and those removed from experiencing their feelings, such an influence may be a useful departure from their introspection and insularity. But even with these, the quality of their interaction, once achieved, has pathological characteristics that need to be explored. Even when patients are emboldened to become emotionally involved, even when this interaction is appropriate, such engagement is not enough to resolve their difficulties. More is needed to achieve reconstructive therapy.

Some group therapists seem to look on emotional interaction as the essence of treatment when it is, for the most part, simply verbal acting out. What is required is free association, the presentation of dreams and fantasies, thoughts as well as feelings, intrapsychic material as well as interaction. This is necessary so that the therapist can then study where, when, and how resistance, transference, and acting out take place. It is necessary so that working through

can be based on insight. It is necessary so that interventions can be based on realistic choices. The affectively compelled group therapist would have his patient, like himself, be regardful only of those sudden and momentary feelings that overwhelm him from time to time. But these feelings are determined by impulse or obsession and inappropriately fulfill the patient's transference expectations. If patients do this with one another, they are gratifying one another's archaic longings instead of resolving them.

Group therapists who are affect-habitués believe that a group member's most profound feelings are not expressed to a leader whose responses are prepared, well-thought-out, and skilled because patients see through such "scheming." The imputation is that reflection in the patient's interest is a cold, dishonest piece of trickery being imposed on him. But draw an analogy between the therapist and a mother. It seems appropriate and necessary for a mother to organize an itinerary for her child, to design a feeding plan, to have a sense of time and of limits, to formulate beforehand a flexible program for the child's best possible future. Her planning does not represent an unfeeling and unrelated attitude. It may be judicious care derived from the mother's tenderness and love.

Consider the therapist whose dedication to group members is experienced most deeply by him, he says, while he sleeps during group sessions because it is then that he is dreaming of them. As a result, he often naps and dreams in the course of group meetings in order to achieve his most profound and rapturous communication with them. Such devotion is generally acknowledged and appreciated by the patients, who demonstrate their gratitude to the exhausted leader by speaking in soft undertones in order not to rouse him from his fatiguing effort to contact them unconscious-to-unconscious. In this transfer of responsibility, the therapist seems to hope to convert the group into the supportive mother while he acts out the part of the dependent child. Or there may be an attempt at fusion with the projected mother in the group with exemption of responsibility. This acting out of archaic hopes exalts and unites the group in love and adoration of the leader as a divining dreamer, one who will wake and tell his oracular and healing vision someday.

The therapist in ecstasy or agony who tries to induce similar feelings in group members is basically neglectful of his responsibilities. He is, in fact, self-seeking but screens his self-indulgence behind a simulated regard for their need to ventilate what they feel. If this is not so, and in some measure it may be unjust to blame the overemotional therapist with such stern judgment, then it would appear that he is quite irrational. Rather than therapist, he is an immature authoritarian who attempts to gain the love of group members by the childlike effort to become a regressed infant. But the inexperienced suckling is incompetent to offer to patients the maturity and skill that good treatment requires. Until he grows up and acquires the responsibility, knowledge, and techniques of psychotherapy, he opposes and repudiates the wearisome necessity to listen to his forebears. He defiantly resists the realistic caution and teaching of more mature minds. As a son, he sees the parent as his adversary; as an employee, his employer; as a patient, his therapist; as an affectivist, intellect.

Individual vs. Group Stimuli

The members of a group provide the patient with more stimuli than does the analyst alone in the dyadic relationship. The analyst is also the focus of more stimulation in the group than in one-to-one treatment. This situation poses a problem. Do these multiple stimuli produce more diversion, more shifting of attention, and less careful examination of each patient than he might receive in individual treatment? It is quite possible. The answer depends in part on the competence, skill, and leadership of the therapist.

In a group, each patient receives not only the analyst's attention but also the critical responses of a number of other members whose observations are insightful. In this respect the patient has the advantage of being stimulated and observed by multiple resources not available to him in the dyad.

Thus the diversity made available by group members may be used to enrich whatever the patient presents, whether fantasy, dream, conflict, or external problem. In the group there may be less focusing than in analytic dyads but more stimulation to a wider canvas of psychopathological and healthy reactivity.

Homogeneity vs. Heterogeneity

The presence of both men and women is a more therapeutic milieu than a unisexual and more homogeneous group. In a group containing both sexes, more of the unconscious psychodynamics, psychopathology, and healthy resources of each patient becomes manifest. The variety in the membership promotes mutual interest, diverse stimulation, complementarity, and multiple transferences. The differences among the patients demand a healthy struggle to cope rationally with divergent points of view, to resolve disagreement in appropriate, reality-bound compromise.

If it is true that heterogeneity facilitates treatment, it is relevant to examine which setting, individual or group, provides more homogeneity. There is more sameness and more consistency of response in dyadic analysis than in group analysis, even if the analyst organizes the group on some homogeneous basis. The group cannot react as a single individual, even though it may at times seem to be doing so. In reality, some members seem more committed to their archaic needs, whereas others struggle more for the healthy alternative. There are myriads of still other differences among all patients. In contrast, the analyst follows a fairly uniform course. His commitment, his value system, his stance, his reactions, his offers of understanding have a particular aim and direction and produce more homogeneity in the dyad than in the group.

It is a formidable task for an analyst to homogenize a group, to impose his authority on an assemblage of patients. The patient in a dyad is much more liable to succumb to his dominations. A therapist may try to impose on a patient a limited responsiveness, such as here-and-now reactivity, or demand that he express only his feeling and not his thoughts or associations. He may circumscribe productions only to historical data, focus on motivation, stress ego functions, or press for strictly conscious and reality-bound material. In doing any of these, he demands of the patient a homogeneous way of operating. Such a fixed way of functioning is not analytic, for it does not facilitate choice. Instead, it promotes repetition-compulsion. The therapist who inflexibly defines what may be explored over time homogenizes and circumscribes treatment.

Isolation vs. Socialization

Isolation and socialization are consequences as well as sources of intrapersonal and interpersonal dynamics. A good many individually but inadequately analyzed patients are poorly adjusted in their relations with groups of people. After extensive individual treatment they sometimes find themselves to be more lonely and unsocialized than before. They may then seek out a group therapist to help them resolve their withdrawal and to promote their socialization. Previously committed to intrapersonal preoccupation, they may be propelled into ever more disengagement. The analyst in groups is aware that patients may socialize in mutually destructive ways that are resistive and acting out. He guards against such abuse of socialization by analyzing these operations and supporting the wholesome qualities of social intercourse.

The feeling of abandonment is more vividly experienced by the patient when he is placed in an analytic group. In individual treatment, he has the therapist all to himself, at least in fantasy, and in reality the illusion is fostered by isolating one patient from the next. A group member repeatedly talks of his sadness, anger, or sense of isolation when the therapist or a meaningful co-patient seems to prefer another member. Because the therapist is less available, because he is not exclusively possessed, the feeling of being isolated recurs more frequently in the group. Therefore, the analyst can more easily pursue the interpersonal dynamics that led to the real and unreal sense of isolation. He can also explore the genetic determinants that led to the intra-

psychic dynamics that now keep the patient in isolation. And the patient has group members with whom he can work toward a more gratifying socialization.

It is always enlightening to the analyst to find how often the problem of isolation presents itself when a patient moves from individual analysis to treatment in a group. The therapist may have been unaware of the extent to which this was a problem. The previous dyadic setting, in which the patient had the analyst to himself, prevented the emergence of this difficulty. The experience in a group vividly promotes the appearance of a sense of isolation for all to see. The patient sets himself apart by reproducing in repetition-compulsion his refusal to participate or by reproducing his competition with a parent or sibling who is favored by another familial figure whose appreciation or affection he wants.

Traditionally, socialization is regarded as a resistive maneuver, and it may so become. This need not be so as long as socialization is examined and analyzed for its resistive components. Socialization is a phenomenon that occurs to some extent in all group therapy. In psychoanalysis in groups, however, the issue of whether socialization is obstructing the analytic process or making it more manageable needs to be explored. It seems to the authors that socialization has a humanizing and a restorative value. But social intercourse may enable patients to resist the search for latent mainsprings. Therefore, the analyst needs to be alert to the way in which patients use the alternate session, the postsession, clique formation, and subgroup dating.

The Alternate Meeting

Many group therapists reject the alternate meeting. They see it largely as encouraging patients to act out. There may be greater opportunity for acting out when alternate meetings are made available, but alternate sessions are not proposed for the purpose of acting out, nor are patients encouraged to act out. They are, in fact, urged not to do so. Attempts are made to analyze imminent acting out. When it takes place, it is analyzed in order to interrupt it. All else failing, it is forbidden.

The alternate meeting has important advantages. One of these is spontaneous mutual support among members of the group, an advantage that appeared quite naturally in the earliest postsessions. At these meetings, thoughts, feelings, and activities emerged that were different from those at regular sessions. By comparing and contrasting behavior at regular and alternate meetings, therapists found quantitative and qualitative differences in the two settings and were able to examine these differences productively.

The authors' appreciation of the value of the alternate session does not mean that they believe group therapy can be successful without a leader. Therapy cannot proceed only in the presence of peers, a group of patients without a therapist. Moreover, the authority vector is present at the alternate meeting, even though the analyst is not physically present. It is a session attended by a group of patients whose assembly exists only as a result of their relationship to the analyst. A group without a leader has little psychotherapeutic potential.

Only the therapist is sufficiently trained to conduct the systematic intervention of treatment. Patients are not expected to be therapists with one another. If they try to assume such inappropriate roles, they are in resistance. They are generally incapable of making the skilled observations required of the therapist. Therefore, treatment in this sense does not go on at the alternate meeting. Patients may attempt to conduct themselves as therapists for one another, but such behavior is usually rejected and resisted. They tend to interact spontaneously. They do not know one another's diagnoses, and they are unaware of what stage of treatment each member is in. The therapist has a plan in mind for the treatment of each member. The patients do not.

The therapist at regular meetings demands that the patients do analytic work. Patients also offer each other insight at alternate sessions, but there the pursuit of mutual understanding and insight is not so intense or concentrated. Patients in the alternate meeting experience one another as

trying to be helpful. This diffused helpfulness is experienced in the regular meeting as well. But under the therapist's influence there is an effort to work more analytically in his presence. He is the primary source of insight and of pressure to give up archaic means. He induces them to apply themselves more vigorously to the task of getting well.

If the analyst tries to use a patient as a co-therapist, he is misusing the patient in countertransference. Whenever the analyst so misuses a group member, the patient may be induced to play this role at alternate meetings as well. But being a co-therapist should be neither his role nor his responsibility. He is in treatment to get well, not to become a therapist. The analyst has no objection to the members being helpful to one another. They do, in fact, repeatedly offer one another useful support and understanding. But whenever a patient compulsively tries to exercise the role of co-therapist, he is in resistance to his more realistic position as patient. Nevertheless, patients often turn to one another for emotional sustenance in anxiety and depression. When the analyst is unavailable—on vacation, for instance—patients are obliged, as at the alternate meeting, to turn to one another for understanding, maintenance, and relief. Such assistance is useful and often insightful. Even at regular meetings, patients offer one another interpretations. The analyst welcomes such expositions as long as they are not pursued compulsively as a way of resisting analysis.

Group Dynamics

There are some positives in homogeneous group responses. Co-patients are often helpful to one another, sustaining in critical situations, compassionate, insightful, and empathic. In spite of variations in their history and character, they frequently identify with and feel for each other. To the degree this takes place, members are constructively homogeneous, and the group leader can endorse such wholesome mutual support and positive interaction. But it does not seem technically possible to incorporate into treatment the idea that, when patients love one another, there is a good reparative result. The therapist cannot in treatment create an atmosphere of love. To try to do so would deny the possibility of technical intervention determined by insight into psychodynamics. It is valuable when patients relate to each other positively and support one another's weakened egos, but such mutual sustenance should not be confused with psychoanalytic treatment.

Anger at Therapist. Occasionally, co-patients support one another in expressing negative feeling toward the therapist. This type of support is extremely productive for those members who are not likely to assert themselves when alone with the analyst. An alliance enables them to do so until they have sufficient ego strength to stand up to the therapist alone. This group dynamic may be encouraged in general, but it seems inappropriate for each patient to experience anger at the group leader at the same time. Nor does it seem at all likely that each member is in that phase of a transference relationship when the expression of negative feeling is indicated.

Demand for Participation. Another example of useful group dynamic pressure occurs when the whole group demands the participation of a silent or withdrawn member. Although such authority directed at a detached patient may, in fact, lead to his engagement, it seems to be an especially nonanalytic means to penetrate resistance. Are there not analytic devices more appropriate than aggressive group demand? Might not an occasional patient take flight in the face of such mass pressure?

A group demand seems dedicated to pressing members to do something. If it appears so, very likely several aggressive patients are leading the pack while the others are submissively following.

Even if the group dynamic demand that a member give up his resistance works under the influence of the united power of the group, the precedent seems dangerous. The idea has too many overtones of brainwashing, of forcing an individual to yield to group demand. The effect may well be de-egotizing and may lead to a split ego.

Therapeutic Value. The authors do not believe that the leader's or the group's pre-occupation with group dynamics is psychoanalytically therapeutic. The group psychodynamicist tends to neglect psychoanalytic confrontations and individual insights for observations about what the group as a group is doing. He may neglect the individual's unconscious psychodynamics and psychopathology.

The leader who is repetitively engaged in pursuing group dynamics tends to homogenize the group, to treat it as a whole. In doing this, the therapist may be motivated by anxiety in coping with a triad or a multivariable condition. He may be more secure in creating the illusion that he is in a dyad. In the dyad, he may be immersed in the illusory security of a relationship with his mother, a transference neurosis. Or he may be in a homosexual relationship with the group homogenized as symbolic father. He may be excluding one parent or the other or disregarding a sibling with whom he is in rivalry.

The group psychodynamicist tends to use group dynamic terms and concepts and to use phrases like "group ego," "group id," "group superego," "group mind," "collective unconscious," "collective consciousness," "group resistance," and "group transference." All these terms are distortions on the part of the leader.

At a workshop in psychoanalysis in groups several years ago, an attending psychoanalyst took issue with the authors' view that emphasis on group dynamics in group analysis was a mystique and was resistive to the analytic process.

How can you say the group in and of itself does not provide a reparative experience? When I was 17, I joined a group of teenagers for a summer at a camp in preparation for a trip to Israel. We studied conversational Hebrew together. We worked and played together. When we were thoroughly prepared, we took a wonderful trip and spent several joyous months on a kibbutz, helping a group of Israelis develop a local program. There I met the girl I fell in love with and married. We have a wonderful family. This inspiring group activity was the greatest experience of my life. It helped me more than my subsequent analysis. It changed me from a shy, introverted, and detached adolescent into an energetic, extroverted, socially involved, and happily married man.

The leader congratulated him on his good fortune in being exposed to such a constructive group of youngsters with a shared, happy ideal. But suppose in his adolescence he had been induced to join another kind of group, a group of addicts or neighborhood gangsters, a group of delinquents or psychopaths. Finding himself in a group dedicated to good social values was partly a choice of his and partly happenstance. A group may be reparative or destructive, but this is a matter of chance and must be distinguished from psychoanalytic therapy, which is a series of technical interventions, such as making the unconscious conscious, working through resistance, and transference.

An emphasis on group dynamics is antianalytic, a distraction from analytic work, because it focuses primarily on the group rather than on the patient. The interpretation of group dynamic phenomena in therapy does not treat the patient. No means has yet been devised to psychoanalyze a group. The individual is not analytically reconstructed by mystical interventions dedicated to treating the group as a whole, despite the ingenuity of Ezriel, for example.

The group psychodynamic view is a mystique because it claims to heal by group cohesion and group atmosphere rather than through the individualized and expert attention and intervention of an analyst. The group is invested with a magically healing power it does not possess. It has no inherent benevolent influence that enables it to apply its magnetic authority. Such a belief in the group is sorcery, incantation. The group dynamicists overvalue cohesion and climate, and they undervalue analysis.

The group dynamicist's dedication to the group leads to a denial of each member's individuality and differences. It tends to promote a pathological homogeneity rather than interactive and complementary heterogeneity. It would influence the patient by group dynamics rather than by understanding. It is repressive-inspirational rather than psychoanalytic. In the group dynamic view, the manifest is seen as the individual patient's unconscious motivation and behavior, and the latent is regarded as the group's activity as a whole. This is, of course, a reversal of the analytic view, in which the group's activity would be conceived of as the manifest and the patient's unconscious contribution to the group's activity as the latent.

Case History

An infantile patient, Bob, monotonously sought maternal support and symbolic nursing from mother figures invested onto co-patients. From his first day in the group, he tried to monopolize meetings with his inordinate demands for reassurance of apparent maternal quality. The group leader saw the members reacting as one, group dynamically, to Bob's archaic pressure. The analyst tried to explore beyond this homogeneous response but was met with resistance. He persisted, nevertheless, in asking each patient to free associate about Bob.

Alan, it turned out, felt under a compulsion to keep Bob talking because, if Bob became silent, Alan remembered an elder sibling whose wrathful silence used to frighten him in childhood. Alan would find relief from his brother's silent hostility by encouraging him to express his anger. In the course of his sibling's ventilation, Alan found that his brother's aggression was quickly dissipated and he himself was relieved of his anxiety. It became clear that he saw Bob as an elder brother who had to be pacified in order to relieve his own tension. So Alan was only manifestly offering Bob a symbolic maternity. On a latent level he was acting out quite subjectively a piece of his earlier life.

When Pamela associated to Bob, she thought he resembled her aggrieved father, whom she felt compelled to sustain and take care of. Underneath, she felt increasing annoyance over this never-ending devotion to her father, a resentment she feared to show in her reluctance to add to his burdens.

Marian in free association to Bob remembered how she, too, longed as a child for more closeness to her mother. She resolved this yearning in part by mothering her dolls, which were stand-ins for her own deprived self. Bob represented this denied infantile self that she supported and nourished in the absence of her own mother. On occasion Bob represented for Marian a younger sibling assigned by her mother to her care.

Kay in her associations saw Bob as her father—miserly, self-depriving, other-depriving, denying Kay the opportunity to gratify most of her rightful inclinations. Kay was generally required to submit to her father's authority. So she felt obliged to yield in the group to Bob's demands.

The other patients, too, were only manifestly offering Bob maternal support. On a latent level, each was acting out a subjective transferential distortion.

Such a denouement is available to any group analyst if he does not settle for the manifest homogeneity of a group response but rather searches for latent personal unconscious material. If the group psychodynamicist misperceives the resistive manifest as latent and central and thereby allows unconscious processes to remain unexposed and basic motivations repressed, then the resistance, distortion, and acting out of group members are animated. By persisting in the examination of latent and individual differentiated psychodynamics in each manifestly maternal member, the therapist discovers a particular transferential maneuver that is not apparent in the group dynamic.

Ego Strength. Whenever a patient has ego weakness, he is inclined to deny his own perceptions, judgment, choices, wishes, and aspirations and to yield to those of the other. Sometimes this other assumes gigantic proportions, especially when it is the homogeneous group dynamic pressure of co-patients. To the extent that a patient has good ego strength, he has the capacity to respect his own ego resources and pursue his own inclinations in the face of group dynamic domination. To the degree that the group leader supports the group dynamic position, he imposes on the individual ego a di-egophrenic problem—a split-ego problem. In doing this, he limits personal development, weakens ego resources, and cultivates borderline pathology.

Health does not come from submission to group fiat. And healthy cohesion does not depend on a denial of individuality and a wholesale acceptance of group standards. It should not be necessary to split one's ego in order to be accepted by a group. Any treatment based on submission to an authoritarian group is dictatorial. Reconstructive change is not achieved by capitulation to a dominating group but by careful analytic work. The patient cannot appropriately avoid conflict by obediently conforming to the common point of view. The authors would rather achieve increasing individual differentiation with mutually acceptable conflict in different points of view and in-

creasing appreciation and acceptance of opposing and complementary positions.

The authors are, therefore, opposed to routine group dynamic interpretations, which do injury to already damaged egos. If the therapist does not recognize individual variations and does not promote each patient's autonomy, if he chooses to make group dynamic observations, he guides the members toward a homogeneity in pathology instead of toward the more wholesome possibility of interactive diversity. He prevents group members from attaining the independence and freedom that are the goals of good treatment. An analyst who endorses group dynamic consensus creates di-egophrenia by not promoting the privilege of each patient to differ with the majority. In so doing, he allows an authoritarian group to dominate the individual. The group psychodynamicist is satisfied with the emergence of group themes. The psychoanalyst is not content with this. He goes beyond the manifest conformity to get to the latent individual uniqueness of each patient.

Combined Therapy

Preliminary Dyadic Sessions. A limited number of individual sessions are useful preparation for the group. These interviews enable patient and analyst to become acquainted, to see whether they find it agreeable to work with each other, to agree on a fee suitable to each, to establish a diagnosis, to see when the patient is free to attend group meetings, and to consider which group would be most suitable for the patient. These early individual sessions give the patient some sense of security with the analyst. He then has some feeling of support when he enters the group of strangers. If a patient requires six to 12 preparatory individual sessions and still seems unready to join a group, the analyst ought to work with him in individual treatment. From time to time in the course of his individual analysis, the question of joining a group may be raised. The patient may at some point show less resistance and indicate his readiness to enter a group.

Concurrent Dyadic and Group Sessions. Some therapists always provide concurrent individual sessions one, two, or even three times a week throughout the group experience. It is doubtful whether these therapists practice analytic group therapy. Such combined therapists tend to make treatment in the group adjunctive to individual therapy. For example, they usually analyze dreams only in dyadic sessions, not in group meetings. Their orientation is primarily one-to-one, derived from their individual analytic orientation and training. They tend, therefore, to homogenize the group members rather than to differentiate them. They are inclined, quite inappropriately, to treat the group en masse or to treat each individual in the group in turn. These procedures limit peer interaction and curtail the emergence of personal and interpersonal material.

Reasons for Combined Therapy. Combined therapy seems to be based on the persuasion that few if any healthy responses are available among patients in a group. As a result, the group meeting is placed in a position subsidiary to the individual session, where real treatment is believed to take place.

Individual sessions can be combined with group meetings if done so discriminatively, selectively, with choice, where indicated. But to employ collateral individual sessions at all times with all patients limits the effectiveness of psychoanalysis in groups. The dyadic meeting may, for example, be used to resist participation in the group. The patient may save his significant reactions and dreams for his private sessions with the analyst.

If the analyst who rejects combined treatment discovers that a patient does not relate to him at group meetings, he may try in the group to analyze this resistance and promote responses to him. Failing in this, he may then ask for dyadic sessions.

In combined therapy there is a tendency to avoid reporting in the group what transpired in individual consultations. If the analyst overestimates the importance of private sessions with him, the patients also begin to devaluate the group experience. The combined therapist may believe that patients cannot expose themselves in depth in the group, when, in fact, the reverse is often true. If he is convinced of the impossibility of depth analysis in the group, he will, of course, provide individual sessions. His conviction begins to permeate the group, and, before long, the members communicate primarily with him in dyads, relate less to each other, and convince him of the rightness of his judgment.

One combined therapist declares that he uses the individual session to relax for a while behind the reclining patient. But the analyst's need for repose is irrelevant to treatment.

For patients inclined to a deeply entrenched transference neurosis or psychosis, the promise of individual consultations usually furthers and dangerously deepens symbiotic needs and is generally contraindicated. Treatment in a group and promotion of peer interaction are effective ways of dealing with the transference neurosis and psychosis.

One combined therapist uses individual sessions to counteract what she refers to as the discontinuity of attention and therapeutic work for the individual patient in the group. But discontinuity is a necessary part of effective treatment. Even in the most intense individual analysis, there is discontinuity between sessions. Interruptions and limits are parts of life and reality to which all must accommodate. If there is an excess of interruption by one member or an excess of yielding to interruption by another, blocker and blocked can be analyzed.

Combined therapists seem to be in conflict about the use and value of the group as a milieu for treatment. In justification for paralleling individual and group sessions, they occasionally use such nebulous words as "cross fertilization," "double exposure," "additive," and "catalytic."

Combined therapists view the group as preparatory, adjunctive, or supplemental to individual analysis. One combined therapist sees regression taking place in individual sessions and maturation taking place at group meetings. A good many combined therapists' view of the group is that it is a medium primarily to excite the emergence of psychopathology, which is then analyzed in the privacy of the analytic cloister. Combined therapists then resist the treatment of the patient in the group.

By so structuring treatment, combined therapists exercise too much authoritative control and limit peer interaction. Therapy becomes too therapist-centered. It rejects peer interaction and is contemptuous of peer potential. It promotes the illusion of therapist omnipotence. Peer interaction is minimized and controlled because it is perceived as largely pathological. The patient is allowed to participate to the extent that he confirms the leader's judgment. The dyadic consultations diminish peer interaction and reinforce hierarchical control.

One combined therapist recently inquired, "Can group therapy harm individual treatment?" This point of view is leader-centered, with help seen as derived largely in the authority vector. But no psychotherapy, whether individual or group, can be effective unless there is also an intensive, interactive, horizontal experience with peers.

The combined therapist presumes the need for authoritative surveillance. He is often overprotective and infantilizing of his patients. He prevents them from exercising their resources in mutual give-and-take. The emphasis in the group is on peer relatedness, on interaction as a movement toward equality in difference, on resolution of the transference cultivated in individual sessions. The necessity for seclusion with the transferential mother invested in the therapist should be gradually worked through, partly by a reduction and final elimination of vertical sessions. Otherwise, a morbid entrenchment of the transference neurosis develops. Peer interaction lessens the possibility of this development and of the imposition of an irrational authoritarianism on the part of the leader. Combined therapy neglects the provocative and reparative reactions of patient to patient. It tends to prevent patients from ventilating their negative feelings toward the leader.

One group analyst believes that associated dyadic sessions are necessary to gratify the patient's oral drives. But such fulfillment of archaic needs is countertransferential and contraindicated, for it tends to embed the transference neurosis.

It is a curious phenomenon that in outpatient clinics group psychotherapy is more prevalent without parallel individual sessions, whereas in private practice combined therapy is generally made available. Some group therapists have confessed that they suggest dyadic hours largely to fill gaps in their appointment schedule. Here the frequency of individual sessions seems to be determined by economic factors more pertinent to the therapist's needs than to those of the patient.

Sometimes a patient is referred for psychoanalysis in groups by an analyst who wishes to continue to treat his analysand at the same time. This arrangement is productive if the two therapists do not compete with each other for the patient or try to prove which one is helping the patient more. It becomes especially productive if the patient shares his experiences in both settings. Occasionally, it may become necessary for the group analyst to refer patients elsewhere for individual sessions if his schedule is full.

The notion that it is important to extract a member from the group in order to intensify transference is frequently a manifest rationalization for latent countertransference. Adequate transference responses, even of a pre-oedipal nature, come to the fore in the group setting itself without the necessity to promote them by providing dyadic hours.

One group therapist admitted that he offered private sessions primarily to his attractive female patients. Another confessed that the patients he liked, he saw individually, and those he did not like, he placed in groups. Still another analyst, with feelings of inadequacy about his competence as a therapist, said that he practiced group therapy because he felt he had so little to offer in dyadic treatment. There are many other countertransferential motivations for insisting on routine individual sessions as well as group meetings—the leader's overprotectiveness, his possessiveness, his wish to seduce the patient, and so on.

Combined treatment may be necessary for some children, for some adolescents, for some acting-out neurotics and psychotics who need supervisory control. The patient may need a one-to-one experience with an analyst who is experienced as a mother figure before he can participate with his peers, whom he may see as father surrogates and sibling surrogates. An already psychotic patient in maternal transference to everyone does better in a group if he does not have extended preparatory or collateral individual sessions. A patient may need a freeing experience with his peers before he can avail himself of a relationship to authority.

Results of Combined Therapy. The choice of therapeutic field offers structural differences that encourage particular kinds of intervention and response. If the leader saves his interpretations for the dyad, patients participate less in the group. The therapist's basic preference for the one-to-one setting leads to his homogenizing the group, making group psychodynamic interpretations, and doing depth analysis in private but not in the group. These results, in turn, lessen peer interaction and limit analysis in the group. Then, since analysands are responsive to the open or latent convictions of the leader, patients save their meaningful, intense, and confused reactions for dyadic meetings, where they tell the analyst their fantasies, dreams, and imagined responses to co-patients.

The nondiscriminative use of private sessions produces resistance. It leads to the members reporting to the analyst rather than to fellow patients their responses to one another. The results are that they develop indirect and devious relationships with one another, they do not see their provocative roles in the group, there is an inhibition of reality-testing, and there is less detailed and active mutual investigation. None of this need occur if the analyst applies his psychoanalytic skills in the group.

Patients in combined treatment often do not make a healthy and swift movement from self-involvement to empathic sensitivity and communication. Too many patients, offered dyadic time, try to misuse it for resistive purposes. As a result, many individual sessions need to be group-centered. The private meeting may be unnecessary if the analyst focuses on new perceptions and insights in the group itself. He is free to return to a particular psychodynamic at a successive group meeting and need not propose a private session to do so. Likewise, the patient should be encouraged to tell group members the transactions that took place in individual meetings.

The conception that the group offers a here-and-now experience and the therapeutic dyad provides a there-and-then experience is a one-dimensional view of treatment. The analyst who permits such homogeneity is allowing his patients to resist the diversified participation necessary to them.

Free Association

Analytically trained therapists are often doubtful about whether patients can associate as freely in a group as in a dyad. True, there are more interruptions of free association in the group. But to look upon unrestrained, unbounded, and indefinite free association as fitting is to misunderstand the function of free association and the nature of analytic treatment. It is better to employ free association selectively, with recognition of when it is expedient. It is neither possible nor advisable to associate freely at all times. Discontinuity and bounds are essential in treatment, as they are in life.

The dyadic analyst may be doubtful of the effectiveness of group analysis because he does not believe the patient can associate freely when he is interrupted by co-patients. In reality, free association may be hindered by co-patients at certain times and helped at others. Where a patient is delving into as-yet-unexplored latent material, he usually stimulates and wins the attention of the other members and is, therefore, emboldened to go on. When he continues to reproduce the same psychopathology in free association, co-patients become disinterested with the recurrence and appropriately try to stay his repetition and ask for a more mutually invigorating alternative. When his free association is moving him to the disclosure of appropriate, noncompulsive possibilities, his fellows are hopefully but quietly attentive, in the expectation that he will have the freedom to make a nonobsessive choice. When his stream of consciousness appears to be running down into estranging autism, co-patients resist his self-destructive and isolating free association.

In dyadic analysis, the therapist interprets the free association of the analysand, whose associations are less free to the extent that he is aware of them. In group analysis, the patient not only freely associates but is required to operate with awareness of the others. Although this obligation may appear to limit the freedom of his stream of consciousness, the demand for mutual awareness promotes his good health. Unrestrained free association without the checking of feedbacks in reality leads to disequilibration and derangement.

In analysis, whether individual or group, the patient is expected to reveal the truth about himself. In the dyad, the analyst is not required to expose himself. In the group, all the members are encouraged to show themselves and interact in an open way. The result is that every patient becomes aware of the effect he has on others in a way that is not available to him in dyadic treatment. Each member finds out what his own provocative role or behavior patterns are.

The group analyst's preoccupation with interruptions of free association may represent his wish to conduct individual analysis in the group setting. But such a commitment prevents the leader from using the good resources of his assembled patients and interferes with proper treatment of them. The interruptive contributions of fellow patients not only clarify the presentation of a given patient but may be used as free associations in themselves. In discussion of a dream, for example, the free associations of various members stir the further exposure of the dreamer's unconscious material. They also give the analyst more hints for understanding the dream and clues to the psychodynamics and psychopathology of the others, which can be multilaterally interpreted.

The analyst's conception of fellow patients' communications as interruptive denies to the group the value of multilateral analysis. Instead, it imposes individual treatment in a group setting and encourages a rivalry to interrupt one another, a competition to be heard by the analyst.

Encouraging patients to enter in with their own free associations, which are also acknowledged and examined, promotes the feeling that all are in analysis rather than just a single member at a time in rotation. It is, therefore, necessary for the analyst to deal with any presented material as inter-actional, so that the number of patient interrelationships is enhanced. In so doing, he augments rather than circumscribes all the streams of consciousness in the group. The analyst's aim to give space to each patient in which to associate freely is commendable. But by limiting the free play of the others, he really hinders the achievement of his goal. In group analysis, all the analysands should be encouraged to be collaborative and active participants.

Dreams

Dreaming and dream analysis are most valuable in treatment, whether in the dyadic or group setting. But dreams are dealt with in different ways in the two climates. In one-to-one therapy, the analysand associates freely to his dream, and the analyst seldom reveals his own associations. They are withheld—or are only partly revealed in a refined product—in his interpretations and other responses. In the group, the dreamer at first associates freely to his dream. Then the co-patients associate to the dream, both as it belongs to the dreamer and as if the dream were their own. Then everyone tries to interpret the dream and the significance of each patient's subjective associations as applicable to himself. In this way the therapist avoids individual analysis of each member's dream in turn and encourages multilateral group analysis. He may enter the interpretive process from time to time to integrate what has been said, to underscore an essence, to make a point more intelligible, or to suggest an exploration of neglected elements in the dream when they seem to be meaningful.

Analysands who evade unconscious processes in the dyad may not present dream material. They justify their opposition by contending that they do not see any value in dream analysis. This resistance can be resolved more readily in the group than in the dyad, for in the group the patients witness another member's presentation of a dream, its analysis, and the member's greater understanding and forward movement in treatment.

Some group therapists do not press for dreams in the group. In fact, they seem to eject the analysis of dreams. But in most groups a number of members quite spontaneously tell their dreams, so it is more difficult for the therapist to discourage them in that setting. He is more obliged to pay them some attention. Even in a group, however, if the analyst frustrates the emergence of dreams, they are likely to be recounted less and less often until they are entirely abandoned.

Transference

Transference Neurosis. A deep transference neurosis is less likely to develop in a group than in a dyad. In individual analysis, the patient is readier to submit, to regress, to accept frustration. In the group, this readiness is less apparent. Besides, the presence of a father figure and sibling surrogates in group members attenuates the formation of deeply symbiotic ties to the analyst as a mother figure. The provision of an alternate meeting further attenuates the possibility of a strong attachment to the therapist. If no alternate sessions are provided or if one or more individual meetings a week with the analyst are routinely used, there is a greater tendency for a transference neurosis to develop. The development of a deep maternal transference is also attenuated by the presence of other members who act as auxiliary egos to enable the patient to free himself from a regressive dependence on the analyst as a mother surrogate.

A large number of patients in groups are borderline psychotic and are already in a transference psychosis to the mother figure that is projected almost everywhere. For these patients there is no need to promote further regression. To do so would produce a further break with reality. For neurotic patients in whom the therapist believes a regression in the service of the ego is indicated, one or more individual sessions a week can be provided to serve such a purpose. But this is not necessary for most patients.

Lateral Transference and Lateral Countertransference. In the therapeutic group, patients may gratify one another's archaic needs in a way that would be inappropriate in individual sessions, where

such behavior on the part of the therapist would be regarded as countertransferential. Patients sometimes bring in food or drink. And on rare occasions some members feel obligated to prepare a dinner for co-patients at an alternate session.

There is a greater likelihood that members will gratify one another's transference expectations in any group therapy than in individual analysis, where the therapist is aware, in general, of the inappropriateness of fulfilling the patient's archaic longings. To distinguish the analyst's countertransference from a member's similar response, the therapist may find it practical to designate such reactions coming from co-patients as lateral, peer, or horizontal countertransference.

Since group members are under no injunction to treat one another therapeutically, their spontaneous and compulsive responses to one another always contain lateral transferential and countertransferential components. If members fulfill in some degree one another's inappropriate expectations, how can they help one another? To the degree that in peer transference and countertransference there is frustration of each other's archaic longings, there is propulsion to other and more mature alternative choices. To the extent that there is regression-inducing fulfillment of horizontal transference expectations, bilateral analysis of the interacting patients is indicated. For the patient who is seeking historically predetermined satisfaction, it becomes necessary to provide insight into the current inappropriateness of his compulsive pursuit of outmoded predilection. For the patient who is obsessively and unconsciously in lateral countertransference, it is necessary to discover the underlying peer transference on which his horizontal countertransference is based. Then it becomes equally possible to work through his present, persistent transferential distortion.

Even what manifestly seems to be a reasonable suggestion from one patient to another, such as a proposal for a more appropriate choice alternative to his pathology, may mask lateral transference and countertransference. It needs, therefore, to be explored for such unconscious content.

A patient is especially likely to step in prematurely between two vigorously disagreeing group members, who are misperceived as contesting members of the nuclear family. His efforts to interrupt the disharmony with pacifying gestures or precipitate analysis are less appropriate to the needs of the antagonists than to his own anxiety over a projected insoluble quarrel in his original family. At the opposite pole is the patient who transferentially detaches himself from any contention among others for fear that he may be accused of taking sides or that he may be caught in the crossfire.

The same kind of anticipatory intervention or disengagement may take place in the face of a positive exchange between co-patients. The interrupting member may be trying to separate the positively engaging members, who are projected as parents or as parent and sibling. He may be hoping to be included. He may wish to exclude one of the partners and to possess the other. Disengaging or retiring members may feel they have no right to be included in loving parental exchange or tender parent-sibling shows of affection.

A patient's lateral transferences and countertransferences make his responses one-dimensional in character. But as long as the group is heterogeneous, as it should be, the multiplicity of the members' peer transferences and countertransferences militates against the fulfillment of archaic longings. The variety of responses in sickness and health leads to a minimal gratification of outdated necessities and to an openness to new ideas. These multiple reactions are influences against any one patient's one-dimensional prevalence in horizontal countertransferential pathology. As a result, it is difficult in the therapeutic group to fulfill a patient's transference needs because the group's heterogeneity makes such varied demands of the individual member.

Transference Dilution. The criticism has been made that depth analysis is not possible in a group because the intensity of transference to the analyst is diluted by the presence of co-patients. It has been the authors' experience that, where regression, as in the transference neurosis, is in the service of the ego, such transference reactions are both achieved and worked through. The intensity of a member's transference neurosis may be diluted by its direction to a co-patient rather than to the analyst, but the experience and resolution of transference aimed at a peer facilitates both its subsequent emergence and ultimate resolution when invested in the group leader. It is as though the prior activation and working through of parental transference directed toward a peer becomes a practice ground for its later emergence and resolution with the therapist. In this sense, transference dilution need not be regarded as a limitation of psychoanalysis in groups but as an asset.

Also, a good many patients enter a group after failures in prolonged individual analysis and are in obvious unresolved transference psychosis after long regressive experiences. For them it becomes necessary, even essential, that the misperception of the therapist in the parental position be diluted by intensified but less noxious peer interaction. Here again, transference dilution is in the service of the ego, and the co-member peers enable the patient to free himself from the intensity of his transference psychosis.

Activity

Acting and Acting Out. Because of his training, the analyst is not likely to act out. There are occasions, however, when he is predisposed by his own or a patient's disequilibrium to act out. If this happens, he loses his reasonable, examining, discerning, and objective role. In the group, he is required, even forced, to retain a regardful and watchful role because the patients sustain one another with refuges in reality. They maintain one another in resisting the inappropriateness of the therapist's acting out.

The members of every therapeutic group sooner or later set bounds on their acting out. Prime movers for this restraint are the wholesome, realistic aspirations in each patient and the prophylactic factors in various ego functions. Another mainspring inheres in the projection of influential power, of living by the rules of law and order, of what is right and wrong, of superego values, which act to curb irrational behavior. The analyst, his attendance at regular meetings, and his vaguely felt presence at alternate sessions or afterward exert a limiting influence as well. The members are aware that their activity will sooner or later be revealed. Apprehension over such an outcome is also a factor in controlling acting out.

Certainly, there is less activity in the dyad than in the group. The essential point is not whether there is more or less activity in one setting than in the other. As long as there are patients in therapy, there will be acting out. The issue rather seems to be that the therapist is alarmed at the prospect of acting out taking place among his patients. In the dyad, acting out is prevented by the analyst, but the patient may act out outside the analytic chamber without the therapist's knowledge for some time. Acting out in the group is more easily exposed and discovered, and it can be more readily worked through.

In psychoanalysis in groups, there is more activity of all kinds than in individual analysis. There is more expression of warmth, affection, helpfulness, anger, aggression, hostility. The analyst is obliged to interrupt an interaction from time to time by offering interpretation, insight, and analysis. On occasion, when analysis fails in its object to limit acting out, he may have to forbid it. At the outset, patients may object to the analyst's denying them in this way and to the imposition of control, but in time the interdiction offers them so much relief from anxiety that they show their appreciation for the limits that are set. A good deal of the activity, however, is not acting out at all but a healthy consequence of wholesome group interaction. Acting out in the group is, in part, a result of intensely affective mutual stimulation. If the therapist persists in his interpretive analysis of what is going on, acting out can be controlled.

Self-Imposed Limits to Acting Out. If the therapist does not intervene to interrupt acting out, even the most dramatic kinds, group members sooner or later set their own limits. In the most seriously disturbed acting-out groups, the members inevitably turn to the analyst and ask him to help them set limits. Ultimately, there

is always such frustration between members who act out that the parties to it inevitably turn to the other patients and the analyst for control and insight. Patients who act out at alternate sessions sooner or later turn to the analyst, asking him to set limits and to seek greater understanding of the nature of their behavior.

A colleague reported a serious acting out in one of his groups. He was at one time a patient in a group, where he was given to a good deal of impulsive motility. If he felt affection for another member, he would rise and embrace him. If he was angry, he would jump from his seat and shake his fist threateningly in a patient's face. Asked to remain in his seat and simply to express in words what he thought or felt, he might, for example, shout at someone:

I'm so mad at you I could kick you in the ass and send you up in the air a hundred yards.

Even his fantasies took on a vigorous motility in his imagination.

The acting out in the group in which he was the therapist took place during the month of August, when he was on vacation. In his absence the group met weekly in alternate sessions.

One of the patients, Arthur, proposed to the other group members that they have a picnic-swim session at a deserted beach. This was agreed to. At the beach Arthur suggested that they disrobe entirely and swim in the nude. The group members resisted except for Bruce, who supported Arthur's proposal. Despite the general opposition, Arthur took his clothes off, and Bruce joined him. Then a third member disrobed, then a fourth. The group dynamic began to prevail, and before long the remaining members were shamed by being called prudes or were otherwise influenced by the aggressive leadership of Arthur and Bruce into joining in the naked swim.

At the next group session at Arthur's house, he proposed to the members that they all urinate in a common pot. Again, Bruce seconded the proposal, and the others resisted. But essentially the same sequence of events occurred, with Arthur taking the leadership, Bruce then taking his turn, and the group going along with varying degrees of conflict about what they were doing.

At a later group meeting, when Arthur proposed that they defecate in the pot, he could not get even Bruce to endorse his suggestion. Without Bruce's support, the group was able to resist Arthur's acting out and prevailed on him not to defecate before them.

When the therapist returned from vacation, each member of the group turned to him for support against Arthur's and Bruce's acting out and asked for some interpretive explanation of what each of them was doing.

It is relevant to note that, when the therapist described regular group sessions, they appeared quite startling to his supervisors. One patient, in a suicidal gesture, would be running toward a window to jump out. Another patient would be in hot pursuit, tackling him to save him. Members seemed in their motility to be reflecting or contagiously getting into the action that the therapist himself exhibited. Yet, despite the therapist's extreme provocation, the group members were able in concert to limit their acting out. This example shows how, even under the most severe stimulation to act inappropriately, a therapeutic group sooner or later controls its acting out.

Such pathological activity in no way typifies regular or alternate meetings. This is the most serious case of acting out the authors know of and is more a reflection of the therapist's inducement than of any characteristic tendency of members to behave this way.

Another illustration of acting out was presented by an analyst who entered a workshop with a view to learning theory and techniques of psychoanalysis in groups. She engaged in discussions with a good deal of interest and vigor. She accepted most of the theoretical formulations presented but expressed some concern and doubt about the value of the alternate meetings. Nevertheless, after some months of training in the workshop, she started her first therapeutic group.

At the workshop meeting after her second group session, she reported with considerable alarm that, at the alternate session without her, her group found one another so interesting that they met all night. She was quite disturbed over this development and questioned the workshop members closely over whether any of them had ever had a similar experience. No one had. On rare occasions, stimulating meetings had lasted until midnight, but alternate sessions generally ran from 8:30 to 10:30 or 11:00 P.M. The workshop members tried to reassure her that the group would surely limit this excess of activity in due course.

At successive workshop meetings for some weeks, the analyst continued to report with mounting anxiety that her suggestions that the members limit their time together were of no avail. Her group continued to meet all night. She asked one of the workshop directors for a private meeting, where she was asked to associate freely to these all-night encounters and her reactions to them. Before long, she recalled how her children had had to be reprimanded at night because they tended, left to their own devices, to stay up very late, too late for their own good, as she said, talking animatedly about all kinds of "nonsense," getting so excited that they were unable to sleep. She then recalled how, when they were at college and returned home on holidays, they would stay up all hours of the night, telling one another of their various college experiences, and how she would again feel called on to interfere and insist on their going to sleep.

She expressed great anxiety that the group members might become psychotic if permitted to engage one another in unconscious processes for many hours. They needed more control, more contact with reality, she said. She told how group members were supporting one another, just as her children did, in criticizing her for trying to limit the time they were spending together. The patients all protested that she was too controlling. They enjoyed their new-found freedom together away from her and enjoyed, as well, their support of one another in confronting her with her need to isolate them from one another in individual sessions. One of the group members expressed their right to these privileges apart from the therapist.

In time, they gradually and at their own pace reduced the time spent at alternate meetings to a reasonable span.

What the group did was in response to the therapist's nonverbalized need to isolate them from one another in individual sessions and in her nonverbally expressed doubts about the appropriateness of the alternate session. Evidently, the therapist was conveying to her patients what she had conveyed to her children—that they relate exclusively to her and not to each other. The patients, like her children, could not rebel until they found one another. But one sees once more how a therapeutic group, left to its own devices, acts in its own interest. Whenever this activity includes some acting out, sooner or later the group limits such pathological behavior. This clinical experience is a reassuring safeguard to analyst and patient alike.

Take another example: Some years ago a group of analysts with some experience in group therapy decided to form a therapeutic group of their own in which they would participate as group analysands but without a formally designated, experienced group analyst. It was reasoned with some logic that there was no need for a trained leader, for they were all clinically experienced therapists with analytic training behind them. For some months, things went fairly well, but angry feelings gradually began to mount.

One day, a member arrived at a group session with a stack of cheap plates. When he became sufficiently annoyed with one of the other members, he would fling a dish at him. At succeeding sessions, everyone arrived with a set of crockery. Fortunately, no one was physically hurt. But the amount of ducking, the dangers, and the ludicrousness of such sessions enabled more sense to prevail. In a calm moment they decided that they would stop their acting out and that they did, indeed, need a leader. The members called on an expert analyst in groups to guide them in subsequent meetings.

Action Groups. In the last 30 years, group therapy has led to movement from lying on the couch to being seated in a circle. And in more recent years there has been a leap into vigorous action. As in youthful circles elsewhere, there is an increasingly anarchic rejection of reasonableness and reality. Whereas psychoanalysis has always sought a controlled, systematic regression in the service of the ego, the disciples of action promote irrational feeling, acting out, and assault on order—all in the name of love. Such destructive activity is a call for infantilism, for regression without thought, in the name of freedom from the bourgeois values of the establishment. This kind of activity is a repudiation of all that years of careful analysis have taught—the necessity for dispassionate study of the patient. It makes a virtue of his illness. It puts pseudolove and its destructiveness above therapeutic reconstruction. It tells people to embrace one another without understanding. It says people can understand nothing. Therefore, they must give up as hopeless their historical aim of knowing one another. All they can do is act—act blindly but feelingfully. This unthinking activity is destructive not only of the other but of the self.

What followers of group-therapy-as-feelingful-action seem not to grasp is that, if feelingful action is the magic road to recovery, there is no further necessity for scrupulous training. Already, the group therapy movement is heavily weighted with dianeticists, scientologists, activists, zenists, and affectivists, who mindlessly lead loving and fighting groups into psychotic acting out. These leaders do not wish to be burdened by what they regard as the formalized disabilities of learning. It is easier to act swiftly and ruthlessly without the handicap of second thoughts or even first ones. What a patient needs, however, is thoughtful consideration. He turns to the analyst for insight, not rebellious exercises. There is serious danger that the group therapy movement will be taken over by the revolutionary know-nothingism of the affect-action promoters, for whom "id is beautiful."

CONCLUSION

The assumption by some dyadic analysts that psychoanalysis in groups cannot be effective because patients are too unaware of each other's realistic necessities and lack the capacity to grasp and deal with their archaic needs is not confirmed by clinical experience. On the contrary, analysands attain in groups an unusual facility for multilateral examination, for insight, and for mutually enhancing conduct.

Until recently, group analysis has been the apprentice, the beneficiary of dyadic analysis. The group analyst has attempted to incorporate in his practice the experience and skills that the dyadic analyst has made available. Now refinements in understanding, new intuitions, and greater clarity derivative of group analysis may well advance, deepen, and improve individual analysis. If dyadic analysts were to become acquainted with the importance and utility of forced interaction, of socializing, of involvement with others, of working through vertical and peer problems, of resolving obsessional concerns with status, of multiple interaction in effecting intrapsychic improvement, and so forth, these factors would not be as overlooked as they now are in individual analytic therapy.

Analytic treatment tries to embody, integrate, and bring into concordance the intrapsychic and the interpersonal. Dyadic and group analysis offer the therapist somewhat different kinds of materials to work with to attain an appropriate harmony between the personal and the interpersonal. In dyadic analysis, the therapist is obliged to deal primarily with intrapsychic data— with the free association, fantasies, dreams, recall, and remembrance of past events and interactions. But in the group, the interactions themselves are presented for scrutiny at the time of their occurrence. In the therapeutic dyad, only the interaction between analysand and therapist is available for study. But in the group, the exchange among members is always within easy reach.

Despite these differences, psychoanalysis is basically the same. Different media provide varying aspects of the interpersonal engagement referred to as the analytic experience. The medium determines, in part, the particular kinds of materials that are used, what needs to be stressed or accented. But the plan to use analysis as a reconstructive experience with the intention of promoting the analysand's chances for positive development are essentially very similar. A congenial unity of skills originating in dyadic analysis and joined with group analysis offers the therapist the opportunity to practice with richer and more extensive means.

This view does not mean that particular structural differences inherent in the two settings do not prevail. Occasionally, these differences have been vaguely referred to as atmosphere. They are, however, more determinate, more specific than the concept of climate. Here are some of the integral characteristics that determine the content and process of group as contrasted with dyadic analysis:

In a group, the attendance of a number of analysands affords the concurrent presence of hierarchical and peer vectors. The therapist is experienced by the patient as more remote, and the patient feels closer to his co-patients. Transference responses are not directed only to the analyst or provoked only by him, and transference is less uniform and entrenched. The multitude of stimulating and animating others in a group makes it more arduous at first to dissect what is appropriate from what is inappropriate in the course of multiple interaction. Nevertheless, the discordant stimuli, whether inciting or sustaining, afford each member many occasions in which he can experience affirmation. In the group, there are more safeguards in reality as well as uncertainties in unreality. At the same time, the analyst's illusions and authenticity are subject to more intensive scrutiny by the members. And the likelihood of the analyst's aggressive or sexual acting out is practically eliminated once he undertakes to practice in a group.

The bilateral, trilateral, and quadrilateral nature of transference responses becomes more apparent in a group milieu. The emotional pitch of co-patient transference is more readily endured than is dyadic transference just because its intensity is diminished in its direction toward a peer. Sometimes mutual peer transferences help keep patients in therapy. Such strong affect directed toward the analyst might impel a patient to escape treatment or to become immobilized. In the group, interpersonal responses are maintained by the members, and the analyst can be the disengaged but active observer. In the group, the patient may withdraw, unless the analyst promotes interaction and requires attendance at alternate meetings. It is more difficult for the patient to remove himself in resistance in the group because other members demand more action, reaction, and interaction. As a consequence, all the relationships of the members are magnified and amplified. As a result of the quantity and quality of animation among the members, the opportunity for more disequilibration and more reconstructive analysis co-exist. The exchange among patients is followed by analysis of intrapsychic material.

In a group, no single member becomes the focus of analytic attention to the exclusion of others. Consideration by the members and the leader moves from one patient to the next so that cyclic oscillation of activity and rest, disinhibition and restitution take place. No member is obliged to engage in only one kind of activity or to play an assigned, homogeneous role. In the analytic dyad, it is difficult to change his repertoire, for he is always in the position of being helped by a helper. In psychoanalysis in groups, he is expected and even required to play a multiplicity of emancipating parts.

REFERENCES

Kadis, A. L., Krasner, J. D., Winick, C., and Foulkes, S. H. *A Practicum of Group Psychotherapy*. Harper and Row, New York, 1963.

Locke, N. *Group Psychoanalysis*. New York University Press, New York, 1961.

Markowitz, M., Schwartz, E., and Liff, Z. Nondidactic methods of group psychotherapy training. Int. J. Group Psychother., *15:* 220, 1965.

Mullan, H., and Rosenbaum, M. *Group Psychotherapy*. Free Press of Glencoe, New York, 1962.

Rosenbaum, M., and Berger, M. *Group Psychotherapy and Group Function*. Basic Books, New York, 1963.

Schwartz, E. K. Leadership and the psychotherapist. In *Topical Problems of Psychotherapy*, p. 72, B. Stokvis, editor. S. Karger, Basel, 1965.

Schwartz, E. K. Group psychotherapy: the individual and the group. Acta Psychother., *13:* 142, 1965.

Schwartz, E. K., and Rabin, H. M. A training group with one non-verbal co-leader. J. Psychoanal. Group., *2:* 35, 1968.

Schwartz, E. K., and Wolf, A. Psychoanalysis in groups: resistances to its use. Amer. J. Psychother., *17:* 457, 1963.

Schwartz, E. K., and Wolf, A. On countertransference in group psychotherapy. J. Psychol., *57:* 131, 1963.

Schwartz, E. K., and Wolf, A. The interpreter in group therapy: conflict resolution through negotiation. Arch. Gen. Psychiat., *18:* 186, 1968.

Wolf, A. Short-term group psychotherapy. In *Short-Term Psychotherapy*, p. 219, L. R. Wolberg, editor. Grune & Stratton, New York, 1965.

Wolf, A. Group psychotherapy. In *Comprehensive Textbook of Psychiatry*, p. 1234, A. M. Freedman and H. I. Kaplan, editors. Williams & Wilkins, Baltimore, 1967.

Wolf, A., and Schwartz, E. K. *Psychoanalysis in Groups*. Grune & Stratton, New York, 1962.

Wolf, A., and Schwartz, E. K. Psychoanalysis in groups: as creative process. Amer. J. Psychoanal., *24:* 46, 1964.

Wolf, A., Schwartz, E. K., McCarty, G. J., and Goldberg, I. A. *Beyond the Couch*. Science House, New York, 1970.

4

Sexual Acting-Out
in the Psychoanalysis of Groups

by Members of The Workshop in Group Psychoanalysis, New York*

INTRODUCTION
AND DEFINITION

Every psychoanalyst has been confronted with behavior that interferes with the movement of the analytic process, with patterns of acting that becloud the recognition of the patient's basic problems. Such obstructive behavior may be said to take place when the patient, instead of verbalizing his feelings, substitutes motor activity. For example, in place of verbalizing his feelings of love and hostility, he may engage in acts of seduction or aggression. The patient who substitutes motor activity for verbal activity in a transference relationship is acting-out. Acting-out has been described as a disturbance of superego control as a result of unusually strong transference reactions. Such reactions are based on an unconscious misunderstanding of present external objects in the sense of the past.

A basic rule of analysis is to provide for free association and free verbalization of

Reprinted with permission from *Int. J. Group Psychother.*, *4*, 1954.

* Members of The Workshop in Group Psychoanalysis included the following participants: Alexander Wolf, M.D., Rachel Bross, M.D., Samuel Flowerman, Ph.D., Janet S. Greene, Ph.D., Asya L. Kadis, M.A., Harold Leopold, M.D., Norman Locke, Ph.D., Irving Milberg, M.D., Hugh Mullan, M.D., Samuel J. Obers, M.D., and Max Rosenbaum, Ph.D.

affect. This rule is broken whenever the patient begins to act out instead of containing his feelings on a verbal level. At that point his actions prevent his gaining insight by means of interpretation and working-through, and the analysis is said to be at a standstill.

In the literature such acting-out is considered to be a common and deplorable occurrence. Emch regards acting-out as a repetition of the past. Loeser and Bry, and Roth, see it in terms of the related phenomenon, transference. Bry regards acting-out as resistance. Weiss, Fenichel, and Kasanin say that acting-out is the reappearance of an inner drive, the expression of or relief from it, that it is unpredictable and irrational. Johnson and Szurek state that the person who acts out is one with a superego defect. Reich has used the term "implusive character" to describe people who act out, and Alexander feels that individuals who need punishment tend to act out. Schmideberg states that patients who act out their conflicts are constitutionally unable to tolerate frustration, as compared with more repressed and inhibited individuals. Aichhorn in his studies of antisocial behavior, and Healy and Bronner, too, pointed out that at times children who act out have identified themselves with the ethical distortions of their parents. Healy and Bronner formulated the concept that the rejected child cannot develop a normal superego that would enable him to control acting-out.

These references in the literature suggest that acting-out is seen as a persistent problem and a therapeutic difficulty. In only a few isolated instances is there admission of the possibility that acting-out may contain a positive element. In no instance does an author indicate that acting-out can be used constructively in the therapeutic process. In the literature, then, acting-out is generally considered obstructive and negative. Sexual acting-out is rarely a subject of discusssion as such.

This chapter is basically concerned with an evaluation of the problem of sexual acting-out in group psychoanalysis with the aim of discovering possible positive elements which do not necessarily doom therapeutic movement to a standstill.

It has been generally agreed, starting with Freud, that successful psychoanalysis is based on the concepts of working-through of resistance and transference. Acting-out may become the expression of and evidence for the transference relationship and is often used by the patient as resistance. The meaning of acting-out can thus always be seen in the frame of the transference relationship. In analysis, the patient displays behavior originally repressed when his conflict was in the making. At this earlier period his characteristic behavior patterns were becoming ingrained into his character structure. Some of the behavior patterns have been compulsively employed over the years at the slightest frustration. Others develop in the course of analysis as an attempt to act out the repressed incestuous or aggressive fantasies of childhood. In both cases, acting-out manifests itself in repetitive, irrational behavior, as an outgrowth of the person's history.

Reasons for Occurrence

In any particular instance, why does acting-out occur? It does so always in the frame of a strong transference relationship, when the impulse is strengthened and the defense is weakened. Prior to therapy, such transference behavior may have been directed at a definite person or persons who have become representatives of some significant figure of the past. Likewise, in therapy, and especially in the group, acting-out may be directed at any member who also becomes a significant figure of the past.

Several factors in the group situation predispose to sexual acting-out. The mixed therapeutic group provides a familial setting, often including for the first time the experience of truly permissive parental figures. The alternate sessions, meetings unattended by the analyst, reinforce this permissive milieu. In such an atmosphere relatively free verbal and nonverbal communication of sexual feelings occurs, often provoked by certain group members. For some individuals such communication is erotically stimulating, particularly under conditions of physical proximity, and the resultant tension may lead to sexual acting-out with members of the same group or with individuals outside the group. There are, of course, significant group reactions that serve to inhibit sexual acting-out. In one group two patients, both married, were on the verge of acting-out sexually, but countertransferences of the other group members, who saw them as parental prototypes, forced them to work through their feelings and prevented them from acting-out.

Group members who act out sexually with one another evoke, in other members of the group, conscious and unconscious feelings that the family pattern is being disrupted by a violation of the incest taboo. The sexual acting-out elicits anxiety in them with respect to their own incestuous feelings. This may in turn lead to constructive working-through, enabling these other group members to resolve their own incestuous conflicts which they have hitherto been unable to face.

Most patients are able, partly because of the accepting group climate, to verbalize their anxieties and aggressive and sexual feelings in the group, thus making these feelings available for analysis. The behavior at alternate meetings is brought up at subsequent sessions. Some members inevitably want to tell "papa" or "mama."

The Group Role

How should the group-analytic process deal with sexual acting-out?

Various attitudes are observed among analysts toward sexual acting-out. Some take the position that their goal is the mobilization of anxiety for therapeutic working-through. It follows that sexual acting-out, which relieves anxiety, should be forestalled. Another therapeutic attitude is neither to prohibit nor to sanction any specific type of behavior. If the therapist takes a stand by expressing either approval or disapproval, he permits himself to be caught up in the unrealistic manipulation with which the patient has been struggling all his life, and the therapist thus defeats his own purposes. It can therefore be seen that in coping with sexual acting-out in group psychoanalysis we seem to be on the horns of a dilemma. If, in the hope of preventing sexual acting-out, we resolutely forbid any physical contact, do we not, like the patient's parents before us, repeat a castrating role that was so damaging in the past? If, on the other hand, we sanction sexual intimacy, do we not encourage sexual acting-out, which reduces anxiety, prevents memories and motives from becoming conscious, and thus postpone behavior integration?

In an effort to avoid this dilemma, the authors' workshop has tried to determine whether the occurrence of sexual acting-out can be used in a constructive way.

With sexual acting-out, as with all behavior in group analysis, the therapist is committed to three endeavors: First, and perhaps foremost, he permits and promotes all affective experiencing within the group. Character defenses against immediate experiencing and resistance to psychoanalysis either crumble or are reinforced for all group members when sexual acting-out is reported in the group. This point will be clarified in a subsequent illustration. Second, the therapist analyzes sexual acting-out historically. This is the analysis of transference components of the event. The family figures in the past and their prototypes in the present, especially among group members, are described. The repetitive nature of the activity and its relative indiscriminateness are brought out. Third, the therapist analyzes sexual behavior in the present. This is the analysis of the vicissitudes of the character structure in its attempt to avoid anxiety by sexual acting-out. Security operations, the unwillingness to change, immaturity, needs for maintaining overidealized concepts of self, etc., are described. The compulsivity of the act is enlarged upon as is the factor of no growth and stasis. The realities of the situation and the consequences of the behavior are brought home to those acting-out and to the group.

Case History 1

The following case is presented to show how the analysis of sexual acting-out aided in the working-through of neurotic conflicts.

Real Sexual Involvement. Two young people—Steve and Ruth—met as patients in a group, were attracted to each other, and began meeting after group sessions. After they had missed two sessions the analyst phoned them. They informed him that they were in love and intended to get married. They felt all their neurotic problems were resolved and that there was no longer any need for group analysis. The therapist invited them to join him in a session before acting on their decision, and in the course of the interview it developed that they had fled treatment with the notion that the group, as the projected original family, would deny them marital and sexual privileges. Accordingly they felt that they had to elope. The analyst assured them that the group as a whole had no negative attitudes toward their establishing a relationship; that if some members objected, it might be due to their own problems; that Steve's and Ruth's flight from the group was based on a neurotic projection that the group as family would object to their marriage; and finally, that while the analyst had no objection to their marriage, it would be wise to look for and work through possible transferences and countertransferences in their feelings for one another. They were then persuaded to return to the group.

Re-examination of Needs. Before long their romance was shaken by reports of Steve's premature ejaculation and Ruth's jealousy of his seeming attentiveness to Jane, another group member. It became clear in time that Steve projected on Ruth maternal qualities that demanded of him self-denying perfection in all activities without sexual privileges, to which he responded with anxious impotence. On Ruth's side she regarded his sexual failure as a rejection of her. When Steve, on occasion, in the course of a group session, directed his attention to Jane, Ruth's sense of rejection was compounded. Steve became for her the father who preferred a more attractive sibling. And Ruth turned from him in hurt and anger. Her resentment became a further threat to Steve, who read into her behavior a growing demand for restricted performance on his part that left him more impotent than ever. His helplessness made Ruth feel still more acutely that Steve, like her father before him, did not really care for her. They climbed an endless and increasingly frustrating tree of transference and countertransference. They were at a seeming impasse.

Response of Other Group Members. All this time members reacted to the relationship according to their own problems. One patient could not bear seeing his "father" and "mother" in disagreement and on the verge of a separation that would leave him abandoned. Jane was delighted to see her "mother" defeated and did her seductive best to win Steve away for herself. Another man assumed his compulsive role of arbitrating any dispute between "father" and "mother" but secretly hoped his "father" would be rejected by his "mother" and expelled from the "family." A voyeur kept urging Steve on to more amorous efforts with Ruth in the hope of hearing more erotically stimulating reports of their incestuous relationship. An analyst (participating as a patient in the group) kept protesting that the group analyst was sponsoring a destructive sexual acting-out by permitting the relationship to go on at all and threatened to quit group analysis for tolerating such unethical practices. A woman who had never had a heterosexual experience threatened to leave the group if Steve and Ruth continued a "disgusting" sexual relationship. It was hard enough for her to *listen* to the group's talk of their sexual experiences without having almost to witness such "horrors" within the body of the "family" itself. A male homosexual was torn between contempt for the weak father in Steve and a wish for him to be the successful, sexual man he hoped to find in his father as an example with whom he could identify. A homosexual woman comforted Ruth and overprotected her, trying all the while to isolate her from Steve.

Working Out the Relationship. Despite these cross-currents of feeling which pulled at Steve and Ruth from all directions, the entire group felt that there was a healthy, hard, and wholesome core of genuine mutual attraction and regard that kept Steve and Ruth close. Despite any transferences of group members which impelled them to separate or bind Steve and Ruth, there existed among them at the same time a wish to see them consummate a good relationship. Over the ensuing months of working-through, Steve began to understand that Ruth's perfectionistic demands and rejection of him, as a figure who preferred Jane, stemmed from and were still related to her attitude to her father. He also perceived that his mother projection on Ruth prevented him from experiencing and expressing all the forbidden incestuous love he had repressed in the past. He thus became able to experience with Ruth all the tenderness he had denied himself in childhood. At one period the analyst became the threatening father who would not allow him Ruth. But this anxiety was gradually dispelled by the analyst's supporting him now in enjoying the woman he loved until she ceased to be mother and became Ruth in her own right.

Ruth, at the beginning of her love for Steve, was stirred emotionally and sexually, as never before in her recollection. Despite this, her presenting problem—an inability to attain orgasm—continued. In the period of Steve's impotence and his seeming interest in Jane, Ruth sank to the depths of despair, feeling again the old hurt of her father's preference for her sister. As Steve developed the historic theme of his struggles with a critical and demanding mother, whose insistence on perfect performance he could never quite satisfy, Ruth wept in sympathy and tenderness for the father and the boy Steve, whom she loved in retrospect, as she loved the man Steve now. Her warmth and understanding helped Steve re-awaken and re-experience his love for her and work through his own transference of the inaccessible mother. Steve's insight into Ruth's projection and his passionate pursuit of her helped her work through the illusion of his preference for a sibling. Finally, the group was able to work through their guilt over incest and their fear of attack by the parent of the same sex by confronting them with the nonfamilial character of their relationship and by encouraging them to gratify their need of one another. Out of their real tenderness for one another and as transference guilt was dispelled, Steve's increasing sexual and social potency developed. Ruth too responded with fully gratifying orgasm and unabashed love for Steve. Ruth and Steve were married before they left the group. All the members attended their wedding.

Resolution. Space does not permit an examination of the development, denouement, and working-through of all the transferences elicited in the various group members by Steve and Ruth. It should be said, however, that in each instance their projected responses became fruitful areas of self-exploration and emotional working-through.

To the authors it seems as if in the process of working-through for Ruth and Steve, there were the usual elements at work: insight into one's transference distortions with attempts in an understanding climate to relate more realistically in the here and now. But the authors believe that the love between Steve and Ruth provided

two elements that facilitated a working-through that need special emphasis. One of these factors was their strong physical, emotional, realistic, and nontransference yearning for one another that kept breaking through the negative, illusory distortions that drove them apart. But for the purposes of this chapter the authors should like to emphasize the second element: the positive aspect of Steve's striving to reach the once inaccessible mother in Ruth and Ruth's equally persistent struggle to express the feelings for her father in Steve. While each was in part sexually acting-out, the experiencing of repressed affect which found a responsive chord in the other became an additional base for a realistic and more mature relationship in the present, freed of transference components. It is in this second factor that we see illustrated the conversion of sexual acting-out into a therapeutic experience.

Case History 2

The following case of acting-out, involving Gertrude, a married woman in her late twenties, and Paul, a few years her junior, comprised only a single traumatic episode and did not result in any protracted relationship.

Background. Gertrude is a well-built woman, dark-haired, with expressive facial features. Prior to her group experience she had two years of individual analysis. Her major complaint was disgust with sexual relations; she experienced vaginismus during intercourse. Her sexual difficulties were associated with a highly derogatory and contemptuous attitude toward her husband. She thought of him as a man "without a penis."

In the group, as a very popular member, she played an active yet manipulative role. Her ready interpretations were astute and intellectual; the same sensitivity expressed itself in a subtle destructive assault that would render fellow group members helpless.

From the outset, Gertrude focused her attention upon Paul, who as an admired, loved, and popular figure had become in many ways the leader of the group. He was very handsome, dramatic, artistic, and capable of expressing his feelings with striking clarity and flavor. Gertrude experienced a strong physical attraction to Paul. She "felt her vagina opening up when looking at him"; he aroused feelings that she had never felt able to experience before. She saw in him her powerful father—an outstanding leader of the community (and the group), the idealized man who could give her an orgasm. She became intent upon seducing Paul. These desires for Paul were related during the regular group sessions when the therapist was present, but it was during alternate meetings that she made active physical overtures to him.

Confrontation. At one of the alternate meetings, when the therapist was away on a brief vacation, Gertrude arranged with Paul to go to his apartment. Upon their arrival, Gertrude immediately headed for the bedroom, and without saying a word, took off her clothes. As Paul looked at her, a large birthmark on her breast struck him, and simultaneously he was overcome by a paralyzing feeling of horror; he was devoid of sexual excitement. Helplessly, he said, "I can't," and left the room in revolt and fear. Gertrude was perplexed at his inability to respond to her, for she knew him to be potent in other relationships. She became intensely angry and they left the apartment separately.

Paul, visibly perturbed, presented the episode at the next regular meeting. He needed relief from his anxiety and found a very sympathetic response from group members. He articulated his anxiety in minute detail; he described the horror, paralysis, and helplessness he had felt in response to Gertrude's actions. Gertrude's initial response to him was one of open indignation, of hurt and desire for revenge. The vividness of Paul's helplessness made her aware that it was she who had rendered him impotent; that she had made her own hero fail. She was confronted, for the first time, with the destructive and hostile role which she had played in heterosexual relations.

As her idol in the group had fallen, so did her original idol, her father. For the first time negative feelings were revealed toward both Paul and father. She reported a memory for the first time that described father as a punitive and as a feared person, and during the following weeks such negative recollections multiplied. The restructured perception of her father produced an important shift in negative affect, away from her husband and toward Paul and her father, with important consequences in her marital relationship. In accepting the hidden negative impulses toward the original love object, she was able to reveal more positive feelings toward her husband—heretofore the object of abuse. Gertrude began to single out her husband as a man strong enough to cope with her aggressions, and she started to regard him as a truly masculine figure.

Working Out the Real Problems. Her acting-out thus led to a revival of her original familial conflict. Unlike the original family, the group could tolerate the actual incestuous conduct, and while some members were very critical, the group as a whole was sufficiently supportive so that her "forbidden" behavior did not result in her being rejected as a person. The group mediated an integration of ambivalent feelings toward love objects between the present and the past.

The episode of acting-out was similarly crucial to Paul's development. One of Paul's major problems was that of succumbing passively to the comfort of an overprotective mother, only to react in impulsive flight when the pressure became intolerable. He lives at home, is being pampered, but in his sudden flights he has twice left the country on extended trips, just "to get away."

Prior to acting-out, Paul became aware of his mother transference to Gertrude. She was an intellectual girl, of similar background, and he felt himself passively succumbing to her seduction, dreading it and warding it off tentatively. Yet the verbal awareness of this transference relationship became insufficient; he repeatedly said, "I know I see here my problem with mother, but what of it?'' Only when the closeness became a physical one was the affect around the repressed mother image revived.

His flight from Gertrude during the acting-out represented a significant re-experiencing of a childhood situation. As Paul related Gertrude's undressing in front of him, he suddenly recalled a memory in which mother called him into a room, lifting her skirt to show him a blue mark on the upper part of her thigh. He also recalled the same feeling of horror he had felt on seeing Gertude's birthmark.

Paul's subsequent recollections of mother assumed a highly concrete, sensuous quality. He began to describe the sensation of mother's body odor, the ''flavor'' of her perfume, the feeling of her breast, the texture of her skin. He suddenly experienced his active desire for mother; but he also suddenly saw mother, not in a protective role, but as a seducer, who, like Gertrude, threatened to paralyze him.

In both Gertrude and Paul, the partner to the acting-out was used as a lever, to loosen up repressed affect which could then be admitted to awareness. The vivid quality of the experience, its sensory and motor aspects, seem to be crucial in bringing about this loosening process. For both patients, though the price may have been momentary hurt and depression, and may have involved temporary regression, acting-out was followed by an unfolding and recovering of repressed experiences.

Evaluation of Case Histories

These cases illustrate that psychoanalytic therapy is most effective when it permits the patient affectively to revive and relive the repressed and painful past. Such a process may entail in some instances an irrational and emotional acting-out. It is the therapist's function to respond to the patient's acting-out—sexually or otherwise —with the warmth and understanding that the patient failed to receive from the original family. In this sense, acting-out can be converted and channeled into a constructive therapeutic experience. Those analysts who

out of their own anxiety forbid any acting-out or who intellectually ''analyze'' it prematurely deny the patient this kind of regression and eventual progressive development.

Some of the authors believe that there are instances in which sexual acting-out may be beneficial to one or both persons in the group-analytic relationship. Sexual contact may be mutually gratifying and therapeutically constructive, even though the experience may represent in part a sexual acting-out. Only if the patient were acting out of pure transference could he be thought of as living through in the present a completely archaic incestuous relationship. But no member of a therapeutic group is so irrational in his interpersonal relations as not to see his associates to some *real* extent. It is this perception of reality with the wholesome possibility of genuine mutual fulfillment that ought not to be tampered with.

The authors do not claim, however, that all sexual acting-out is necessarily therapeutic. We could just as easily provide illustrations of its potentially destructive aspects. Nor do we profess that sexual acting-out necessarily terminates in every instance like a Cinderella story. Steve's and Ruth's marriage is more the exception than the rule, even though in a few other instances sexual acting-out in therapy groups has also led to good marriages. More frequently it is instrumental in improving a marital relationship that has been threatening to break up. Some sexual acting-out has led in analysis to misunderstanding, hurt, and separation of the partners.

The authors' goals, as in all analysis, are largely directed at the resolution of resistance and transference. We are in no way blind to the possibility that seeming affection may screen hostility. However, the authors do maintain that the destructive aspects of sexual acting-out are complemented by equally constructive potentials, which, while they commonly do not end in a lasting affinity, may yet be used to work through conflicts, thus facilitating closer, mutual understanding.

We say, then, that there exists in all

sexual acting-out, despite its archaic component, a creative striving for mutual fulfillment, which, if experienced and worked through in a therapeutic atmosphere, may lead to a realistic, adult relationship.

The successful working-through of sexual acting-out is contingent in large measure upon the therapist's conscious and unconscious reactions to the patients' behavior. The therapist's attitudes and feelings toward sexual acting-out is thus of the utmost importance.

The Analyst's Attitude

As the authors have noted, sexual acting-out may occur, but whether it is reported so that it can be analyzed depends largely on the analyst's attitude. When acting-out is sexual in nature, it often heightens the therapist's anxiety. This anxiety may evoke in him the same restrictive patterns the patient had already experienced from parent, church, and society. To such a therapist, the patients may become children who are not allowed the many expressions of sexual feelings, interests, or curiosities. Another danger is an overprotective attitude on the part of the analyst, also resulting from unrecognized countertransference feelings. The patient in this circumstance is denied intimate relationship with any other person because of the therapist's own needs.

The analyst's value system, his cultural compliance, his neurotic desires and fears engendered by his unresolved sexual adjustment, will determine his attitude toward the sexuality of his patients. The therapist, for example, may use the sexual behavior in the group to reassure himself regarding his own wishes for promiscuity, or he may use it voyeuristically to obtain vicarious satisfaction. In these instances the analyst is bent upon remaining free from anxiety and utilizes any security operation open to him. The rigid, restrictive, authoritative analyst will discourage any kind of extragroup socialization: he will regard alternate meetings as a therapeutic danger to his patients as well as a rebellious threat to himself. He has to maintain a watchful,

moralistic eye over his "children's" behavior and keep them obedient. It seems that these attitudes of the analyst do not have bearing solely on the patient's acting-out but also on the whole structure of his total approach and planning of therapy.

Summary

In summary, sexual acting-out may be forbidden; it may be permitted; it may be encouraged. It may also be analyzed before it occurs or after it has taken place. The authors' experience has been that if forbidden, it takes place in secret without the analyst's knowledge. The therapist is treated with the same distrust and rebellion as is the parent. An adequate working-through becomes impossible with a substitute who is as denying as the original parent. If the therapist can sense that an imminent sexual acting-out is going to be destructive to a patient or another group member who may be involved, the most therapeutic approach is to analyze it in advance and prevent its occurrence. The authors are particularly on guard with adolescents, potential delinquents, and prepsychotics. We are not yet in a position to make specific predictions in regard to the prognostic implications of acting-out in relation to particular diagnostic categories. This is a task for further research.

In those instances in which patients report sexual acting-out, we have no alternative but to analyze it after it has taken place. We do not encourage or discourage any involvement between two patients. We do not *choose* to have sexual acting-out in our group. We encourage our patients to adopt as a plan of action the phrase: "*Talk out rather than act out.*" However, we are aware that sexual acting-out occurs, as does any neurotic manifestation. We deal with the anxiety with which the sexual problem is fraught, discovering how all of us have been more afraid of expressing love than hate. We try to work within the framework of verbalized transference and countertransference. If, however, any acting-out occurs, whether sexual or not, we enlist it on the side of therapy.

REFERENCES

Aichhorn, A. *Wayward Youth.* Viking Press, New York, 1935.

Alexander, F. The neurotic character. Int. J. Group Psychother., 11, 1930.

Bry, T. Acting out in group psychotherapy, Int. J. Group Psychother., *3:* 42, 1953.

Emch, M. On the need to know, as related to identification and acting out. Int. J. Group Psychoanal., *25:* 13, 1944.

Fenichel, O. *The Psychoanalytic Theory of Neurosis.* Norton, New York, 1945.

Fenichel, O. Neurotic acting out. Psychoanal. Rev., *32:* 10, 1945.

Freud, S. *An Outline of Psychoanalysis,* Norton, New York, 1949.

Healy, W., and Bronner, A. *New Lights on Delinquency and Its Treatment.* Yale University Press, New Haven, 1936.

Johnson, A., and Szurek, S. A. The genesis of antisocial acting out in children and adults. Psychoanal. Quart., *21:* 58, 1952.

Kasanin, J. S. Neurotic acting out as a basis for sexual promiscuity in women. Psychoanal. Rev., 31, 1944.

Loeser, L., and Bry, T. The position of the group therapist in transference and countertransference: An Experimental Study. Int. J. Group Psychother., *3:* 389, 1953.

Reich, W. *Der Triebhafte Charakter,* Internationaler psychoanalytischer Verlag, Wien, 1925.

Roth, N. The acting out of transferences. Psychoanal. Rev., *39:* 67, 1952.

Schmideberg, M. The mode of operation of psychoanalytic therapy. Int. J. Group Psychother., *19:* 310, 1938.

Weiss, E. Emotional memories and acting out. Psychoanal. Quart., *11:* 123, 1942.

Glossary*

Aberration, mental. Pathological deviation from normal thinking. Mental aberration is not related to a person's intelligence. *See also* Mental illness.

Abreaction. A process by which repressed material, particularly a painful experience or a conflict, is brought back to consciousness. In the process of abreacting, the person not only recalls but relives the repressed material, which is accompanied by the appropriate affective response. *See also* Catharsis.

Accelerated interaction. An alternate term for marathon group session that was introduced by one of its co-developers, Frederick Stoller. *See also* Group marathon.

Accountability. The responsibility a member has for his actions within a group and the need to explain to other members the motivations for his behavior.

Acid. Slang for lysergic acid diethylamide (LSD).

Acrophobia. Fear of high places.

Acting out. An action rather than a verbal response to an unconscious instinctual drive or impulse that brings about temporary partial relief of inner tension. Relief is attained by reacting to a present situation as if it were the situation that originally gave rise to the drive or impulse. *See also* Therapeutic crisis.

Actional-deep approach. Group procedure in which communication is effected through various forms of nonverbal behavior as well as or in place of language to produce character change. It is a technique used in psychodrama. *See also* Actional-superficial approach, Activity group therapy, Verbal-deep approach, Verbal-superficial approach.

Actional-superficial approach. Group procedure in which specific activities and verbal communication are used for limited goals. Verbal interchange and patient-to-patient interaction are of relatively minor therapeutic significance, and the groups are usually large. *See also* Actional-deep approach, Verbal-deep approach, Verbal-superficial approach.

Action group (A-group). Group whose purpose is to discuss a problem—community, industrial, or organizational—and to formulate a program of action. Emphasis is put on problem-solving rather than on developing awareness of self and group process. *See also* T-group.

Active therapist. Type of therapist who makes no effort to remain anonymous but is forceful and expresses his personality definitively in the therapy setting. *See also* Passive therapist.

Activity group therapy. A type of group therapy introduced and developed by S. R. Slavson and designed for children and young adolescents, with emphasis on emotional and active interaction in a permissive, nonthreatening atmosphere. The therapist stresses reality-testing, ego-strengthening, and action interpretation. *See also* Actional-deep approach; Activity-interview method; Bender, Lauretta; Play therapy.

Activity-interview method. Screening and diagnostic technique used with children. *See also* Activity group therapy.

Actualization. Process of mobilizing one's potentialities or making them concrete. *See also* Individuation.

---

* Edited by Ernesto A. Amaranto, M.D.

I

Adaptational approach. An approach used in analytic group therapy. Consonant with Sandor Rado's formulations on adaptational psychodynamics, the group focuses on the maladaptive patterns used by patients in the treatment sessions, on how these patterns developed, and on what the patients must do to overcome them and stabilize their functioning at self-reliant, adult levels. New methods of adaptation are practiced by the group members in the therapeutic sessions and later in their regular interpersonal relationships. *See also* Social adaptation.

Adapted Child. In transactional analysis, the primitive ego state that is under the parental influence. The adapted Child is dependent, unexpressive, and constrained. *See also* Natural Child.

Adler, Alfred (1870–1937). Viennese psychiatrist and one of Freud's original followers. Adler broke off from Freud and introduced and developed the concepts of individual psychology, inferiority complex, and overcompensation. A pioneer in group psychotherapy, he believed that the sharing of problems takes precedence over confidentiality. He also made contributions in the understanding of group process. *See also* Individual psychology, Masculine protest.

Adolescence. Period of growth from puberty to maturity. The beginning of adolescence is marked by the appearance of secondary sexual characteristics, usually at about age 12, and the termination is marked by the achievement of sexual maturity at about age 20. *See also* Psychosexual development.

Adult. In transactional analysis, an ego state oriented toward objective, autonomous data-processing and estimating. It is essentially a computer, devoid of feeling. It is also known as neopsychic function.

Affect. Emotional feeling tone attached to an object, idea, or thought. The term includes inner feelings and their external manifestations. *See also* Inappropriate affect, Mood.

Affect, blunted. A disturbance of affect manifested by dullness of externalized feeling tone. Observed in schizophrenia, it is one of that disorder's fundamental symptoms, according to Eugen Bleuler.

Affection phase. Last stage of group treatment. In this phase the members experience reasonable equality with the therapist and dwell on affectionate contact with each other in a give-and-take atmosphere rather than dwelling on dependency or aggression. *See also* Inclusion phase, Power phase.

Affective interaction. Interpersonal experience and exchange that are emotionally charged.

Affectualizing. In transactional analysis, the expression of emotions or feelings in group or individual treatment as part of a pasttime or game. It is distinguished from the expression of authentic feelings, which are characteristic of intimacy.

Afro-American. American Negro of African ancestry. This term has significance for blacks who seek a deeper and more positive sense of identity with their African heritage. *See also* Black separatism.

After-session. Group meeting of patients without the therapist. It is held immediately after a regular therapist-led session. *See also* Alternate session, Premeeting.

Agency. The striving and need to achieve in a person. Agency manifests itself in self-protection, the urge to master, self-expansion, and repression of thought, feeling, and impulse. *See also* Communion.

Aggression. Forceful, goal-directed behavior that may be verbal or physical. It is the motor counterpart of the affects of rage, anger, and hostility.

Aggressive drive. Destructive impulse directed at oneself or another. It is also known as the death instinct. According to contemporary psychoanalytic psychology, it is one of the two basic drives; sexual drive is the other one. Sexual drive operates on the pleasure-pain principle, whereas aggressive drive operates on the repetition-compulsion principle. *See also* Aggression, Libido theory.

Agitation. State of anxiety associated with severe motor restlessness.

Agnosia. Disturbance of perception characterized by inability to recognize a stimulus and interpret the significance of its memory impressions. It is observed in patients with organic brain disease and in certain schizophrenics, hysterics, and depressed patients.

Agoraphobia. Fear of open places. *See also* Claustrophobia.

Agranulocytosis. A rare, serious side effect, occurring with some of the psychotropic drugs. The condition is characterized by sore throat, fever, a sudden sharp decrease in white blood cell count, and a marked reduction in number of granulocytes.

A-group. *See* Action group.

Alcoholics Anonymous (A.A.) An organization of alcoholics formed in 1935. It uses certain group methods, such as inspirational-supportive techniques, to help rehabilitate chronic alcoholics.

Algophobia. Fear of pain.

Allergic jaundice. *See* Jaundice, allergic.

Alliance. *See* Therapeutic alliance, Working alliance.

Allport's group relations theory. Gordon W. Allport's theory that a person's behavior is influenced by his personality and his need to conform to social forces. It illustrates the interrelationship between group therapy and social psychology. For example, dealing with bigotry in a therapy group enhances the opportunity for therapeutic experiences because it challenges the individual patient's need to conform to earlier social determinants or to hold on to familiar but restrictive aspects of his personality.

Alternate session. Scheduled group meeting held without the therapist. Such meetings are held on a regular basis in between therapist-led sessions. Use of this technique was originated by Alexander Wolf. *See also* After-session, Premeeting.

Alternating role. Pattern characterized by periodic switching from one type of behavior to another. For example, in a group, alternating role is observed among members who switch from the role of the recipient of help to the giver of help.

Alternating scrutiny. *See* Shifting attention.

Altruism. Regard for and dedication to the welfare of others. The term was originated by Auguste Comte (1798–1857), a French philosopher. In psychiatry the term is closely linked with ethics and morals. Freud recognized altruism as the only basis for the development of community interest; Bleuler equated it with morality.

Ambivalence. Presence of strong and often overwhelming simultaneous contrasting attitudes, ideas, feelings, and drives toward an object, person, or goal. The term was coined by Eugen Bleuler, who differentiated three types: affective, intellectual, and ambivalence of the will.

Amnesia. Disturbance in memory manifested by partial or total inability to recall past experiences.

Amphetamine. A central nervous system stimulant. Its chemical structure and action are closely related to ephedrine and other sympathomimetic amines. *See also* Sympathomimetic drug.

Anal erotism. *See* Anal phase.

Anal phase. The second stage in psychosexual development. It occurs when the child is between the ages of one and three. During this period the infant's activities, interests, and concerns are centered around his anal zone, and the pleasurable experience felt around this area is called anal erotism. *See also* Genital phase, Infantile sexuality, Latency phase, Oral phase, Phallic phase.

Analysis. *See* Psychoanalysis.

Analysis in depth. *See* Psychoanalysis.

Analysis of transference. *See* Psychoanalysis.

Analytic psychodrama. Psychotherapy method in which a hypothesis is tested on a stage to verify its validity. The analyst sits in the audience and observes. Analysis of the material is made immediately after the scene is presented.

Anchor. Point at which the patient settles down to the analytic work involved in the therapeutic experience.

Antianxiety drug. Drug used to reduce pathological anxiety and its related symptoms without influencing cognitive or perceptual disturbance. It is also known as a minor tranquilizer and a psycholeptic drug. Meprobamate derivatives and diazepoxides are typical antianxiety drugs.

Anticholinergic effect. Effect due to a blockade of the cholinergic (parasympathetic and somatic) nerves. It is often seen as a side effect of phenothiazine therapy. Anticholinergic effects include dry mouth and blurred vision. *See also* Paralytic ileus.

Antidepressant drug. Drug used in the treatment of pathological depression. It is also known as a thymoleptic drug and a psychic energizer. The two main classes of antidepressant drugs are the tricyclic drugs and the monoamine oxidase inhibitors. *See also* Hypertensive crisis, Monoamine oxidase inhibitor, Tinnitus, Tricyclic drug.

Antimanic drug. Drug, such as lithium, used to alleviate the symptoms of mania. Lithium is particularly effective in preventing relapses in manic-depressive illness. Other drugs with antimanic effects are haloperidol and chlorpromazine.

Antiparkinsonism drug. Drug used to relieve the symptoms of parkinsonism and the extrapyramidal side effects often induced by antipsychotic drugs. The antiparkinsonism drug acts by diminishing muscle tone and involuntary movements. Antiparkinsonism agents include benztropine, procyclidine, biperiden, and trihexphenidyl. *See also* Cycloplegia, Mydriasis.

Antipsychotic drug. Drug used to treat psychosis, particularly schizophrenia. It is also known as a major tranquilizer and a neuroleptic drug. Phenothiazine derivatives, thioxanthene derivatives, and butyrophenone derivatives are typical antipsychotic drugs. *See also* Autonomic side effect, Dyskinesia, Extrapyramidal effect, Major tranquilizer, Parkinsonismlike effect, Reserpine, Tardive oral dyskinesia.

Antirepression device. Technique used in encounter groups and therapeutic groups to break through the defense of repression. In encounter groups, such techniques are frequently nonverbal and involve physical contact between group members. In therapeutic groups, dream analysis, free association, and role-playing are some antirepression techniques.

Anxiety. Unpleasurable affect consisting of psychophysiological changes in response to an intrapsychic conflict. In contrast to fear, the danger or threat in anxiety is unreal. Physiological changes consist of increased heart rate, disturbed breathing, trembling, sweating, and vasomotor changes. Psychological changes consist of an uncomfortable feeling of impending danger accompanied by overwhelming awareness of being powerless, inability to perceive the unreality of the threat, prolonged feeling of tension, and exhaustive readiness for the expected danger. *See also* Basic anxiety, Fear.

Apathetic withdrawal. *See* Withdrawal.

Apathy. Want of feeling or affect; lack of interest and emotional involvement in one's surroundings. It is observed in certain types of schizophrenia and depression.

Apgar scores. Measurements taken one minute and five minutes after birth to determine physical normality in the neonate. The scores are based on color, respiratory rate, heart beat, reflex action, and muscle tone. Used routinely, they are particularly useful in detecting the effects on the infant of drugs taken by the pregnant mother.

Aphasia. Disturbance in speech due to organic brain disorder. It is characterized by inability to express thoughts verbally. There are several types of aphasia: (1) motor aphasia—inability to speak, although understanding remains; (2) sensory aphasia—inability to comprehend the meaning of words or use of objects; (3) nominal aphasia—difficulty in finding the right name for an object; (4) syntactical aphasia—inability to arrange words in proper sequence.

Apperception. Awareness of the meaning and significance of a particular sensory stimulus as modified by one's own experiences, knowledge, thoughts, and emotions. *See also* Perception.

Archeopsychic function. *See* Child.

Arteriosclerotic cardiovascular disease. A metabolic disturbance characterized by degenerative changes involving the blood vessels of the heart and other arteries, mainly the arterioles. Fatty plaques, deposited within the blood vessels, gradually obstruct the flow of blood. Organic brain syndrome may develop when cerebral arteries are involved in the degenerative process.

Ataractic drug. *See* Major tranquilizer.

Ataxia. Lack of coordination, either physical or mental. In neurology it refers to loss of muscular coordination. In psychiatry the term intrapsychic ataxia refers to lack of coordination between feelings and thoughts; the disturbance is found in schizophrenia.

Atmosphere. *See* Therapeutic atmosphere.

Attention. Concentration; the aspect of consciousness that relates to the amount of effort exerted in focusing on certain aspects of an experience.

Attitude. Preparatory mental posture with which one receives stimuli and reacts to them. Group therapy often involves itself in defining for the group members their attitudes that have unconsciously dominated their reactions.

Auditory hallucination. False auditory sensory perception.

Authenticity. Quality of being authentic, real, and valid. In psychological functioning and personality, it applies to the conscious feelings, perceptions, and thoughts that a person expresses and communicates. It does not apply to the deeper, unconscious layers of the personality. *See also* Honesty.

Authority figure. A real or projected person in a position of power; transferentially, a projected parent.

Authority principle. The idea that each member of an organizational hierarchy tries to comply with the presumed or fantasied wishes of those above him while those below him try to comply with his wishes. *See also* Hierarchical vector, Political therapist, Procedural therapist.

Autism. *See* Autistic thinking.

Autistic thinking. A form of thinking in which the thoughts are largely narcissistic and egocentric, with emphasis on subjectivity rather than objectivity and without regard for reality. The term is used interchangeably with autism and dereism. *See also* Narcissism.

Autoerotism. Sexual arousal of self without the participation of another person. The term, introduced by Havelock Ellis, is at present used interchangeably with masturbation. In psychoanalysis, autoerotism is considered a primitive phase in object-relationship development, preceding the narcissistic stage. In narcissism there is a love object, but there is no love object in autoerotism.

Autonomic side effect. Disturbance of the autonomic nervous system, both central and peripheral. It may be a result of the use of anti-psychotic drugs, particularly the phenothiazine derivatives. The autonomic side effects include hypotension, hypertension, blurred vision, nasal congestion, and dryness of the mouth. *See also* Mydriasis.

Auxiliary ego. In psychodrama, a person, usually a member of the staff, trained to act out different roles during a psychodramatic session to intensify the therapeutic situation. The trained auxiliary ego may represent an important figure in the patient's life. He may express the patient's unconscious wishes and attitudes or portray his unacceptable self. He may represent a delusion, hallucination, symbol, ideal, animal, or object that makes the patient's psychodramatic world real, concrete, and tangible. *See also* Ego model Hallucinatory psychodrama, Mirror, Multiple double.

Auxiliary therapist. Co-therapist. *See also* Co-therapy.

Back-home group. Collection of persons that a patient usually lives with, works with, and socializes with. It does not include the members of his therapy group. *See also* Expanded group.

Bag. Slang for area of classification, interest, or skill. Bringing together members of a group with different bags makes it initially difficult to achieve a feeling of group cohesiveness but later provides the potential for more productive interchange and deeper cohesiveness.

Basic anxiety. As conceptualized by Karen Horney, the mainspring from which neurotic trends get their intensity and pervasiveness. Basic anxiety is characterized by vague feelings of loneliness, helplessness, and fear of a potentially hostile world. *See also* Anxiety, Fear.

Basic skills training. The teaching of leadership functions, communication skills, the use of group processes, and other interpersonal skills. National Training Laboratories' groups include this training as part of the T-group process. *See also* East-Coast-style T-group.

Behavioral group psychotherapy. A type of group therapy that focuses on overt and objectively observable behavior rather than on thoughts and feelings. It aims at symptomatic improvement and the elimination of suffering and maladaptive habits. Various conditioning and anxiety-eliminating techniques derived from learning theory are combined with didactic discussions and techniques adapted from other systems of treatment.

Behind-the-back technique. An encounter group procedure in which a patient talks about himself and then turns his back and listens while the other participants discuss him as if he were physically absent. Later he "returns" to the group to participate in further discussions of his problems.

Bender, Lauretta (1897–). American psychiatrist who has done extensive work in the fields of child psychiatry, neurology, and psychology. She employed group therapy, particularly activity group therapy, with inpatient children in the early 1940's.

Berne, Eric (1910–1970). American psychiatrist. He was the founder of transactional analysis, which is used in both individual and group therapy. *See also* Transactional group psychotherapy.

Bestiality. Sexual deviation in which a person engages in sexual relations with an animal.

Bieber, Irving (1908–). American psychiatrist and psychoanalyst who has done extensive work in the field of homosexuality. He originated the first major scientific study of male homosexuality published as *Homosexuality; A Psychoanalytic Study.*

Bio-energetic group psychotherapy. A type of group therapy developed by Alexander Lowen that directly involves the body and mobilizes energy processes to facilitate the expression of feeling. Verbal interchange and a variety of exercises are designed to improve and coordinate physical functioning with mental functioning.

Bion, Walter R. British psychoanalyst of the Kleinian school. He introduced concepts dealing largely with the group as a whole. He was one of the European workers who demonstrated the use of open wards in mental hospitals and who developed the concept of therapeutic milieu. *See also* Leaderless therapeutic group, Pairing, Therapeutic community.

Bisexuality. Existence of the qualities of both sexes in the same person. Freud postulated that both biologically and psychologically the sexes differentiated from a common core, that differentiation between the two sexes was relative rather than absolute, and that regression to the common core occurs to varying degrees in both normal and abnormal conditions. An adult person who engages in bisexual behavior is one who is sexually attracted to and has contact with members of both sexes. He is also known in lay terms as an AC-DC person. *See also* Heterosexuality, Homosexuality, Latent homosexuality, Overt homosexuality.

Black separatism. Philosophy that blacks, in order to develop a positive identity, must establish cultural, socioeconomic, and political systems that are distinctively black and separate from white systems. *See also* Afro-American.

Blank screen. Neutral backdrop on which the patient projects a gamut of transferential irrationalities. The passivity of the analyst allows him to act as a blank screen.

Blind self. The behavior, feelings, and motivations of a person known to others but not to himself. The blind self is one quadrant of the Johari Window, a diagrammatic concept of human behavior. *See also* Hidden self, Public self, Undeveloped potential.

Blind spot. Area of someone's personality that he is totally unaware of. These unperceived areas are often hidden by repression so that he can avoid painful emotions. In both group and individual therapy, such blind spots often appear obliquely as projected ideas, intentions, and emotions.

Blind walk. A technique used in encounter groups to help a member experience and develop trust. As a group exercise, each member picks a partner; one partner closes his eyes, and the other leads him around, keeping him out of dangerous places. The partners then reverse roles. Later, the group members discuss their reactions to the blind walk.

Blocking. Involuntary cessation of thought processes or speech because of unconscious emotional factors. It is also known as thought deprivation.

Blunted affect. *See* Affect, blunted.

Body-contact-exploration maneuver. Any physical touching of another person for the purpose of becoming more aware of the sensations and emotions aroused by the experience. The technique is used mainly in encounter groups.

Boundary. Physical or psychological factor that separates relevant regions in the group structure. An external boundary separates the group from the external environment. A major internal boundary distinguishes the group leader from the members. A minor internal boundary separates individual members or subgroups from one another.

Brainwashing. Any technique designed to manipulate human thought or action against the desire, will, or knowledge of the person involved. It usually refers to systematic efforts to indoctrinate nonbelievers. *See also* Dog-eat-dog period, Give-up-itis.

Breuer, Josef (1842–1925). Viennese physician with wide scientific and cultural interests. His collaboration with Freud in studies of cathartic therapy were reported in *Studies on Hysteria* (1895). He withdrew as Freud proceeded to introduce psychoanalysis, but he left important imprints on that discipline, such as the concepts of the primary and secondary process.

Brill, A. A. (1874–1948). First American analyst (1908). Freud gave him permission to translate several of his most important works. He was active in the formation of the New York Psychoanalytic Society (1911) and remained in the forefront of propagators of psychoanalysis as a lecturer and writer throughout his life.

Brooding compulsion. *See* Intellectualization.

Bull session. Informal group meeting at which members discuss their opinions, philosophies, and personal feelings about situations and people. Such groups are leaderless, and no attempt is made to perceive group process, but the cathartic value is often great. It is also known as a rap session.

Burned-out anergic schizophrenic. A chronic schizophrenic who is apathetic and withdrawn, with minimal florid psychotic symptoms but with persistent and often severe schizophrenic thought processes.

Burrow, Trigant L. (1875–1951). American student of Freud and Jung who coined the term group analysis and later developed a method called phyloanalysis. Much of Burrow's work was based on his social views and his opinion that individual psychotherapy places the therapist in too authoritarian a role to be therapeutic. He formed groups of patients, students, and colleagues who, living together in a camp, analyzed their interactions.

Catalepsy. *See* Cerea flexibilitas.

Cataphasia. *See* Verbigeration.

Cataplexy. Temporary loss of muscle tone, causing weakness and immobilization. It can be precipitated by a variety of emotional states.

Catecholamine. Monoamine containing a catechol group that has a sympathomimetic property. Norepinephrine, epinephrine, and dopamine are common catecholamines.

Category method. Technique used in structured interactional group psychotherapy. Members are asked to verbally rate one another along a variety of parameters—such as appearance, intelligence, and relatedness.

Catharsis. Release of ideas, thoughts, and repressed materials from the unconscious, accompanied by an affective emotional response and release of tension. Commonly observed in the course of treatment, both individual and group, it can also occur outside therapy. *See also* Abreaction, Bull session, Conversational catharsis.

Cathexis. In psychoanalysis, a conscious or unconscious investment of the psychic energy of a drive in an idea, a concept, or an object.

Cerea flexibilitas. Condition in which a person maintains the body position he is placed into. It is a pathological symptom observed in severe cases of catatonic schizophrenia. It is also known as waxy flexibility or catalepsy.

Chain-reaction phenomenon. Group therapy situation in which information is passed from one group to another, resulting in a loss of confidentiality. This phenomenon is common when members of different groups socialize together.

Chemotherapy. *See* Drug therapy.

Child. In transactional analysis, an ego state that is an archaic relic from an early period of the person's life. It is also known as archeopsychic function. *See also* Adapted Child, Natural Child.

Chlorpromazine. A phenothiazine derivative used primarily as an antipsychotic agent and in the treatment of nausea and vomiting. The drug was synthesized in 1950 and was used in psychiatry for the first time in 1952. At present, chlorpromazine is one of the most widely used drugs in medical practice.

Circumstantiality. Disturbance in the associative thought processes in which the patient digresses into unnecessary details and inappropriate thoughts before communicating the central idea. It is observed in schizophrenia, obsessional disturbances, and certain cases of epileptic dementia. *See also* Tangentiality, Thought process disorder.

Clarification. In transactional analysis, the attainment of Adult control by a patient who understands what he is doing, knows what parts of his personality are involved in what he is doing, and is able to control and decide whether or not to continue his games. Clarification contributes to stability by assuring the patient that his hidden Parent and Child ego states can be monitored by his Adult ego state. *See also* Decontamination, Interpretation.

Class method. Group therapy method that is lecture-centered and designed to enlighten patients as to their condition and provide them with motivations. Joseph Pratt, a Boston physician, first used this method at the turn of the century to help groups of tuberculous patients understand their illness. *See also* Didactic technique, Group bibliotherapy, Mechanical group therapy.

Claustrophobia. Fear of closed places. *See also* Agoraphobia.

Client-centered psychotherapy. A form of psychotherapy, formulated by Carl Rogers, in which the patient or client is believed to possess the ability to improve. The therapist merely helps him clarify his own thinking and feeling. The client-centered approach in both group and individual therapy is democratic, unlike the psychotherapist-centered treatment methods. *See also* Group-centered psychotherapy, Nondirective approach.

Closed group. Treatment group into which no new members are permitted once it has begun the treatment process. *See also* Open group.

Clouding of consciousness. Disturbance of consciousness characterized by unclear sensory perceptions.

Coexistent culture. Alternative system of values, perceptions, and patterns for behavior. The group experience leads to an awareness of other systems as legitimate alternatives to one's own system.

Cognition. Mental process of knowing and becoming aware. One of the ego functions, it is closely associated with judgment. Groups that study their own processes and dynamics use more cognition than do encounter groups, which emphasize emotions. It is also known as thinking.

Cohesion. *See* Group cohesion.

Cold turkey. Abrupt withdrawal from opiates without the benefit of methadone or other drugs. The term was originated by drug addicts to describe their chills and consequent goose flesh. This type of detoxification is generally used by abstinence-oriented therapeutic communities.

Collaborative therapy. A type of marital therapy in which treatment is conducted by two therapists, each of whom sees one spouse. They may confer occasionally or at regular intervals. This form of treatment affords each analyst a double view of his patient—the way in which one patient reports to his analyst and the way in which the patient's mate sees the situation as reported to the analyst's colleague. *See also* Combined therapy, Concurrent therapy, Conjoint therapy, Family therapy, Group marital therapy, Marriage therapy, Quadrangular therapy, Square interview.

Collective experience. The common emotional experiences of a group of people. Identification, mutual support, reduction of ego defenses, sibling transferences, and empathy help integrate the individual member into the group and accelerate the therapeutic process. S. R. Slavson, who coined the phrase, warned against letting the collective experience submerge the individuality of the members or give them an opportunity to escape from their own autonomy and responsibility.

Collective family transference neurosis. A phenomenon observed in a group when a member projects irrational feelings and thoughts onto other members as a result of transferring the family psychopathology from early childhood into the therapeutic group situation. The interpretation and analysis of this phenomenon is one of the cornerstones of psychoanalytic group therapy. *See also* Lateral transference, Multiple transference.

Collective unconscious. Psychic contents outside the realm of awareness that are common to mankind in general, not to one person in particular. Jung, who introduced the term, believed that the collective unconscious is inherited and derived from the collective experience of the species. It transcends cultural differences and explains the analogy between ancient mythological ideas and the primitive archaic projections observed in some patients who have never been exposed to these ideas.

Coma. A profound degree of unconsciousness with minimal or no detectable responsiveness to stimuli. It is seen in conditions involving the brain—such as head injury, cerebral hemorrhage, thrombosis and embolism, and cerebral infection—in such systemic conditions as diabetes, and in drug and alcohol intoxication. In psychiatry, comas may be seen in severe catatonic states.

Coma vigil. A profound degree of unconsciousness in which the patient's eyes remain open but there is minimal or no detectable evidence of responsiveness to stimuli. It is seen in acute brain syndromes secondary to cerebral infection.

Combined therapy. A type of psychotherapy in which the patient is in both individual and group treatment with the same or two different therapists. In marriage therapy, it is the combination of married couples group therapy with either individual sessions with one spouse or conjoint sessions with the marital pair. *See also* Collaborative therapy, Concurrent therapy, Conjoint therapy, Co-therapy, Family therapy, Group marital therapy, Marriage therapy, Quadrangular therapy, Square interview.

Coming on. A colloquial term used in transactional analysis groups to label an emerging ego state. For example, when a patient points his finger and says "should," he is coming on Parent.

Command automation. Condition closely associated with catalepsy in which suggestions are followed automatically.

Command negativism. *See* Negativism.

Common group tension. Common denominator of tension arising out of the dominant unconscious fantasies of all the members in a group.

Each member projects his unconscious fantasy onto the other members and tries to manipulate them accordingly. Interpretation by the group therapist plays a prominent role in bringing about change.

Communion. The union of one living thing with another or the participation of a person in an organization. It is a necessary ingredient in individual and group psychotherapy and in sensitivity training. Both the leader-therapist and the patient-trainee must experience communion for a successful learning experience to occur. *See also* Agency.

Communion-oriented group psychotherapy. A type of group therapy that focuses on developing a spirit of unity and cohesiveness rather than on performing a task.

Community. *See* Therapeutic community.

Community psychiatry. Psychiatry focusing on the detection, prevention, and early treatment of emotional disorders and social deviance as they develop in the community rather than as they are perceived and encountered at large, centralized psychiatric facilities. Particular emphasis is placed on the environmental factors that contribute to mental illness.

Compensation. Conscious or, usually, unconscious defense mechanism by which a person tries to make up for an imagined or real deficiency, physical or psychological or both.

Competition. Struggle for the possession or use of limited goods, concrete or abstract. Gratification for one person largely precludes gratification for another.

Complementarity of interaction. A concept of bipersonal and multipersonal psychology in which behavior is viewed as a response to stimulation and interaction replaces the concept of reaction. Each person in an interactive situation plays both a provocative role and a responsive role.

Complex. A group of inter-related ideas, mainly unconscious, that have a common affective tone. A complex strongly influences the person's attitudes and behavior. *See also* God complex, Inferiority complex, Mother Superior complex, Oedipus complex.

Composition. Make-up of a group according to

sex, age, race, cultural and ethnic background, and psychopathology.

Compulsion. Uncontrollable impulse to perform an act repetitively. It is used as a way to avoid unacceptable ideas and desires. Failure to perform the act leads to anxiety. *See also* Obsession.

Conation. That part of a person's mental life concerned with his strivings, instincts, drives, and wishes as expressed through his behavior.

Concretization of living. As used in psychodrama, the actualization of life in a therapeutic setting, integrating time, space, reality, and cosmos.

Concurrent therapy. A type of family therapy in which one therapist handles two or more members of the same family but sees each member separately. *See also* Collaborative therapy, Combined therapy, Conjoint therapy, Family therapy, Group marital therapy, Marriage therapy, Quadrangular therapy, Square interview.

Conditioning. Procedure designed to alter behavioral potential. There are two main types of conditioning—classical and operant. Classical or Pavlovian conditioning pairs two stimuli—one adequate, such as offering food to a dog to produce salivation, and the other inadequate, such as ringing a bell, which by itself does not have an effect on salivation. After the two stimuli have been paired several times, the dog responds to the inadequate stimulus (ringing of bell) by itself. In operant conditioning, a desired activity is reinforced by giving the subject a reward every time he performs the act. As a result, the activity becomes automatic without the need for further reinforcement.

Confabulation. Unconscious filling of gaps in memory by imagining experiences that have no basis in fact. It is common in organic brain syndromes. *See also* Paramnesia.

Confidentiality. Aspect of medical ethics in which the physician is bound to hold secret all information given him by the patient. Legally, certain states do not recognize confidentiality and can require the physician to divulge such information if needed in a legal proceeding. In group psychotherapy this ethic is adhered to by the members as well as by the therapist.

Confirmation. In transactional analysis, a re-

confrontation that may be undertaken by the patient himself. *See also* Confrontation.

Conflict. Clash of two opposing emotional forces. In a group, the term refers to a clash between group members or between the group members and the leader, a clash that frequently reflects the inner psychic problems of individual members. *See also* Extrapsychic conflict, Intrapsychic conflict.

Conflict-free area. Part of one's personality or ego that is well-integrated and does not cause any conflicts, symptoms, or displeasure. Conflict-free areas are usually not analyzed in individual analysis, but they become obvious in the interaction of an analytic group, where they can then be analyzed.

Confrontation. Act of letting a person know where one stands in relationship to him, what one is experiencing, and how one perceives him. Used in a spirit of deep involvement, this technique is a powerful tool for changing relationships; used as an attempt to destroy another person, it can be harmful. In group and individual therapy, the value of confrontation is likely to be determined by the therapist. *See also* Encounter group, Existential group psychotherapy.

Confusion. Disturbance of consciousness manifested by a disordered orientation in relation to time, place, or person.

Conjoint therapy. A type of marriage therapy in which a therapist sees the partners together in joint sessions. This situation is also called triadic or triangular, since two patients and one therapist work together. *See also* Collaborative therapy, Combined therapy, Concurrent therapy, Family therapy, Group marital therapy, Marriage therapy, Quadrangular therapy, Square interview.

Conscious. One division of Freud's topographical theory of the mind. The content of the conscious is within the realm of awareness at all times. The term is also used to describe a function of organic consciousness. *See also* Preconscious, Unconscious.

Consciousness. *See* Sensorium.

Consensual validation. The continuous comparison of the thoughts and feelings of group members toward one another that tend to modify and correct interpersonal distortions. The term was introduced by Harry Stack Sullivan. Previously, Trigant Burrow referred to consensual observation to describe this process, which results in effective reality-testing.

Contact situation. Encounter between individual persons or groups in which the interaction patterns that develop represent the dynamic interplay of psychological, cultural, and socioeconomic factors.

Contagion. Force that operates in large groups or masses. When the level of psychological functioning has been lowered, some sudden upsurge of anxiety can spread through the group, speeded by a high degree of suggestibility. The anxiety gradually mounts to panic, and the whole group may be simultaneously affected by a primitive emotional upheaval.

Contamination. In transactional analysis, a state in which attitudes, prejudices, and standards that originate in a Parent or Child ego state become part of the Adult ego state's information and are treated as accepted facts. *See also* Clarification, Decontamination.

Contemporaneity. Here-and-now.

Contract. Explicit, bilateral commitment to a well-defined course of action. In group or individual therapy, the therapist-patient contract is to attain the treatment goal.

Conversational catharsis. Release of repressed or suppressed thoughts and feelings in group and individual psychotherapy as a result of verbal interchange.

Conversion. An unconscious defense mechanism by which the anxiety that stems from an intrapsychic conflict is converted and expressed in a symbolic somatic symptom. Seen in a variety of mental disorders, it is particularly common in hysterical neurosis.

Cooperative therapy. *See* Co-therapy.

Co-patients. Members of a treatment group exclusive of the therapist and the recorder or observer. Co-patients are also known as patient peers.

Coprolalia. The use of vulgar, obscene, or dirty words. It is observed in some cases of schizophrenia. The word is derived from the Greek words *kopros* (excrement) and *lalia* (talking). *See also* Gilles de la Tourette's disease.

Corrective emotional experience. Re-exposure, under favorable circumstances, to an emotional situation that the patient could not handle in the past. As advocated by Franz Alexander, the therapist temporarily assumes a particular role to generate the experience and facilitate reality-testing.

Co-therapy. A form of psychotherapy in which more than one therapist treat the individual patient or the group. It is also known as combined therapy, cooperative therapy, dual leadership, multiple therapy, and three-cornered therapy. *See also* Role-divided therapy, Splitting situation.

Counterdependent person. *See* Nontruster.

Countertransference. Conscious or unconscious emotional response of the therapist to the patient. It is determined by the therapist's inner needs rather than by the patient's needs, and it may reinforce the patient's earlier traumatic history if not checked by the therapist.

Co-worker. Professional or paraprofessional who works in the same clinical or institutional setting.

Creativity. Ability to produce something new. Silvano Arieti describes creativity as the tertiary process, a balanced combination of primary and secondary processes, whereby materials from the id are used in the service of the ego.

Crisis-intervention group psychotherapy. Group therapy aimed at decreasing or eliminating an emotional or situational crisis.

Crisis, therapeutic. *See* Therapeutic crisis.

Crystallization. In transactional analysis, a statement of the patient's position from the Adult of the therapist to the Adult of the patient. *See also* Ego state.

Cultural conserve. The finished product of the creative process; anything that preserves the values of a particular culture. Without this repository of the past, man would be forced to create the same forms to meet the same situations day after day. The cultural conserve also entices new creativity.

Cultural deprivation. Restricted participation in the culture of the larger society.

Current material. Data from present interpersonal experiences. *See also* Genetic material.

Cyclazocine. A narcotic antagonist that blocks the effects of heroin but does not relieve heroin craving. It has been used experimentally with a limited number of drug addicts in research programs.

Cycloplegia. Paralysis of the muscles of accommodation in the eye. It is observed at times as an autonomic side effect of phenothiazine and antiparkinsonism drugs.

Dance therapy. Nonverbal communication through rhythmic body movements, used to rehabilitate people with emotional or physical disorders. Pioneered by Marian Chase in 1940, this method is used in both individual and group therapy.

Data. *See* Current material, Genetic material.

Death instinct. *See* Aggressive drive.

Decision. In transactional analysis, a childhood commitment to a certain existential position and life style. *See also* Script analysis.

Decompensation. In medical science, the failure of normal functioning of an organ, as in cardiac decompensation; in psychiatry, the breakdown of the psychological defense mechanisms that maintain the person's optimal psychic functioning. *See also* Depersonalization.

Decontamination. In transactional analysis, a process whereby a person is freed of Parent or Child contaminations. *See also* Clarification.

Defense mechanism. Unconscious intrapsychic process. Protective in nature, it is used to relieve the anxiety and conflict arising from one's impulses and drives. *See also* Compensation, Conversion, Denial, Displacement, Dissociation, Idealization, Identification, Incorporation, Intellectualization, Introjection, Projection, Rationalization, Reaction formation, Regression, Repression, Sublimation, Substitution, Symbolization, Undoing.

Defensive emotion. Strong feeling that serves as a screen for a less acceptable feeling, one that would cause a person to experience anxiety if it appeared. For example, expressing the emotion of anger is often more acceptable to a group member than expressing the fear that his anger covers up. In this instance, anger is defensive.

Déjà entendu. Illusion of auditory recognition. *See also* Paramnesia.

Déjà vu. Illusion of visual recognition in which a new situation is incorrectly regarded as a repetition of a previous experience. *See also* Paramnesia.

Delirium. A disturbance in the state of consciousness that stems from an acute organic reaction characterized by restlessness, confusion, disorientation, bewilderment, agitation, and affective lability. It is associated with fear, hallucinations, and illusions.

Delusion. A false fixed belief not in accord with one's intelligence and cultural background. Types of delusion include:
Delusion of control. False belief that one is being manipulated by others.
Delusion of grandeur. Exaggerated concept of one's importance.
Delusion of infidelity. False belief that one's lover is unfaithful; it is derived from pathological jealousy.
Delusion of persecution. False belief that one is being harrassed.
Delusion of reference. False belief that the behavior of others refers to oneself; a derivation from ideas of reference in which the patient falsely feels that he is being talked about by others.
Delusion of self-accusation. False feeling of remorse.
Paranoid delusion. Oversuspiciousness leading to false persecutory ideas or beliefs.

Dementia. Organic loss of mental functioning.

Denial. An unconscious defense mechanism in which an aspect of external reality is rejected. At times it is replaced by a more satisfying fantasy or piece of behavior. The term can also refer to the blocking of awareness of internal reality. It is one of the primitive or infantile defenses.

Dependence on therapy. Patient's pathological need for therapy, created out of the belief that he cannot survive without it.

Dependency. A state of reliance on another

for psychological support. It reflects needs for security, love, protection, and mothering.

Dependency phase. *See* Inclusion phase.

Depersonalization. Sensation of unreality concerning oneself, parts of oneself, or one's environment. It is seen in schizophrenics, particularly during the early stages of decompensation. *See also* Decompensation.

Depression. In psychiatry, a morbid state characterized by mood alterations, such as sadness and loneliness; by low self-esteem associated with self-reproach; by psychomotor retardation and, at times, agitation; by withdrawal from interpersonal contact and, at times, a desire to die; and by such vegetative symptoms as insomnia and anorexia. *See also* Grief.

Derailment. *See* Tangentiality.

Derealization. Sensation of distorted spatial relationships. It is seen in certain types of schizophrenia.

Dereism. Mental activity not concordant with logic or experience. This type of thinking is commonly observed in schizophrenic states.

Detoxification. Removal of the toxic effects of a drug. It is also known as detoxication. *See also* Cold turkey, Methadone.

Diagnostic and Statistical Manual of Mental Disorders. A handbook for the classification of mental illnesses. Formulated by the American Psychiatric Association, it was first issued in 1952 (DSM-I). The second edition (DSM-II), issued in 1968, correlates closely with the World Health Organization's *International Classification of Diseases.*

Dialogue. Verbal communication between two or more persons.

Didactic psychodrama. Psychodrama used as a teaching method. It is used with persons involved in the care of psychiatric patients to teach them how to handle typical conflicts.

Didactic technique. Group therapeutic method given prominence by J. M. Klapman that emphasizes the tutorial approach. The group therapist makes use of outlines, texts, and visual aids to teach the group about themselves and

their functioning. *See also* Class method, Group bibliotherapy, Mechanical group therapy.

Differentiation. *See* Individuation.

Dilution of transference. Partial projection of irrational feelings and reactions onto various group members and away from the leader. Some therapists do not believe that dilution of transference occurs. *See also* Multiple transference, Transference.

Dipsomania. Morbid, irrepressible compulsion to drink alcoholic beverages.

Directive-didactic approach. Group therapy approach characterized by guided discussions and active direction by the therapist. Various teaching methods and printed materials are used, and autobiographical material may be presented. Such an approach is common with regressed patients in mental institutions.

Discussion model of group psychotherapy. A type of group therapy in which issues, problems, and facts are deliberated, with the major emphasis on rational understanding.

Disinhibition. Withdrawal of inhibition. Chemical substances such as alcohol can remove inhibitions by interfering with functions of the cerebral cortex. In psychiatry, disinhibition leads to the freedom to act on one's own needs rather than to submit to the demands of others.

Displacement. An unconscious defense mechanism by which the affective component of an unacceptable idea or object is transferred to an acceptable one.

Disposition. Sum total of a person's inclinations as determined by his mood.

Dissociation. An unconscious defense mechanism by which an idea is separated from its accompanying affect, as seen in hysterical dissociative states; an unconscious process by which a group of mental processes are split off from the rest of a person's thinking, resulting in an independent functioning of this group of processes and thus a loss of the usual inter-relationships.

Distortion. Misrepresentation of reality. It is based on historically determined motives.

Distractability. Inability to focus one's attention.

Diversified reality. A condition in a treatment situation that provides various real stimuli with which the patient may interact. In a group, the term refers to the variety of personalities of the co-members, in contrast with the one personality of the analyst in the dyadic relationship.

Doctor-patient relationship. Human interchange that exists between the person who is sick and the person who is selected because of training and experience to heal.

Dog-eat-dog period. Early stage of Communist brainwashing of American prisoners during the Korean War. During this period, as described by former Army psychiatrist William Mayer, the Communists encouraged each prisoner to be selfish and to do only what was best for himself. *See also* Give-up-itis.

Dominant member. The patient in a group who tends to monopolize certain group sessions or situations.

Double. *See* Mirror.

Double-bind. Two conflicting communications from another person. One message is usually nonverbal and the other verbal. For example, parents may tell a child that arguments are to be settled peacefully and yet battle with each other constantly. The concept was formulated by Gregory Bateson.

Double-blind study. A study in which one or more drugs and a placebo are compared in such a way that neither the patient nor the persons directly or indirectly involved in the study know which is being given to the patient. The drugs being investigated and the placebo are coded for identification.

Dream. Mental activity during sleep that is experienced as though it were real. A dream has both a psychological and a biological purpose. It provides an outlet for the release of instinctual impulses and wish fulfillment of archaic needs and fantasies unacceptable in the real world. It permits the partial resolution of conflicts and the healing of traumata too overwhelming to be dealt with in the waking state. And it is the guardian of sleep, which is indispensable for the proper functioning of mind and body during the waking state. *See also* Hypnagogic hallucination, Hypnopompic hallucination, Paramnesia.

Dreamy state. Altered state of consciousness likened to a dream situation. It is accompanied by hallucinations—visual, auditory, and olfactory—and is believed to be associated with temporal lobe lesions. *See also* Marijuana.

Drive. A mental constituent, believed to be genetically determined, that produces a state of tension when it is in operation. This tension or state of psychic excitation motivates the person into action to alleviate the tension. Contemporary psychoanalysts prefer to use the term drive rather than Freud's term, instinct. *See also* Aggressive drive, Instinct, Sexual drive.

Drop-out. Patient who leaves group therapy against the therapist's advice.

Drug therapy. The use of chemical substances in the treatment of illness. It is also known as chemotherapy. *See also* Maintenance drug therapy.

DSM. *See Diagnostic and Statistical Manual of Mental Disorders.*

Dual leadership. *See* Co-therapy.

Dual therapy. *See* Co-therapy.

Dyad. A pair of persons in an interactional situation—such as husband and wife, mother and father, co-therapists, or patient and therapist.

Dyadic session. Psychotherapeutic session involving only two persons, the therapist and the patient.

Dynamic reasoning. Forming all the clinical evidence gained from free-associative anamnesis into a psychological reconstruction of the patient's development. It is a term used by Franz Alexander.

Dyskinesia. Involuntary, stereotyped, rhythmic muscular activity, such as a tic or a spasm. It is sometimes observed as an extrapyramidal side effect of antipsychotic drugs, particularly the phenothiazine derivatives. *See also* Tardive oral dyskinesia.

Dystonia. Extrapyramidal motor disturbance consisting of uncoordinated and spasmodic movements of the body and limbs, such as arching of the back and twisting of the body and neck. It is observed as a side effect of phenothiazine drugs and other major tranquilizers. *See also* Tardive oral dyskinesia.

East-Coast-style T-group. Group that follows the traditional National Training Laboratories orientation by developing awareness of group process. The first T-groups were held in Bethel, Maine. *See also* Basic skills training, West-Coast-style T-group.

Echolalia. Repetition of another person's words or phrases. It is a psychopathological symptom observed in certain cases of schizophrenia, particularly the catatonic types. Some authors consider this behavior to be an attempt by the patient to maintain a continuity of thought processes. *See also* Gilles de la Tourette's disease.

Echopraxia. Imitation of another person's movements. It is a psychopathological symptom observed in some cases of catatonic schizophrenia.

Ecstasy. Affect of intense rapture.

Ego. One of the three components of the psychic apparatus in the Freudian structural framework. The other two components are the id and the superego. Although the ego has some conscious components, many of its operations are automatic. It occupies a position between the primal instincts and the demands of the outer world, and it therefore serves to mediate between the person and external reality. In so doing, it performs the important functions of perceiving the needs of the self, both physical and psychological, and the qualities and attitudes of the environment. It evaluates, coordinates, and integrates these perceptions so that internal demands can be adjusted to external requirements. It is also responsible for certain defensive functions to protect the person against the demands of the id and the superego. It has a host of functions, but adaptation to reality is perhaps the most important one. *See also* Reality-testing.

Ego-coping skill. Adaptive method or capacity developed by a person to deal with or overcome a psychological or social problem.

Ego defense. *See* Defense mechanism.

Ego ideal. Part of the ego during its development that eventually fuses with the superego. It is a social as well as a psychological concept, reflecting the mutual esteem as well as the dis-illusionment in child-parent and subsequent relationships.

Egomania. Pathological self-preoccupation or self-centeredness. *See also* Narcissism.

Ego model. A person on whom another person patterns his ego. In a group, the therapist or a healthier member acts as an ego model for members with less healthy egos. In psychodrama, the auxiliary ego may act as the ego model.

Ego state. In Eric Berne's structural analysis, a state of mind and its related set of coherent behavior patterns. It includes a system of feelings directly related to a given subject. There are three ego states—Parent, Adult, and Child.

Eitingon, Max (1881–1943). Austrian psychoanalyst. An emissary of the Zurich school, he gained fame as the first person to be analyzed by Freud—in a few sessions in 1907. Later he became the first chief of the Berlin Psychoanalytic Clinic, a founder of the Berlin Psychoanalytic Institute, and a founder of the Palestine Psychoanalytic Society.

Elation. Affect characterized by euphoria, confidence, and enjoyment. It is associated with increased motor activity.

Electrocardiographic effect. Change seen in recordings of the electrical activity of the heart. It is observed as a side effect of phenothiazine derivatives, particularly thioridazine.

Electroconvulsive treatment. *See* Shock treatment.

Emotion. *See* Affect.

Emotional deprivation. Lack of adequate and appropriate interpersonal or environmental experiences or both, usually in the early developmental years. Emotional deprivation is caused by poor mothering or by separation from the mother.

Emotional insight. *See* Insight.

Emotional support. Encouragement, hope, and inspiration given to one person by another. Members of a treatment group often empathize with a patient who needs such support in order to try a new mode of behavior or to face the truth.

Empathy. Ability to put oneself in another person's place, get into his frame of reference, and understand his feelings and behavior objectively. It is one of the major qualities in a successful therapist, facilitator, or helpful group member. *See also* Sympathy.

Encounter group. A form of sensitivity training that emphasizes the experiencing of individual relationships within the group and minimizes intellectual and didactic input. It is a group that focuses on the present rather than concerning itself with the past or outside problems of its members. J. L. Moreno introduced and developed the idea of the encounter group in 1914. *See also* Here-and-now approach, Intervention laboratory, Nonverbal interaction, Task-oriented group.

Encountertapes. Tape recordings designed to provide a group with guidelines for progressive interaction in the absence of a leader. They are copyrighted by the Bell & Howell Company and are available commercially from their Human Development Institute in Atlanta, Georgia.

Epileptic dementia. A form of epilepsy that is accompanied by progressive mental and intellectual impairment. Some believe that the circulatory disturbances during epileptic attacks cause nerve cell degeneration and lead to dementia.

Epinephrine. A sympathomimetic agent. It is the chief hormone secreted by the adrenal medulla. In a state of fear or anxiety, the physiological changes stem from the release of epinephrine. Also known as adrenaline, it is related to norepinephrine, a substance presently linked with mood disturbances in depression.

Eros. *See* Sexual drive.

Erotomania. Pathological preoccupation with sexual activities or fantasies.

Esalen massage. A particular type of massage taught and practiced at the Esalen Institute, a growth center at Big Sur, California. The massage lasts between one and a half and three hours and is intended to be an intimate, loving communion between the participants. A variation is the massage of one person by a group. The massage is given without words.

Ethnocentrism. Conviction that one's own group is superior to other groups. It impairs one's ability to evaluate members of another group realistically or to communicate with them on an open, equal, and person-to-person basis.

Euphoria. An altered state of consciousness characterized by an exaggerated feeling of well-being that is inappropriate to apparent events. It is often associated with opiate, amphetamine, or alcohol abuse.

Evasion. Act of not facing up to or of strategically eluding something. It consists of suppressing an idea that is next in a thought series and replacing it with another idea closely related to it. Evasion is also known as paralogia and perverted logic.

Exaltation. Affect consisting of intense elation and feelings of grandeur.

Exhibitionism. A form of sexual deviation characterized by a compulsive need to expose one's body, particularly the genitals.

Existential group psychotherapy. A type of group therapy that puts the emphasis on confrontation, primarily in the here-and-now interaction, and on feeling experiences rather than on rational thinking. Less attention is put on patient resistances. The therapist is involved on the same level and to the same degree as the patients. *See also* Encounter group.

Expanded group. The friends, immediate family, and interested relatives of a group therapy patient. They are the people with whom he has to relate outside the formal therapy group. *See also* Back-home group.

Experiencing. Feeling emotions and sensations as opposed to thinking; being involved in what is happening rather than standing back at a distance and theorizing. Encounter groups attempt to bring about this personal involvement.

Experiential group. *See* Encounter group.

Experiential stimulator. Anything that stimulates an emotional or sensory response. Several techniques, many of them nonverbal, have been developed for encounter groups to accomplish this stimulation. *See also* Behind-the-back technique, Blind walk.

Extended family therapy. A type of family therapy that involves family members, beyond the nuclear family, who are closely associated with it and affect it. *See also* Network, **Social** network therapy, Visitor.

Exteropsychic function. *See* Parent.

Extrapsychic conflict. Conflict that arises between the person and his environment. *See also* Intrapsychic conflict.

Extrapyramidal effect. Bizarre, involuntary motor movement. It is a central nervous system side effect sometimes produced by antipsychotic drugs. *See also* Dyskinesia.

Extratherapeutic contact. Contact between group members outside of a regularly scheduled group session.

Facilitator. Group leader. He may be the therapist or a patient who emerges during the course of an encounter and who channels group interaction. He is also known as the session leader.

Fag hag. Slang, derogatory expression often used by homosexuals to describe a woman who has become part of a homosexual social circle and has assumed a central role as a mother figure.

Family neurosis. Emotional maladaptation in which a person's psychopathology is unconsciously inter-related with that of the other members of his family.

Family therapy. Treatment of a family in conflict. The whole family meets as a group with the therapist and explores its relationships and process. The focus is on the resolution of current reactions to one another rather than on individual members. *See also* Collaborative therapy, Combined therapy, Concurrent therapy, Conjoint therapy, Extended family therapy, Group marital therapy, Marriage therapy, Quadrangular therapy, Square interview.

Fantasy. Day dream; fabricated mental picture or chain of events. A form of thinking dominated by unconscious material and primary processes, it seeks wish-fulfillment and immediate solutions to conflicts. Fantasy may serve as the matrix for creativity or for neurotic distortions of reality.

Father surrogate. Father substitute. In psychoanalysis, the patient projects his father image onto another person and responds to that person unconsciously in an inappropriate and unrealistic manner with the feelings and attitudes he had toward the original father.

Fausse reconnaissance. False recognition. *See also* Paramnesia.

Fear. Unpleasurable affect consisting of psychophysiological changes in response to a realistic threat or danger to one's existence. *See also* Anxiety.

Federn, Paul (1871–1950). Austrian psychoanalyst, one of Freud's earliest followers, and the last survivor of the original Wednesday Evening Society. He made important original contributions to psychoanalysis—such as the concepts of flying dreams and ego feeling—and was instrumental in saving the minutes of the Vienna Psychoanalytic Society for subsequent publication.

Feedback. Expressed response by one person or a group to another person's behavior. *See also* Sociometric feedback, Transaction.

Feeling-driven group. A group in which little or no attention is paid to rational processes, thinking, or cognition and where the expression of all kinds of emotion is rewarded. *See also* Affectualizing, Encounter group, Existential group psychotherapy.

Ferenczi, Sandor (1873–1933). Hungarian psychoanalyst, one of Freud's early followers, and a brilliant contributor to all aspects of psychoanalysis. His temperament was more romantic than Freud's, and he came to favor more active and personal techniques, to the point that his adherence to psychoanalysis during his last years was questioned.

Field theory. Concept postulated by Kurt Lewin that a person is a complex energy field in which all behavior can be conceived of as a change in some state of the field during a given unit of time. Lewin also postulated the presence within the field of psychological tensions—states of readiness or preparation for action. The field theory is concerned essentially with the present field, the here-and-now. The theory has been applied by various group psychotherapists.

Fliess, Wilhelm (1858–1928). Berlin nose and throat specialist. He shared an early interest with Freud in the physiology of sex and entered into a prolonged correspondence that figures importantly in the records of Freud's self-analysis. Freud was influenced by Fliess's concept of bisexuality and his theory of the periodicity of the sex functions.

Focal-conflict theory. Theory elaborated by Thomas French in 1952 that explains the current behavior of a person as an expression of his method of solving currently experienced personality conflicts that originated very early in his life. He constantly resonates to these early-life conflicts.

Focused exercise. Technique used particularly in encounter groups to help participants break through their defensive behavior and express such specific emotional reactions as anger, affection, and joy. A psychodrama, for instance, may focus on a specific problem that a group member is having with his wife. In playing out both his part and her part, he becomes aware of the emotion he has been blocking.

Folie à deux. Emotional illness shared by two persons. If it involves three persons, it is referred to as *folie à trois*, etc.

Forced interaction. Relationship that occurs in a group when the therapist or other members demand that a particular patient respond, react, and be active. *See also* Structured interactional group psychotherapy.

Ford negative personal contacts with Negroes scale. A scale that measures whites' negative social contacts with blacks. *See also* Kelley desegregation scale, Rosander anti-Negro behavior scale, Steckler anti-Negro scale, Steckler anti-white scale.

Ford negative personal contacts with whites scale. A scale that measures blacks' negative personal contacts with whites. It helps assess the extent to which negative social contacts influence prejudiced attitudes, thus contributing to the theoretical basis for the employment of inter-racial group experiences to reduce prejudice. *See also* Kelley desegregation scale, Rosander anti-Negro behavior scale, Steckler anti-Negro scale, Steckler anti-white scale.

Formal operations. Jean Piaget's label for the complete development of a person's logical thinking capacities.

Foulkes, S. H. (1923–). English psychiatrist and one of the organizers of the group therapy movement in Great Britain. His work combines Moreno's ideas—the here-and-now, the socio-genesis, the social atom, the psychological network—with psypchoanalytic views. He stresses the importance of group-as-a-whole phenomena. *See also* Group analytic psychotherapy, Network.

Free association. Investigative psychoanalytic technique devised by Freud in which the patient seeks to verbalize, without reservation or censor, the passing contents of his mind. The conflicts that emerge while fulfilling this task constitute resistances that are the basis of the analyst's interpretations. *See also* Antirepression device, Conflict.

Free-floating anxiety. Pervasive, unrealistic fear that is not attached to any idea or alleviated by symptom substitution. It is observed particularly in anxiety neurosis, although it may be seen in some cases of latent schizophrenia.

Freud, Sigmund (1856–1939). Austrian psychiatrist and the founder of psychoanalysis. With Josef Breuer, he explored the potentialities of cathartic therapy, then went on to develop the analytic technique and such fundamental concepts of mental phenomena as the unconscious, infantile sexuality, repression, sublimation, superego, ego, and id formation and their applications throughout all spheres of human behavior.

Fulfillment. Satisfaction of needs that may be either real or illusory.

Future projection. Psychodrama technique wherein the patient shows in action how he thinks his future will shape itself. He, sometimes with the assistance of the director, picks the point in time, the place, and the people, if any, he expects to be involved with at that time.

Galactorrhea. Excessive or spontaneous flow of milk from the breast. It may be a result of the endocrine influence of phenothiazine drugs.

Gallows transaction. A transaction in which a person with a self-destructive script smiles while narrating or engaging in a self-destructive act. His smile evokes a smile in the listener, which is in essence an encouragement for self-destruction. *See also* Hamartic script.

Game. Technique that resembles a traditional game in being physical or mental competition conducted according to rules but that is used in the group situation as an experiential learning device. The emphasis is on the process of the game rather than on the objective of the game. A game in Eric Berne's transactional analysis refers to an orderly sequence of social maneuvers with an ulterior motive and resulting in a psychological payoff for the players. *See also* Hit-and-run game, Million-dollar game, Pastime, Survival, Transactional group psychotherapy.

Game analysis. In transactional analysis, the analysis of a person's social interactions that are not honest and straightforward but are contaminated with pretenses for personal gain. *See also* Script analysis, Structural analysis.

Genetic material. Data out of the personal history of the patient that are useful in developing an understanding of the psychodynamics of his present adaptation. *See also* Current material.

Genital phase. The final stage of psychosexual development. It occurs during puberty. In this stage the person's psychosexual development is so organized that he can achieve sexual gratification from genital-to-genital contact and has the capacity for a mature, affectionate relationship with someone of the opposite sex. *See also* Anal phase, Infantile sexuality, Latency phase, Oral phase, Phallic phase.

Gestalt therapy. Type of psychotherapy that emphasizes the treatment of the person as a whole—his biological component parts and their organic functioning, his perceptual configuration, and his inter-relationships with the outside world. Gestalt therapy, developed by Frederic S. Perls, can be used in either an individual or a group therapy setting. It focuses on the sensory awareness of the person's here-and-now experiences rather than on past recollections or future expectations. Gestalt therapy employs role-playing and other techniques to promote the patient's growth process and to develop his full potential. *See also* Nonverbal interaction.

Gilles de la Tourette's disease. A rare illness that has its onset in childhood. The illness, first described by a Paris physician, Gilles de la Tourette, is characterized by involuntary muscular movements and motor incoordination accompanied by echolalia and coprolalia. It is considered by some to be a schizophrenic condition.

Give-up-itis. Syndrome characterized by a giving up of the desire to live. The alienation, isolation, withdrawal, and eventual death associated

with this disease syndrome were experienced by many American prisoners during the Korean War, particularly in the early stages of Communist brainwashing. *See also* Dog-eat-dog period.

Go-around. Technique used in group therapy, particularly in structured interactional group psychotherapy, in which the therapist requires that each member of the group respond to another member, a theme, an association, etc. This procedure encourages participation of all members in the group.

God complex. A belief, sometimes seen in therapists, that one can accomplish more than is humanly possible or that one's word should not be doubted. The God complex of the aging psychoanalyst was first discussed by Ernest Jones, Freud's biographer. *See also* Mother Superior complex.

Gould Academy. Private preparatory school in Bethel, Maine, that has been used during summers as the site of the human relations laboratories run by the National Educational Association.

Grief. Alteration in mood and affect consisting of sadness appropriate to a real loss. *See also* Depression.

Group. *See* Therapeutic group.

Group action technique. Technique used in group work to help the participants achieve skills in interpersonal relations and improve their capacity to perform certain tasks better on the job or at home; technique, often involving physical interaction, aimed at enhancing involvement or communion within a new group.

Group analysand. A person in treatment in a psychoanalytically oriented group.

Group analytic psychotherapy. A type of group therapy in which the group is used as the principal therapeutic agent and all communications and relationships are viewed as part of a total field of interaction. Interventions deal primarily with group forces rather than with individual forces. S. H. Foulkes applied the term to his treatment procedure in 1948. It is also known as therapeutic group analysis. *See also* Phyloanalysis, Psychoanalytic group psychotherapy.

Group apparatus. Those people who preserve order and ensure the survival of a group. The internal apparatus deals with members' proclivities in order to maintain the structure of the group and strengthen cohesion. The therapist usually serves as his own apparatus in a small therapy group; in a courtroom, a bailiff ensures internal order. The external apparatus deals with the environment in order to minimize the threat of external pressure. The therapist usually acts as his own external apparatus by setting the time and place for the meetings and making sure that outsiders do not interfere; in a war, combat forces act as the external apparatus.

Group bibliotherapy. A form of group therapy that focuses on the use of selected readings as stimulus material. Outside readings and oral presentations of printed matter by therapist and patients are designed to encourage verbal interchange in the sessions and to hold the attention of severely regressed patients. This approach is used in the treatment of large groups of institutionalized patients. *See also* Class method, Didactic technique, Mechanical group therapy.

Group-centered psychotherapy. A short-term, nonclinical form of group therapy developed by followers of Carl Rogers and based on his client-centered method of individual treatment. The therapist maintains a nonjudgmental attitude, clarifies the feelings expressed in the sessions, and communicates empathic understanding and respect. The participants are not diagnosed, and uncovering techniques are not employed.

Group climate. Atmosphere and emotional tone of a group therapy session.

Group cohesion. Effect of the mutual bonds between members of a group as a result of their concerted effort for a common interest and purpose. Until cohesiveness is achieved, the group cannot concentrate its full energy on a common task. *See also* Group growth.

Group dynamics. Phenomena that occur in groups; the movement of a group from its inception to its termination. Interactions and interrelations among members and between the members and the therapist create tension, which maintains a constantly changing group equilibrium. The interactions and the tension they create are highly influenced by individual members' psychological make-up, unconscious instinctual drives, motives, wishes, and fantasies. The understanding and effective use of group dynamics is essential in group treatment. It is also known as

group process. *See also* Group mobility, Psychodynamics.

Group grope. Belittling reference to procedures used in certain encounter groups. The procedures are aimed at providing emotional release through physical contact.

Group growth. Gradual development of trust and cohesiveness in a group. It leads to awareness of self and of other group process and to more effective coping with conflict and intimacy problems. *See also* Group cohesion.

Group history. Chronology of the experiences of a group, including group rituals, group traditions, and group themes.

Group inhibition. *See* Group resistance.

Group marathon. Group meeting that usually lasts from eight to 72 hours, although some sessions last for a week. The session is interrupted only for eating and sleeping. The leader works for the development of intimacy and the open expression of feelings. The time-extended group experience culminates in intense feelings of excitement and elation. Group marathon was developed by George Bach and Frederick Stoller. *See also* Accelerated interaction, Nude marathon, Too-tired-to-be-polite phenomenon.

Group marital therapy. A type of marriage therapy that makes use of a group. There are two basic techniques: (1) Inviting the marital partner of a group member to a group session. The other group members are confronted with the neurotic marriage pattern, which gives them new insights and awareness. (2) Placing a husband and wife together in a traditional group of patients. This method seems indicated if the spouses are unable to achieve meaningful intimacy because they fear the loss of their individual identity at an early phase of the marriage, before a neurotic equilibrium is established. *See also* Collaborative therapy, Combined therapy, Concurrent therapy, Conjoint therapy, Family therapy, Quadrangular therapy, Square interview.

Group mind. Autonomous and unified mental life in an assemblage of people bound together by mutual interests. It is a concept used by group therapists who focus on the group as a unit rather than on the individual members.

Group mobility. Spontaneity and movement in

the group brought about by changes in the functions and roles of individual members, relative to their progress. *See also* Group dynamics.

Group-on-group technique. Device used in T-groups wherein one group watches another group in action and then gives feedback to the observed group. Frequently, one group breaks into two sections, each taking turns in observing the other. The technique is intended to sharpen the participants' observation of individual behavior and group process.

Group phenomenon. *See* Group dynamics.

Group pressure. Demand by group members that individual members submit and conform to group standards, values, and behavior.

Group process. *See* Group dynamics.

Group psychotherapy. A type of psychiatric treatment that involves two or more patients participating together in the presence of one or more psychotherapists, who facilitate both emotional and rational cognitive interaction to effect changes in the maladaptive behavior of the members. *See also* Behavioral group psychotherapy, Bio-energetic group psychotherapy, Client-centered psychotherapy, Communion-oriented group psychotherapy, Crisis-intervention group psychotherapy, Existential group psychotherapy, Group analytic psychotherapy, Group bibliotherapy, Group-centered psychotherapy, Individual therapy, Inspirational-supportive group psychotherapy, Psychoanalytic group psychotherapy, Repressive-inspirational group psychotherapy, Social network therapy, Structured interactional group psychotherapy, Traditional group therapy, Transactional group psychotherapy.

Group resistance. Collective natural aversion of the group members toward dealing with unconscious material, emotions, or old patterns of defense.

Group ritual. Tradition or activity that any group establishes to mechanize some of its activities.

Group stimulus. Effect of several group members' communicating together. Each member has a stimulating effect on every other member, and the total stimulation is studied for therapeutic purposes. *See also* Transactions.

Group therapy. *See* Group psychotherapy.

Group tradition. Activity or value established historically by a group. It determines in part the group's manifest behavior.

Group value. Relative worth or standard developed by and agreed on by the members of a group.

Guilt. Affect associated with self-reproach and need for punishment. In psychoanalysis, guilt refers to a neurotic feeling of culpability that stems from a conflict between the ego and the superego. It begins developmentally with parental disapproval and becomes internalized as conscience in the course of superego formation. Guilt has normal psychological and social functions, but special intensity or absence of guilt characterizes many mental disorders, such as depression and antisocial personality. Some psychiatrists distinguish shame as a less internalized form of guilt.

Gustatory hallucination. False sense of taste.

Hallucination. A false sensory perception without a concrete external stimulus. It can be induced by emotional and by organic factors, such as drugs and alcohol. Common hallucinations involve sights or sounds, although any of the senses may be involved. *See also* Auditory hallucination, Gustatory hallucination, Hypnagogic hallucination, Hypnopompic hallucination, Kinesthetic hallucination, Lilliputian hallucination, Tactile hallucination, Visual hallucination.

Hallucinatory psychodrama. A type of psychodrama wherein the patient portrays the voices he hears and the visions he sees. Auxiliary egos are often called on to enact the various phenomena expressed by the patient and to involve him in interaction with them, so as to put them to a reality test. The intended effect on the patient is called psychodramatic shock.

Hallucinogenic drug. *See* Psychotomimetic drug.

Hamartic script. In transactional analysis, a life script that is self-destructive and tragic in character. *See also* Gallows transaction, Script, Script antithesis, Script matrix.

Healthy identification. Modeling of oneself, consciously or unconsciously, on another person who has sound psychic make-up. The identification has constructive purposes. *See also* Imitation.

Herd instinct. Desire to belong to a group and to participate in social activities. Wilfred Trotter used the term to indicate the presence of a hypothetical social instinct in man. In psychoanalysis, herd instinct is viewed as a social phenomenon rather than as an instinct. *See also* Aggressive drive, Sexual drive.

Here-and-now. Contemporaneity. *See also* There-and-then.

Here-and-now approach. A technique that focuses on understanding the interpersonal and intrapersonal responses and reactions as they occur in the on-going treatment session. Little or no emphasis is put on past history and experiences. *See also* Encounter group, Existential group psychotherapy.

Heterogeneous group. A group that consists of patients from both sexes, a wide age range, differing psychopathologies, and divergent socioeconomic, racial, ethnic, and cultural backgrounds. *See also* Homogeneous group.

Heterosexuality. Sexual attraction or contact between opposite-sex persons. The capacity for heterosexual arousal is probably innate, biologically programmed, and triggered in very early life, perhaps by olfactory modalities, as seen in lower animals. *See also* Bisexuality, Homosexuality.

Hidden self. The behavior, feelings, and motivations of a person known to himself but not to others. It is a quadrant of the Johari Window, a diagrammatic concept of human behavior. *See also* Blind self, Public self, Undeveloped potential.

Hierarchical vector. Thrust of relating to the other members of a group or to the therapist in a supraordinate or subordinate way. It is the opposite of relating as peers. It is also known as vertical vector. *See also* Authority principle, Horizontal vector, Political therapist.

Hit-and-run game. Hostile or nonconstructive aggressive activity indiscriminately and irresponsibly carried out against others. *See also* Game, Million dollar game, Survival.

Homogeneous group. A group that consists of patients of the same sex, with similarities in their psychopathology, and from the same age range and socioeconomic, racial, ethnic, and cultural background. *See also* Heterogeneous group.

Homosexuality. Sexual attraction or contact between same-sex persons. Some authors distinguish two types: overt homosexuality and latent homosexuality. *See also* Bisexuality, Heterosexuality, Inversion, Lesbianism.

Homosexual panic. Sudden, acute onset of severe anxiety, precipitated by the unconscious fear or conflict that one may be a homosexual or act out homosexual impulses. *See also* Homosexuality.

Honesty. Forthrightness of conduct and uprightness of character; truthfulness. In therapy, honesty is a value manifested by the ability to communicate one's immediate experience, including inconsistent, conflicting, or ambivalent feelings and perceptions. *See also* Authenticity.

Hook. In transactional analysis, to switch one's transactions to a new ego state. For example, a patient's Adult ego state is hooked when he goes to the blackboard and draws a diagram.

Horizontal vector. Thrust of relating to the therapist or other members of the group as equals. It is also known as peer vector. *See also* Authority principle, Hierarchical vector, Political therapist.

House encounter. Group meeting of all the persons in a treatment facility. Such a meeting is designed to deal with specific problems within the therapeutic community that affect its functioning, such as poor morale and poor job performances.

Hydrotherapy. External or internal use of water in the treatment of disease. In psychiatry, the use of wet packs to calm an agitated psychotic patient was formerly a popular treatment modality.

Hyperactivity. Increased muscular activity. The term is commonly used to describe a disturbance found in children that is manifested by constant restlessness and movements executed at a rapid rate. The disturbance is believed to be due to brain damage, mental retardation, emotional disturbance, or physiological disturbance. It is also known as hyperkinesis.

Hyperkinesis. *See* Hyperactivity.

Hypermnesia. Exaggerated degree of retention and recall. It is observed in schizophrenia, the manic phase of manic-depressive illness, organic brain syndrome, drug intoxication induced by amphetamines and hallucinogens, hypnosis, and febrile conditions. *See also* Memory.

Hypertensive crisis. Severe rise in blood pressure that can lead to intracranial hemorrhage. It is occasionally seen as a side effect of certain antidepressant drugs.

Hypnagogic hallucination. False sensory perception that occurs just before falling asleep. *See also* Hypnopompic hallucination.

Hypnodrama. Psychodrama under hypnotic trance. The patient is first put into a hypnotic trance. During the trance he is encouraged to act out the various experiences that torment him.

Hypnopompic hallucination. False sensory perception that occurs just before full wakefulness. *See also* Hypnagogic hallucination.

Hypnosis. Artificially induced alteration of consciousness of one person by another. The subject responds with a high degree of suggestibility, both mental and physical, during the trancelike state.

Hypochondriasis. Exaggerated concern with one's physical health. The concern is not based on real organic pathology.

Hypotension, orthostatic. *See* Orthostatic hypotension.

Hysterical anesthesia. Disturbance in sensory perception characterized by absence of sense of feeling in certain areas of the body. It is observed in certain cases of hysterical neurosis, particularly the conversion type, and it is believed to be a defense mechanism.

Id. Part of Freud's concept of the psychic apparatus. According to his structural theory of mental functioning, the id harbors the energy that stems from the instinctual drives and desires of a person. The id is completely in the unconscious realm, unorganized and under the influence of the primary processes. *See also* Conscious, Ego, Preconscious, Primary process, Superego, Unconscious.

Idealization. A defense mechanism in which a

person consciously or, usually, unconsciously overestimates an attribute or an aspect of another person.

Ideas of reference. Misinterpretation of incidents and events in the outside world as having a direct personal reference to oneself. Occasionally observed in normal persons, ideas of reference are frequently seen in paranoid patients. *See also* Projection.

Ideational shield. An intellectual, rational defense against the anxiety a person would feel if he became vulnerable to the criticisms and rejection of others. As a result of his fear of being rejected, he may feel threatened if he criticizes another person—an act that is unacceptable to him. In both group and individual therapy, conditions are set up that allow the participants to lower this ideational shield.

Identification. An unconscious defense mechanism in which a person incorporates into himself the mental picture of an object and then patterns himself after this object; seeing oneself as like the person used as a pattern. It is distinguished from imitation, a conscious process. *See also* Healthy identification, Imitation, Role.

Identification with the aggressor. An unconscious process by which a person incorporates within himself the mental image of a person who represents a source of frustration from the outside world. A primitive defense, it operates in the interest and service of the developing ego. The classical example of this defense occurs toward the end of the oedipal stage, when the male child, whose main source of love and gratification is the mother, identifies with his father. The father represents the source of frustration, being the powerful rival for the mother; the child cannot master or run away from his father, so he is obliged to identify with him. *See also* Psychosexual development.

Idiot. *See* Mental retardation.

I-It. Philosopher Martin Buber's description of damaging interpersonal relationships. If a person treats himself or another person exclusively as an object, he prevents mutuality, trust, and growth. When pervasive in a group, I-It relationships prevent human warmth, destroy cohesiveness, and retard group process. *See also* I-Thou.

Ileus, paralytic. *See* Paralytic ileus.

Illusion. False perception and misinterpretation of an actual sensory stimulus.

Illustration. In transactional analysis, an anecdote, simile, or comparison that reinforces a confrontation or softens its potentially undesirable effects. The illustration may be immediate or remote in time and may refer to the external environment or to the internal situation in the group.

Imbecile. *See* Mental retardation.

Imitation. In psychiatry, a conscious act of mimicking another person's behavior pattern. *See also* Healthy identification, Identification.

Impasse. *See* Therapeutic impasse.

Improvement scale. In transactional analysis, a quantitative specification of a patient's position in terms of improvement in the course of therapy.

Improvisation. In psychodrama, the acting out of problems without prior preparation.

Impulse. Unexpected, instinctive urge motivated by conscious and unconscious feelings over which the person has little or no control. *See also* Drive, Instinct.

Inappropriate affect. Emotional tone that is out of harmony with the idea, object, or thought accompanying it.

Inclusion phase. Early stage of group treatment. In this phase, each group member's concern focuses primarily on belonging and being accepted and recognized, particularly by the therapist. It is also known as the dependency stage. *See also* Affection phase, Power phase.

Incorporation. An unconscious defense mechanism in which an object representation is assimilated into oneself through symbolic oral ingestion. One of the primitive defenses, incorporation is a special form of introjection and is the primary mechanism in identification.

Individual psychology. Holistic theory of personality developed by Alfred Adler. Personality development is explained in terms of adaptation to the social milieu (life style), strivings toward perfection motivated by feelings of inferiority, and the interpersonal nature of the person's problems. Individual psychology is applied in

group psychotherapy and counseling by Adlerian practitioners.

Individual therapy. A type of psychotherapy in which a professionally trained psychotherapist treats one patient who either wants relief from disturbing symptoms or improvement in his ability to cope with his problems. This one therapist-one patient relationship, the traditional dyadic therapeutic technique, is opposed to other techniques that deal with more than one patient. *See also* Group psychotherapy, Psychotherapy.

Individuation. Differentiation; the process of molding and developing the individual personality so that it is different from the rest of the group. *See also* Actualization.

Infantile dynamics. Psychodynamic integrations, such as the Oedipus complex, that are organized during childhood and continue to exert unconsciously experienced influences on adult personality.

Infantile sexuality. Freudian concept regarding the erotic life of infants and children. Freud observed that, from birth, infants are capable of erotic activities. Infantile sexuality encompasses the overlapping phases of psychosexual development during the first five years of life and includes the oral phase (birth to 18 months), when erotic activity centers around the mouth; the anal phase (ages one to three), when erotic activity centers around the rectum; and the phallic phase (ages two to six), when erotic activity centers around the genital region. *See also* Psychosexual development.

Inferiority complex. Concept, originated by Alfred Adler, that everyone is born with inferiority or a feeling of inferiority secondary to real or fantasied organic or psychological inadequacies. How this inferiority or feeling of inferiority is handled determines a person's behavior in life. *See also* Masculine protest.

Infra reality. Reduced actuality that is observed in certain therapeutic settings. For example, according to J. L. Moreno, who coined the term, the contact between doctor and patient is not a genuine dialogue but is an interview, research situation, or projective test.

Injunction. In transactional analysis, the instructions given by one ego state to another, usually the Parent ego state to the Child ego state, that become the basis of the person's life script decisions. *See also* Permission, Program, Role, Script analysis.

Inner-directed person. A person who is self-motivated and autonomous and is not easily guided or influenced by the opinions and values of other people. *See also* Other-directed person.

Insight. Conscious awareness and understanding of one's own psychodynamics and symptoms of maladaptive behavior. It is highly important in effecting changes in the personality and behavior of a person. Most therapists distinguish two types: (1) intellectual insight—knowledge and awareness without any change of maladaptive behavior; (2) emotional or visceral insight—awareness, knowledge, and understanding of one's own maladaptive behavior, leading to positive changes in personality and behavior.

Inspirational-supportive group psychotherapy. A type of group therapy that focuses on the positive potential of members and stresses reinforcement for accomplishments or achievements. *See also* Alcoholics Anonymous.

Instinct. A biological, species-specific, genetically determined drive to respond in an automatic, complex, but organized way to a particular stimulus. *See also* Drive, Impulse.

Institute of Industrial Relations. A department of the Graduate School of Business Administration at the University of California at Los Angeles. It has conducted sensitivity training laboratories for business and professional people for nearly 20 years.

Insulin coma therapy. A form of psychiatric treatment originated by Manfred Sakel in which insulin is administered to the patient to produce coma. It is used in certain types of schizophrenia. *See also* Shock treatment.

Intellectual insight. *See* Insight.

Intellectualization. An unconscious defense mechanism in which reasoning or logic is used in an attempt to avoid confrontation with an objectionable impulse or affect. It is also known as brooding or thinking compulsion.

Intelligence. Capacity for understanding, recalling, mobilizing, and integrating constructively what one has learned and for using it to meet new situations.

Intensive group process. Group process designed to evoke a high degree of personal interaction and involvement, often accompanied by the expression of strong or deep feelings.

Interaction. *See* Transaction.

Interpersonal conflict. *See* Extrapsychic conflict.

Interpersonal psychiatry. Dynamic-cultural system of psychoanalytic therapy based on Harry Stack Sullivan's interpersonal theory. Sullivan's formulations were couched in terms of a person's interactions with other people. In group psychotherapy conducted by practitioners of this school, the focus is on the patients' transactions with one another.

Interpersonal skill. Ability of a person in relationship with others to express his feelings appropriately, to be socially responsible, to change and influence, and to work and create. *See also* Socialization.

Interpretation. A psychotherapeutic technique used in psychoanalysis, both individual and group. The therapist conveys to the patient the significance and meaning of his behavior, constructing into a more meaningful form the patient's resistances, defenses, transferences, and symbols (dreams). *See also* Clarification.

Interpretation of Dreams, The. Title of a book by Freud. Published in 1899, this work was a major presentation not only of Freud's discoveries about the meaning of dreams—hitherto regarded as outside scientific interest—but also of his concept of a mental apparatus that is topographically divided into unconscious, preconscious, and conscious areas.

Interracial group. *See* Heterogeneous group.

Intervention laboratory. Human relations laboratory, such as an encounter group or training group, especially designed to intervene and resolve some group conflict or crisis.

Intrapersonal conflict. *See* Intrapsychic conflict.

Intrapsychic ataxia. *See* Ataxia.

Intrapsychic conflict. Conflict that arises from the clash of two opposing forces within oneself.

It is also known as intrapersonal conflict. *See also* Extrapsychic conflict.

Introjection. An unconscious defense mechanism in which a psychic representation of a loved or hated object is taken into one's ego system. In depression, for example, the emotional feelings related to the loss of a loved one are directed toward the introjected mental representation of the loved one. *See also* Identification, Incorporation.

Inversion. Synonym for homosexuality. Inversion was the term used by Freud and his predecessors. There are three types: absolute, amphigenous, and occasional. *See also* Homosexuality, Latent homosexuality, Overt homosexuality.

I-Thou. Philosopher Martin Buber's conception that man's identity develops from true sharing by persons. Basic trust can occur in a living partnership in which each member identifies the particular real personality of the other in his wholeness, unity, and uniqueness. In groups, I-Thou relationships promote warmth, cohesiveness, and constructive group process. *See also* I-It.

Jamais vu. False feeling of unfamiliarity with a real situation one has experienced. *See also* Paramnesia.

Jaundice, allergic. Yellowish staining of the skin and deeper tissues accompanied by bile in the urine secondary to a hypersensitivity reaction. An obstructive type of jaundice, it is occasionally detected during the second to fourth week of phenothiazine therapy.

Johari Window. A schematic diagram used to conceptualize human behavior. It was developed by Joseph (Jo) Luft and Harry (Hari) Ingham at the University of California at Los Angeles in 1955. The diagram is composed of quadrants, each representing some aspect of a person's behavior, feelings, and motivations. *See also* Blind self, Hidden self, Public self, Undeveloped potential.

Jones, Ernest (1879–1958). Welsh psychoanalyst and one of Freud's early followers. He was an organizer of the American Psychoanalytic Association in 1911 and the British Psychoanalytical Society in 1919 and a founder and long-time editor of the journal of the International Psychoanalytical Association. He was the author of many valuable works, the most important of which is his three-volume biography of Freud.

Judgment. Mental act of comparing or evaluating choices within the framework of a given set of values for the purpose of electing a course of action. Judgment is said to be intact if the course of action chosen is consistent with reality; judgment is said to be impaired if the chosen course of action is not consistent with reality.

Jung, Carl Gustav (1875–1961). Swiss psychiatrist and psychoanalyst. He founded the school of analytic psychology. *See also* Collective unconscious.

Karate-chop experience. A technique used in encounter groups to elicit aggression in timid or inhibited participants in a humorous way. The timid one stands facing a more aggressive member. Both make violent pseudokarate motions at each other, without making physical contact but yelling "Hai!" as loudly as possible at each stroke. After this exercise, the group members discuss the experience.

Kelley desegregation scale. A scale designed to measure the attitudes of whites toward blacks in the area of school integration. The scale provides a rough measure of racial prejudice and may be of help in ascertaining the effects on prejudice of participation in an interracial group. *See also* Ford negative personal contacts with Negroes scale, Ford negative personal contacts with whites scale, Rosander anti-Negro behavior scale, Steckler anti-Negro scale, Steckler anti-white scale.

Kinesthetic hallucination. False perception of muscular movement. An amputee may feel movement in his missing limb; this phenomenon is also known as phantom limb.

Kinesthetic sense. Sensation in the muscles as differentiated from the senses that receive stimulation from outside the body.

Kleptomania. Pathological compulsion to steal. In psychoanalytic theory, it originates in the infantile stage of psychosexual development.

Latency phase. Stage of psychosexual development extending from age five to the beginning of adolescence at age 12. Freud's work on ego psychology showed that the apparent cessation of sexual preoccupation during this period stems from a strong, aggressive blockade of libidinal and sexual impulses in an effort to avoid the dangers of the oedipal relationships. During the latency period, boys and girls are inclined to choose friends and join groups of their own sex. *See also* Identification with the aggressor, Psychosexual development.

Latent homosexuality. Unexpressed conscious or unconscious homoerotic wishes that are held in check. Freud's theory of bisexuality postulated the existence of a constitutionally determined, though experientially influenced, instinctual masculine-feminine duality. Normally, the opposite-sex component is dormant, but a breakdown in the defenses of repression and sublimation may activate latent instincts and result in overt homoeroticism. Many writers have questioned the validity of a universal latent homoeroticism. *See also* Bisexuality, Homosexuality, Overt homosexuality.

Lateral transference. Projection of long-range attitudes, values, and emotions onto the other members of the treatment group rather than onto the therapist. The patient sees other members of the group, co-patients, and peers in terms of his experiences in his original family. *See also* Collective family transference neurosis, Multiple transference.

Leaderless therapeutic group. An extreme form of nondirective group, conducted primarily for research purposes, such as the investigations of intragroup tensions by Walter R. Bion. On occasion, the therapist interacts verbally in a nonauthoritarian manner, but he generally functions as a silent observer—withholding explanations, directions, and support.

Leadership function. *See* Leadership role.

Leadership role. Stance adopted by the therapist in conducting a group. There are three main leadership roles: authoritarian, democratic, and laissez-faire. Any group—social, therapeutic, training, or task-oriented—is primarily influenced by the role practiced by the leader.

Leadership style. *See* Leadership role.

Lesbianism. Female homosexuality. About 600 B.C. on the island of Lesbos in the Aegean Sea, the poetess Sappho encouraged young women to engage in mutual sex practices. Lesbianism is also known as Sapphism. *See also* Bisexuality, Homosexuality, Latent homosexuality, Overt homosexuality.

Lewin, Kurt (1890–1946). German psychologist who emigrated to the United States in 1933. His work on the field theory has been useful in the experimental study of human behavior in a social situation. He was one of the early workers who helped develop the National Training Laboratories.

Libido theory. Freudian theory of sexual instinct, its complex process of development, and its accompanying physical and mental manifestations. Before Freud's introduction and completion of the dual-instinct theory (sexual and aggressive) in 1920, all instinctual manifestations were related to the sexual instinct, making for some confusion at that time. Current psychoanalytic practice assumes the existence of two instincts: sexual (libido) and aggressive (death). *See also* Aggressive drive, Sexual drive.

Life instinct. *See* Sexual drive.

Life lie. A contrary-to-fact conviction around which a person structures his life philosophy and attitudes.

Life line. A group technique in which each member is asked to draw a line representing his life, beginning with birth and ending with death. Comparison and discussion usually reveal that the shape and slope of the lines are based on a variety of personally meaningful parameters, such as maturity and academic achievement.

Lifwynn Foundation. Organization established by Trigant Burrow in 1927 as a social community in which the participants examined their interactions in the daily activities in which they were engaged. Lifwynn is currently under the direction of Hans Syz, M.D., in Westport, Conn.

Lilliputian hallucination. False perception that persons are reduced in size. *See also* Micropsia.

Lobotomy. Neurosurgical procedure in which one or more nerve tracts in a lobe of the cerebrum are severed. Prefrontal lobotomy is the ablation of one or more nerve tracts in the prefrontal area of the brain. It is used in the treatment of certain severe mental disorders that do not respond to other treatments.

Locus. Place of origin.

Logorrhea. Copious, pressured, coherent speech. It is observed in manic-depressive illness, manic type. Logorrhea is also known as tachylogia, verbomania, and volubility.

LSD (lysergic acid diethylamide). A potent psychotogenic drug discovered in 1942. LSD produces psychoticlike symptoms and behavior changes—including hallucinations, delusions, and time-space distortions.

Lysergic acid diethylamide. *See* LSD.

Macropsia. False perception that objects are larger than they really are. *See also* Micropsia.

Maintenance drug therapy. A stage in the course of chemotherapy. After the drug has reached its maximal efficacy, the dosage is reduced and sustained at the minimal therapeutic level that will prevent a relapse or exacerbation.

Major tranquilizer. Drug that has antipsychotic properties. The phenothiazines, thioxanthenes, butyrophenones, and reserpine derivatives are typical major tranquilizers, which are also known as ataractics, neuroleptics, and antipsychotics. *See also* Dystonia, Minor tranquilizer.

Maladaptive way. Poorly adjusted or pathological behavior pattern.

Mannerism. Stereotyped involuntary activity that is peculiar to a person.

MAO inhibitor. *See* Monoamine oxidase inhibitor.

Marathon. *See* Group marathon.

Marijuana. Dried leaves and flowers of *Cannabis sativa* (Indian hemp). It induces somatic and psychic changes in man when smoked or ingested in sufficient quantity. The somatic changes include increased heart rate, rise in blood pressure, dryness of the mouth, increased appetite, and occasional nausea, vomiting, and diarrhea. The psychic changes include dreamy-state level of consciousness, disruptive chain of ideas, perceptual disturbances of time and space, and alterations of mood. In strong doses, marijuana can produce hallucinations and, at times, paranoid ideas and suspiciousness. It is also known as pot, grass, weed, tea, and Mary Jane.

Marital counseling. Process whereby a trained counselor helps married couples resolve problems that arise and trouble them in their relationship. The theory and techniques of this approach were first developed in social agencies as part of family casework. Husband and wife are seen by the same worker in separate and joint counseling sessions, which focus on immediate family problems.

Marital therapy. *See* Marriage therapy.

Marriage therapy. A type of family therapy that involves the husband and the wife and focuses on the marital relationship, which affects the individual psychopathology of the partners. The rationale for this method is the assumption that psychopathological processes within the family structure and in the social matrix of the marriage perpetuate individual pathological personality structures, which find expression in the disturbed marriage and are aggravated by the feedback between partners. *See also* Collaborative therapy, Combined therapy, Concurrent therapy, Conjoint therapy, Family therapy, Group marital therapy, Marital counseling, Quadrangular therapy, Square interview.

Masculine identity. Well-developed sense of gender affiliation with males.

Masculine protest. Adlerian doctrine that depicts a universal human tendency to move from a passive and feminine role to a masculine and active role. This doctrine is an extension of his ideas about organic inferiority. It became the prime motivational force in normal and neurotic behavior in the Adlerian system. *See also* Adler, Alfred; Inferiority complex.

Masculinity-femininity scale. Any scale on a psychological test that assesses the relative masculinity or femininity of the testee. Scales vary and may focus, for example, on basic identification with either sex or preference for a particular sex role.

Masochism. A sexual deviation in which sexual gratification is derived from being maltreated by the partner or oneself. It was first described by an Austrian novelist, Leopold von Sacher-Masoch (1836–1895). *See also* Sadism, Sadomasochistic relationship.

Masturbation. *See* Autoerotism.

Mattress-pounding. A technique used in encounter groups to mobilize repressed or suppressed anger. A group member vents his resentments by beating the mattress with his fists and yelling. Frequently, the mattress becomes in fantasy a hated parent, sibling, or spouse. After this exercise, the group members discuss their reactions. *See also* Pillow-beating.

Maximal expression. Utmost communication. In psychodrama, it is the outcome of an involved sharing by the group of the three portions of the session: the warm-up, the action, and the postaction. During the action period the patient is encouraged to express all action and verbal communication to the limit. To this end, delusions, hallucinations, soliloquies, thoughts, and fantasies are allowed to be part of the production.

Mechanical group therapy. A form of group therapy that makes use of mechanical devices. As applied in the early 1950's, it required neither a group nor a therapist. An example of this form of therapy is the playing of brief recorded messages over the loudspeaker system of a mental hospital; the same statement, bearing on some elementary principle of mental health, is frequently repeated to secure general acceptance. *See also* Class method, Didactic technique, Group bibliotherapy.

Megalomania. Morbid preoccupation with expansive delusions of power and wealth.

Melancholia. Old term for depression that is rarely used at the present time. As used in the term involutional melancholia, it refers to a morbid state of depression and not to a symptom.

Memory. Ability to revive past sensory impressions, experiences, and learned ideas. Memory includes three basic mental processes: registration—the ability to perceive, recognize, and establish information in the central nervous system; retention—the ability to retain registered information; and recall—the ability to retrieve stored information at will. *See also* Amnesia, Hypermnesia, Paramnesia.

Mental aberration. *See* Aberration, mental.

Mental illness. Psychiatric disease included in the list of mental disorders in the *Diagnostic and Statistical Manual of Mental Disorders* published by the American Psychiatric Association and in the *Standard Nomenclature of Diseases and Operations* approved by the American Medical Association.

Mental retardation. Subnormal general intellectual functioning, which may be evident at birth or may develop during childhood. Learning, social adjustment, and maturation are impaired, and emotional disturbance is often present. The degree of retardation is commonly measured in terms of I.Q.: borderline (68–85), mild (52–67), moderate (36–51), severe (20–35), and profound (under 20). Obsolescent terms that are still used occasionally are idiot (mental age of less than three years), imbecile (mental age of three to seven years), and moron (mental age of eight years).

Methadone. Methadone hydrochloride, a long-acting synthetic narcotic developed in Germany as a substitute for morphine. It is used as an analgesic and in detoxification and maintenance treatment of opiate addicts.

Methadone maintenance treatment. Long-term use of methadone on a daily basis to relieve narcotic craving and avert the effects of narcotic drugs.

Micropsia. False perception that objects are smaller than they really are. *See also* Lilliputian hallucination, Macropsia.

Milieu therapy. Treatment that emphasizes appropriate socioenvironmental manipulation for the benefit of the patient. The setting for milieu therapy is usually the psychiatric hospital.

Million-dollar game. Group game designed to explore the psychological meaning of money and to encourage free, creative thinking. The group is told that it has a million dollars, which is to be used productively in any way, as long as the endeavor actively involves all members of the group. *See also* Game, Hit-and-run game, Survival.

Minnesota Multiphasic Personality Inventory. Questionnaire type of psychological test for ages 16 and over with 550 true-false statements that are coded in 14 scales, ranging from a social scale to a schizophrenia scale. Group and individual forms are available.

Minor tranquilizer. Drug that diminishes tension, restlessness, and pathological anxiety without any antipsychotic effect. Meprobamate and diazepoxides are typical minor tranquilizers, which are also known as psycholeptics. *See also* Major tranquilizer.

Minutes of the Vienna Psychoanalytic Society. Diary of Freud's Wednesday Evening Society (after 1910, the Vienna Psychoanalytic Society) as recorded by Otto Rank, the paid secretary between 1906 and 1915.

Mirror. In psychodrama, the person who represents the patient, copying his behavior and trying to express his feelings in word and movement, showing the patient as if in a mirror how other people experience him. The mirror may exaggerate, employing techniques of deliberate distortion in order to arouse the patient to come forth and change from a passive spectator into an active participant. The mirror is also known as the double. *See also* Auxiliary ego.

Mirroring. A group process by which a person sees himself in the group by the reflections that come back to him in response to the way he presents himself. The image may be true or distorted, depending on the level of truth at which the group is functioning at the time. Mirroring has been used as an exercise in encounter group therapy and as a laboratory procedure in the warming-up period of the psychodrama approach.

Mixed-gender group. *See* Heterogeneous group.

MMPI. *See* Minnesota Multiphasic Personality Inventory.

Mobility. *See* Group mobility.

Monoamine oxidase inhibitor. Agent that inhibits the enzyme monoamine oxidase (MAO), which oxidizes such monoamines as norepinephrine and serotonin. Some of the MAO inhibitors are highly effective as antidepressants. *See also* Tricyclic drug.

Monomania. Morbid mental state characterized by preoccupation with one subject. It is also known as partial insanity.

Mood. Feeling tone that is experienced by a person internally. Mood does not include the external expression of the internal feeling tone. *See also* Affect.

Mood swing. Oscillation of a person's emotional feeling tone between periods of euphoria and depression.

Moron. *See* Mental retardation.

Moses and Monotheism. Title of a book by Freud published in 1939. In this book, Freud undertook a historical but frankly speculative reconstruction of the personality of Moses and examined the concept of monotheism and the abiding effect of the patriarch on the character of the Jews. One of Freud's last works, it bears the imprint of his latter-day outlook and problems.

Mother Superior complex. Tendency of a therapist to play the role of the mother in his relations with his patients. The complex often leads to interference with the therapeutic process. *See also* God complex.

Mother surrogate. Mother substitute. In psychoanalysis, the patient projects his mother image onto another person and responds to that person unconsciously in an inappropriate and unrealistic manner with the feelings and attitudes he had toward the original mother.

Motivation. Force that pushes a person to act to satisfy a need. It implies an incentive or desire that influences the will and causes the person to act.

Mourning. *See* Grief.

Multibody situation. Group situation. The term was originally used in the description of the evolution of social interaction in human beings from narcissism through the dyadic relationship to the three-body constellation of the Oedipus complex to the multibody situation prevailing in groups.

Multiple double. Several representations of the patient, each portraying a part of him—one as he is now, another as he was (for instance, five years ago), another at a crucial moment in his life (for example, when his mother died), a fourth how he may be 20 years hence. The multiple representations of the patient are presented in sequence, each continuing where the last left off. *See also* Auxiliary ego.

Multiple ego states. Many psychological stages, relating to different periods of one's life or to different depths of experience. These states may be of varying degrees of organization and complexity, and they may or may not be capable of being called to awareness consecutively or simultaneously.

Multiple interaction. Group behavior in which many members participate in the transactions, both verbal and nonverbal, at any one moment in the session.

Multiple intragroup transference. *See* Multiple transference.

Multiple reactivity. A phenomenon in which many group members respond in a variety of ways to the provocative role or stimulation afforded by one patient's behavior.

Multiple therapy. *See* Co-therapy.

Multiple transferences. Feelings and attitudes originally held toward members of one's family that become irrationally attached to the therapist and various group members simultaneously. *See also* Collective family transference neurosis, Lateral transference.

Mutism. *See* Stupor.

Mutual support. Expressions of sympathy, understanding, and affection that group members give to one another. *See also* Pairing.

Mydriasis. Dilatation of the pupil. The condition sometimes occurs as an autonomic side effect of phenothiazine and antiparkinsonism drugs.

Nalline test. The use of Nalline, a narcotic antagonist, to determine abstinence from opiates. An injection of Nalline precipitates withdrawal symptoms if opiates have been used recently. The most important use for Nalline, however, is as an antidote in the treatment of opiate overdose.

Narcissism. Self-love. It is linked to autoerotism but is devoid of genitality. The word is derived from Narcissus, a Greek mythology figure who fell in love with his own reflected image. In psychoanalytic theory, it is divided into primary narcissism and secondary narcissism. Primary narcissism refers to the early infantile phase of object relationship development, when the child has not differentiated himself from the outside world. All sources of pleasure are unrealistically recognized as coming from within himself, giving him a false sense of omnipotence.

Secondary narcissism is the type of narcissism that results when the libido once attached to external love objects is redirected back to the self. *See also* Autistic thinking, Autoerotism.

Narcotic hunger. A physiological craving for a drug. It appears in abstinent narcotic addicts.

National Training Laboratories. Organization started in 1947 at Bethel, Maine, to train professionals who work with groups. Interest in personal development eventually led to sensitivity training and encounter groups. The organization is now called the NTL Institute for Applied Behavioral Science. *See also* Basic skills training, East Coast style T-group.

Natural Child. In transactional analysis, the autonomous, expressive, archaic Child ego state that is free from parental influence. *Se also* Adapted Child.

Natural group. Group that tends to evolve spontaneously in human civilization, such as a kinship, tribal, or religious group. In contrast are various contrived groups or aggregates of people who meet for a relatively brief time to achieve some goal.

Negativism. Verbal or nonverbal opposition to outside suggestions and advice. It is also known as command negativism.

Neologism. New word or condensation of several words formed by patient in an effort to express a highly complex idea. It is often seen in schizophrenia.

Neopsychic function. *See* Adult.

Network. The persons in the patient's environment with whom he is most intimately connected. It frequently includes the nuclear family, the extended family, the orbit of relatives and friends, and work and recreational contacts. S. H. Foulkes believes that this dynamically interacting network has a fundamental significance in the production of illness in the patient. *See also* Extended family therapy, Social network therapy, Visitor.

Neuroleptic. *See* Antipsychotic drug, Major tranquilizer.

Neurosis. Mental disorder characterized by anxiety. The anxiety may be experienced and expressed directly, or, through an unconscious psychic process, it may be converted, displaced, or somatized. Although neuroses do not manifest depersonalization or overt distortion of reality, they can be severe enough to impair a person's functioning. The neuroses, also known as psychoneuroses, include the following types: anxiety neurosis, hysterical neurosis, phobic neurosis, obsessive-compulsive neurosis, depressive neurosis, neurasthenic neurosis, depersonalization neurosis, and hypochondriacal neurosis.

Nondirective approach. Technique in which the therapist follows the lead of the patient in the interview rather than introducing his own theories and directing the course of the interview. This method is applied in both individual and group therapy, such as Carl Rogers' client-centered and group-centered therapy. *See also* Passive therapist.

Nontruster. A person who has a strong unfilled need to be nurtured but whose early experience was one of rejection or overprotection. As a defense against repetition of this experience, he develops an overly strong show of independence. Sometimes this independence is manifested in group therapy by a member's constant rejection of support and of attempts by other members to get close to him. *See also* Outsider.

Nonverbal interaction. Technique used without the aid of words in encounter groups to promote communication and intimacy and to bypass verbal defenses. Many exercises of this sort are carried out in complete silence; in others, the participants emit grunts, groans, yells, cries, or sighs. Gestalt therapy pays particular attention to nonverbal expression.

Norepinephrine. A catecholamine that functions as a neurohumoral mediator liberated by postganglionic adrenergic nerves. It is also present in the adrenal medulla and in many areas in the brain, with the highest concentration in the hypothalamus. A disturbance in the metabolism of norepinephrine is considered to be an important factor in the etiology of depression. *See also* Serotonin.

Nuclear family. Immediate members of a family, including the parents and the children. *See also* Extended family therapy, Network, Social network therapy, Visitor.

Nuclear group member. *See* Therapist surrogate.

Nude marathon. Encounter group in which members assemble for an emotional experience of prolonged duration (from a minimum of eight hours to a couple of days), with the added factor of physical nakedness as members go about their activities. The theory is that clothes are themselves defenses against openness, that they connote limiting roles and result in stereotyped responses from others, and that they allow participants to avoid facing conflicts about their own bodies. *See also* Group marathon, Sensory-experiential group.

Nymphomania. Morbid, insatiable need in women for sexual intercourse. *See also* Satyriasis.

Observer. Person who is included but is generally not an active participant in therapy sessions. His observations are later discussed in posttherapy meetings with the staff or supervisor. *See also* Recorder.

Observer therapist. *See* Passive therapist.

Obsession. Persistent idea, thought, or impulse that cannot be eliminated from consciousness by logical effort. *See also* Compulsion.

Oedipus complex. A distinct group of associated ideas, aims, instinctual drives, and fears that are generally observed in children when they are from three to six years of age. During this period, which coincides with the peak of the phallic phase of psychosexual development, the child's sexual interest is attached chiefly to the parent of the opposite sex and is accompanied by aggressive feelings and wishes for the parent of the same sex. One of Freud's most important concepts, the Oedipus complex was discovered in 1897 as a result of his self-analysis. *See also* Totem and Taboo.

Ogre. In structural analysis, the Child ego state in the father that supersedes the nurturing Parent and becomes a pseudo-Parent.

One-gender group. *See* Homogeneous group.

Open group. Treatment group in which new members are continuously added as other members leave. *See also* Closed group.

Oral dyskinesia, tardive. *See* Tardive oral dyskinesia.

Oral phase. The earliest stage in psychosexual development. It lasts through the first 18 months of life. During this period, the oral zone is the center of the infant's needs, expression, and pleasurable erotic experiences. It has a strong influence on the organization and development of the child's psyche. *See also* Anal phase, Genital phase, Infantile sexuality, Latency phase, Phallic phase.

Orientation. State of awareness of one's relationships and surroundings in terms of time, place, and person.

Orthostatic hypotension. Reduction in blood pressure brought about by a shift from a recumbent to an upright position. It is observed as a side effect of several psychotropic drugs.

Other-directed person. A person who is readily influenced and guided by the attitudes and values of other people. *See also* Inner-directed person.

Outsider. In group therapy, a member who feels alienated and isolated from the group. Such a person has usually experienced repetitive rejection in his early life and is wary of trusting people in the present. Often much effort is required by the group and the therapist before the outsider trusts someone. *See also* Nontruster.

Overt homosexuality. Behaviorally expressed homoeroticism as distinct from unconsciously held homosexual wishes or conscious wishes that are held in check. *See also* Homosexuality, Latent homosexuality.

Pairing. Term coined by Walter R. Bion to denote mutual support between two or more group members who wish to avoid the solution of their problems. The term is often used more loosely to denote an attraction between two group members.

Panic. An acute, intense attack of anxiety associated with personality disorganization. Some writers use the term exclusively for psychotic episodes of overwhelming anxiety. *See also* Homosexual panic.

Pantomime. Gesticulation; psychodrama without the use of words.

Paralogia. *See* Evasion.

Paralytic ileus. Intestinal obstruction of the nonmechanical type, secondary to paralysis of the bowel wall, that may lead to fecal retention.

It is a rare anticholinergic side effect of phenothiazine therapy.

Paramnesia. Disturbance of memory in which reality and fantasy are confused. It is observed in dreams and in certain types of schizophrenia and organic brain syndromes. *See also* Confabulation, Déjà entendu, Déjà vu, Fausse reconnaissance, Jamais vu, Retrospective falsification.

Paranoid delusion. *See* Delusion.

Parent. In transactional analysis, an ego state borrowed from a parental figure. It is also known as exteropsychic function.

Parental rejection. Denial of affection and attention to a child by one or both parents. The child in turn develops great affect hunger and hostility, which is directed either outwardly in the form of tantrums, etc., or inwardly toward himself in the form of allergies, etc.

Parkinsonism. Syndrome characterized by rhythmical muscular tremors known as pill rolling accompanied by spasticity and rigidity of movement, propulsive gait, droopy posture, and masklike facies. It is usually seen in later life as a result of arteriosclerotic changes in the basal ganglia.

Parkinsonismlike effect. Symptom that is a frequent side effect of antipsychotic drugs. Typical symptoms are motor retardation, muscular rigidity, alterations of posture, tremor, and autonomic nervous system disturbances. *See also* Phenothiazine derivative.

Partial insanity. *See* Monomania.

Passive therapist. Type of therapist who remains inactive but whose presence serves as a stimulus for the patient in the group or individual treatment setting. *See also* Active therapist, Leaderless therapeutic group, Nondirective approach.

Pastime. In transactional analysis, semistereotyped set of transactions dealing with a certain topic. Unlike Berne's term game, a pastime has no ulterior motive and no psychological payoff.

Patient peers. *See* Co-patients.

Patty-cake exercise. An encounter group technique that involves the palm-to-palm contact made by children in the game of patty-cake. This type of contact is familiar and does not usually arouse much anxiety in participants, yet it allows people to bypass verbal defenses in getting to know each other. After this exercise, the group members discuss their reactions. Also called Hand-dance.

Pecking order. Sequence of hierarchy or authority in an organization or social group. *See also* Hierarchical vector.

Peer co-therapist. Therapist who is equal in status to the other therapist treating a group and who relates to him on an equal level.

Peer-group phenomenon. Interaction or reaction of a person with a group of equals. These phenomena include activities he does within the group that he would probably not do individually outside the group.

Peer identification. Unconscious process that occurs in a group when one member incorporates within himself the qualities and attributes of another member. It usually occurs in members with low self-esteem who would like to feel at one with members who have improved.

Peer vector. *See* Horizontal vector.

Perception. Mental process by which data—intellectual, sensory, and emotional—are organized meaningfully. Through perception, a person makes sense out of the many stimuli that bombard him. It is one of the many ego functions. Therapy groups and T-groups aim to expand and alter perception in ways conducive to the development of the potential of each participant. *See also* Agnosia, Apperception, Clouding of consciousness, Ego, Hallucination, Hysterical anesthesia, Memory.

Perceptual expansion. Development of one's ability to recognize and interpret the meaning of sensory stimuli through associations with past experiences with similar stimuli. Perceptual expansion through the relaxation of defenses is one of the goals in both individual and group therapy.

Permission. In transactional analysis, a therapeutic transaction designed to permanently neutralize the parental injunctions.

Personal growth laboratory. A sensitivity training laboratory in which the primary emphasis is on each participant's potentialities for creativity, empathy, and leadership. In such a laboratory the facilitator encourages most modalities of experience and expression—such as art, sensory stimulation, and intellectual, emotional, written, oral, verbal, and nonverbal expression. *See also* National Training Laboratories.

Personality. Habitual configuration of behavior of a person, reflecting his physical and mental activities, attitudes, and interests and corresponding to the sum total of his adjustment to life.

Personality disorder. Mental disorder characterized by maladaptive patterns of adjustment to life. There is no subjective anxiety, as seen in neurosis, and no disturbance in the capacity to recognize reality, as seen in psychosis. The types of personality disorders include passive-aggressive, antisocial, schizoid, hysterical, paranoid, cyclothymic, explosive, obsessive-compulsive, asthenic, and inadequate.

Perversion. Deviation from the expected norm. In psychiatry it commonly signifies sexual perversion. *See also* Sexual deviation.

Perverted logic. *See* Evasion.

Peter Principle. Theory that man tends to advance to his level of incompetence. The idea was popularized in a book of the same name by Laurence J. Peter and Raymond Hull.

Phallic overbearance. Domination of another person by aggressive means. It is generally associated with masculinity in its negative aspects.

Phallic phase. The third stage in psychosexual development. It occurs when the child is from two to six years of age. During this period, the child's interest, curiosity, and pleasurable experiences are centered around the penis in boys and the clitoris in girls. *See also* Anal phase, Genital phase, Infantile sexuality, Latency phase, Oral phase.

Phantasy. *See* Fantasy.

Phantom limb. *See* Kinesthetic hallucination.

Phenothiazine derivative. Compound derived from phenothiazine. It is particularly known for its antipsychotic property. As a class, the phenothiazine derivatives are among the most widely used drugs in medical practice, particularly in psychiatry. Chlorpromazine, triflupromazine, fluphenazine, perphenazine, and thioridazine are some examples of phenothiazine derivatives. *See also* Anticholinergic effect, Autonomic side effect, Electrocardiographic effect, Mydriasis, Paralytic ileus, Parkinsonismlike effect.

Phobia. Pathological fear associated with some specific type of stimulus or situation. *See also* Acrophobia, Agoraphobia, Algophobia, Claustrophobia, Xenophobia, Zoophobia.

Phyloanalysis. A means of investigating disorders of human behavior, both individual and collective, resulting from impaired tensional processes that affected the organism's internal reaction as a whole. Trigant Burrow adopted the word to replace his earlier term, group analysis, which he first used in 1927 to describe the social participation of many persons in their common analysis. Because group analysis was confused with group psychotherapy of the analytic type, Burrow changed his nomenclature to phyloanalysis.

Pillow-beating. A technique used in encounter groups to elicit pent-up rage in a group member who needs to release it in a physical way. The member beats the pillow and yells angry words until he gets tired. The acceptance of his anger by the group is considered therapeutic. After this exercise, the group members discuss their reactions. *See also* Mattress-pounding.

Placebo. Inert substance prepared to resemble the active drug being tested in experimental research. It is sometimes used in clinical practice for a psychotherapeutic effect. The response to the placebo may represent the response due to the psychological effect of taking a pill and not to any pharmacological property.

Play therapy. Type of therapy used with children, usually of preschool and early latency ages. The patient reveals his problems on a fantasy level with dolls, clay, and other toys. The therapist intervenes opportunely with helpful explanations about the patient's responses and behavior in language geared to the child's comprehension. *See also* Activity group therapy.

Political therapist. A therapist who gives strong weight to the personalities of those above him as far as they impinge on his professional activities. He pays particular attention to the personal and historical aspects of authority. *See also* Authority principle, Hierarchical vector, Procedural therapist.

Popular mind. The primitive, fickle, suggestible, impulsive, uncritical type of mind that Le Bon felt was characteristic of the mass. He was referring to the unorganized crowds who lack leadership.

Postsession. *See* After-session.

Power phase. Second stage in group treatment. In this phase members start expressing anger and hostility—usually directed at the leader, sometimes directed at other members—in an attempt to achieve individuation and autonomy. *See also* Affection phase, Inclusion phase.

Pratt, Joseph H. Boston physician born in 1842 generally considered to be the first pioneer in group psychotherapy in America. He is known for his work with tuberculous patients (1900–1906). He formed discussion groups to deal with the physical aspects of tuberculosis. Later, these groups began discussing the emotional problems that stemmed from the illness. *See also* Class method.

Preconscious. In psychoanalysis, one of the three divisions of the psyche according to Freud's topographical psychology. The preconscious includes all ideas, thoughts, past experiences, and other memory impressions that can be consciously recalled with effort. *See also* Conscious, Unconscious.

Prefrontal lobotomy. *See* Lobotomy.

Prejudice. Adverse judgment or opinion formed without factual knowledge. Elements of irrational suspicion or hatred are often involved, as in racial prejudice.

Premeeting. Group meeting of patients without the therapist. It is held immediately before the regular therapist-led session and is also referred to as warming-up session and presession. *See also* After-session, Alternate session.

Preoccupation of thought. *See* Trend of thought.

Pressure cooker. Slang phrase to describe the high degree of group involvement and emotional pitch sought by certain intensive groups, such as marathon groups.

Primal father. Hypothetical head of the tribe. He is depicted by Freud in *Totem and Taboo* as slain by his sons, who subsequently devour him in a cannibalistic rite. Later, he is promoted to a god. The son who murders him is the prototype of the tragic hero, and the memory of the crime is perpetuated in the conscience of the individual and of the culture.

Primal scene. In psychoanalysis, the real or fantasied observation by a child of sexual intercourse, particularly between his parents.

Primary process. In psychoanalysis, the mental process directly related to the functions of the id and characteristic of unconscious mental activity. The primary process is marked by unorganized, illogical thinking and by the tendency to seek immediate discharge and gratification of instinctual demands. *See also* Secondary process.

Probe. An encounter technique designed for a specific purpose—for instance, to determine motivation for admission to treatment. The technique is commonly used in such drug rehabilitation centers as Odyssey House.

Procedural therapist. A therapist who places the most weight on the written word, on formal rules and regulations, and on the hierarchical system. *See also* Authority principle, Political therapist.

Process-centered group. Group whose main purpose is to study the dynamics of the group itself—how it operates and through what stages it progresses. Such groups often ask the question, "What's going on here?" rather than the encounter group question, "What are you experiencing or feeling?" *See also* Group analytic psychotherapy, Group-centered psychotherapy.

Program. In transactional analysis, the teaching by one of the parents of how best to comply with the script injunction.

Projection. Unconscious defense mechanism in which a person attributes to another the ideas, thoughts, feelings, and impulses that are part of his inner perceptions but that are unacceptable to him. Projection protects the person from anxiety arising from an inner conflict. By externalizing whatever is unacceptable, the person deals with it as a situation apart from himself. *See also* Blind spot, Future projection.

Projective method. Group treatment proce-

dure that uses the spontaneous creative work of the patients. For example, group members make and analyze drawings, which are often expressions of their underlying emotional problems.

Protagonist. In psychodrama, the patient who is the focal point of a psychodramatic session. He is asked to be himself, to portray his own private world on the stage.

Pseudoauthenticity. False or copied expression of thoughts and feelings.

Pseudocollusion. Sense of closeness, relationship, or cooperation that is not real but is based on transference.

Psychic determinism. Freudian adaptation of the concept of causality. It states that all phenomena or events have antecedent causes that operate on an unconscious level, beyond the control of the person involved.

Psychoactive drug. Drug that alters thoughts, feelings, or perceptions. Such a drug may help a person in either individual or group therapy overcome depression, anxiety, or rigidity of thought and behavior while he learns new methods of perceiving and responding.

Psychoanalysis. Freud's method of psychic investigation and form of psychotherapy. As a technique for exploring the mental processes, psychoanalysis includes the use of free association and the analysis and interpretation of dreams, resistances, and transferences. As a form of psychotherapy, it uses the investigative technique, guided by Freud's libido and instinct theories and by ego psychology, to gain insight into a person's unconscious motivations, conflicts, and symbols and thus to effect a change in his maladaptive behavior. Several schools of thought are loosely referred to as psychoanalytic at present. Psychoanalysis is also known as analysis in depth.

Psychoanalytically oriented group psychotherapy. *See* Psychoanalytic group psychotherapy.

Psychoanalytic group psychotherapy. A major method of group psychotherapy, pioneered by Alexander Wolf and based on the operational principles of individual psychoanalytic therapy. Analysis and interpretation of a patient's transferences, resistances, and defenses are modified to take place in a group setting. Although strictly designating treatment structured to produce significant character change, the term encompasses the same approach in groups conducted at more superficial levels for lesser goals. *See also* Collective family transference neurosis, Discussion model of group psychotherapy, Verbal-deep approach.

Psychoanalytic treatment. *See* Psychoanalysis.

Psychodrama. Psychotherapy method originated by J. L. Moreno in which personality make-up, interpersonal relationships, conflicts, and emotional problems are explored by means of dramatic methods. The therapeutic dramatization of emotional problems includes: (1) protagonist or patient, the person who presents and acts out his emotional problems with the help of (2) auxiliary egos, persons trained to act and dramatize the different aspects of the patient that are called for in a particular scene in order to help him express his feelings, and (3) director, leader, or therapist, the person who guides those involved in the drama for a fruitful and therapeutic session. *See also* Actional-deep approach, Analytic psychodrama, Concretization of living, Didactic psychodrama, Hallucinatory psychodrama, Hypnodrama, Improvisation, Maximal expression, Mirror, Re-enactment, Regressive-reconstructive approach, Role-playing, Role reversal, Self-realization.

Psychodramatic director. Leader of a psychodrama session. The director has three functions: producer, therapist, and analyst. As producer, he turns every clue the patient offers into dramatic action. As therapist, he attacks and shocks the patient at times, laughs and jokes with him at times, and becomes indirect and passive at times. As analyst, he interprets and elicits responses from the audience.

Psychodramatic shock. *See* Hallucinatory psychodrama.

Psychodynamics. Science of the mind, its mental processes, and affective components that influence human behavior and motivations. *See also* Group dynamics, Infantile dynamics.

Psychological defense system. *See* Defense mechanism.

Psychological procedure. Any technique intended to alter a person's attitude toward and perception of himself and others. *See also* Group psychotherapy, Psychoanalysis, Psychotherapy.

Psychomotor stimulant. Drug that arouses the patient through its central excitatory and analeptic properties. Amphetamine and methylphenidate are drugs in this class.

Psychopathology. Branch of science that deals with morbidity of the mind.

Psychophysiological disorder. Mental disorder characterized by physical symptoms of psychic origin. It usually involves a single organ system innervated by the autonomic nervous system. The physiological and organic changes stem from a sustained emotional disturbance.

Psychosexual development. Maturation and development of the psychic phase of sexuality from birth to adult life. Its phases are oral, anal, phallic, latency, and genital. *See also* Identification with the aggressor, Infantile sexuality.

Psychosis. Mental disorder in which a person's mental capacity, affective response, and capacity to recognize reality, communicate, and relate to others are impaired enough to interfere with his capacity to deal with the ordinary demands of life. The psychoses are subdivided into two major classifications according to their origin—psychoses associated with organic brain syndromes and functional psychoses.

Psychosomatic illness. *See* Psychophysiological disorder.

Psychosurgery. *See* Lobotomy.

Psychotherapy. Form of treatment for mental illness and behavioral disturbances in which a trained person establishes a professional contract with the patient and through definite therapeutic communication, both verbal and nonverbal, attempts to alleviate the emotional disturbance, reverse or change maladaptive patterns of behavior, and encourage personality growth and development. Psychotherapy is distinguished from such other forms of psychiatric treatment as the use of drugs, surgery, electric shock treatment, and insulin coma treatment. *See also* Growth psychotherapy, Individual therapy, Psychoanalysis.

Psychotomimetic drug. Drug that produces psychic and behavioral changes that resemble psychosis. Unlike other drugs that can produce organic psychosis as a reaction, a psychotomimetic drug does not produce overt memory impairment. It is also known as a hallucinogenic drug. Lysergic acid diethylamide (LSD), tetrahydrocannabinol, and mescaline are examples of psychotomimetic drugs.

Psychotropic drug. Drug that affects psychic function and behavior. Also known as a phrenotropic drug, it may be classified as an antipsychotic drug, antidepressant drug, antimanic drug, antianxiety drug, or hallucinogenic drug. *See also* Agranulocytosis, Orthostatic hypotension.

Public self. The behavior, feelings, and motivations of a person known both to himself and to others. It is a quadrant of the Johari Window, a diagrammatic concept of human behavior. *See also* Blind self, Hidden self, Undeveloped potential.

Quadrangular therapy. A type of marital therapy that involves four people: the married pair and each spouse's therapist. *See also* Collaborative therapy, Combined therapy, Concurrent therapy, Conjoint therapy, Family therapy, Group marital therapy, Marriage therapy, Square interview.

Rank, Otto (1884–1939). Austrian psychoanalyst. He was one of Freud's earliest followers and the long-time secretary and recorder of the minutes of the Vienna Psychoanalytic Society. He wrote such fundamental works as *The Myth of the Birth of the Hero*. He split with Freud on the significance of the birth trauma, which he used as a basis of brief psychotherapy.

Rapport. Conscious, harmonious accord that usually reflects a good relationship between two persons. In a group, rapport is the presence of mutual responsiveness, as evidenced by spontaneous and sympathetic reaction to each other's needs, sentiments, and attitudes. *See also* Countertransference, Transference.

Rap session. *See* Bull session.

Rationalization. An unconscious defense mechanism in which an irrational behavior, motive, or feeling is made to appear reasonable. Ernest Jones introduced the term.

Reaction formation. An unconscious defense mechanism in which a person develops a socialized attitude or interest that is the direct antithesis of some infantile wish or impulse in the unconscious. One of the earliest and most unstable defense mechanisms, it is closely related to repression; both are defenses against impulses or urges that are unacceptable to the ego.

Reality. The totality of objective things and factual events. Reality includes everything that is perceived by a person's special senses and is validated by other people.

Reality-testing. Fundamental ego function that consists of the objective evaluation and judgment of the world outside the self. By interacting with his animate and inanimate environment, a person tests its real nature as well as his own relation to it. How the person evaluates reality and his attitudes toward it are determined by early experiences with the significant persons in his life. *See also* Ego.

Recall. Process of remembering thoughts, words, and actions of a past event in an attempt to recapture what actually happened. It is part of a complex mental function known as memory. *See also* Amnesia, Hypermnesia.

Recathexis. In transactional analysis, the experiencing of different ego states.

Recognition. *See* Memory.

Reconstructive psychotherapy. A form of therapy that seeks not only to alleviate symptoms but to produce alterations in maladaptive character structures and to expedite new adaptive potentials. This aim is achieved by bringing into consciousness an awareness of and insight into conflicts, fears, inhibitions, and their derivatives. *See also* Psychoanalysis.

Recorder. Person who takes notes during the group or individual therapy session. Also referred to as the recorder-observer, he generally does not participate in therapy. *See also* Observer.

Re-enactment. In psychodrama, the acting out of a past experience as if it were happening in the present so that a person can feel, perceive, and act as he did the first time.

Registration. *See* Memory.

Regression. Unconscious defense mechanism in which a person undergoes a partial or total return to earlier patterns of adaptation. Regression is observed in many psychiatric conditions, particularly schizophrenia.

Regressive-reconstructive approach. A psychotherapeutic procedure in which regression is made an integral element of the treatment process. The original traumatic situation is reproduced to gain new insight and to effect significant personality change and emotional maturation. *See also* Psychoanalysis, Reconstructive psychotherapy.

Reik, Theodor (1888–1969). Psychoanalyst and early follower of Freud, who considered him one of his most brilliant pupils. Freud's book, *The Question of Lay Analysis* was written to defend Reik's ability to practice psychoanalysis without medical training. Reik made many valuable contributions to psychoanalysis on the subjects of religion, masochism, and technique. *See also* Third ear.

Relatedness. Sense of sympathy and empathy with regard to others; sense of oneness with others. It is the opposite of isolation and alienation.

Reparenting. A technique evolved in transactional analysis for the treatment of schizophrenia. The patient is first regressed to a Child ego state, and then missing Parent transactions are supplied and contaminations corrected.

Repeater. Group member who has had experience in another group.

Repetitive pattern. Continual attitude or mode of behavior characteristic of a person and performed mechanically or unconsciously.

Repression. An unconscious defense mechanism in which a person removes from consciousness those ideas, impulses, and affects that are unacceptable to him. A term introduced by Freud, it is important in both normal psychological development and in neurotic and psychotic symptom formation. Freud recognized two kinds of repression: (1) repression proper—the repressed material was once in the conscious domain; (2) primal repression—the repressed material was never in the conscious realm. *See also* Suppression.

Repressive-inspirational group psychotherapy. A type of group therapy in which discussion is intended to bolster patients' morale and help them avoid undesired feelings. It is used primarily with large groups of seriously regressed patients in institutional settings.

Reserpine. An alkaloid extracted from the root of the *Rauwolfia serpentina* plant. It is used primarily as an antihypertensive agent. It was formerly used as an antipsychotic agent because of its sedative effect.

Residential treatment facility. A center where the patient lives and receives treatment appropriate for his particular needs. A children's residential treatment facility ideally furnishes both educational and therapeutic experiences for the emotionally disturbed child.

Resistance. A conscious or unconscious opposition to the uncovering of the unconscious. Resistance is linked to underlying psychological defense mechanisms against impulses from the id that are threatening to the ego. *See also* Group resistance.

Resonance. Unconscious response determined by early life experiences. In a group, a member may respond by fantasizing at a particular level of psychosexual development when another member functions regressively at that level. The unconscious sounding board is constructed in the first five years of life. *See also* Focal-conflict theory.

Retardation. Slowness of development or progress. In psychiatry there are two types, mental retardation and psychomotor retardation. Mental retardation refers to slowness or arrest of intellectual maturation. Psychomotor retardation refers to slowness or slackened psychic activity or motor activity or both; it is observed in pathological depression.

Retention. *See* Memory.

Retrospective falsification. Recollection of false memory. *See also* Paramnesia.

Review session. Meeting in which each member reviews with the group his goals and progress in treatment. It is a technique used in structured interactional group psychotherapy.

Ritual. Automatic activity of psychogenic or cultural origin. *See also* Group ritual.

Role. Pattern of behavior that a person takes. It has its roots in childhood and is influenced by significant people with whom the person had primary relationships. When the behavior pattern conforms with the expectations and demands of other people, it is said to be a complementary role. If it does not conform with the demands and expectation of others, it is known as noncomplementary role. *See also* Identification, Injunction, Therapeutic role.

Role-divided therapy. Therapeutic arrangement in a co-therapy situation when each therapist takes on a specific function in treatment. For example, one therapist may take the role of a provocateur, while the other takes the role of a passive observer and interpreter. *See also* Splitting situation.

Role limit. Boundary placed on the therapist or the patient by virtue of his conscious position in the therapy group. The patient plays the patient, and the therapist plays the therapist; there is no reversal of roles.

Role model. In a therapeutic community or methadone program, an ex-addict who, because of his successful adjustment and similarity of experience with the patient population, becomes a source of positive identification and a tangible proof of success. *See also* Ego model.

Role-playing. Psychodrama technique in which a person is trained to function more effectively in his reality roles—such as employer, employee, student, and instructor. In the therapeutic setting of psychodrama, the protagonist is free to try and to fail in his role, for he is given the opportunity to try again until he finally learns new approaches to the situation he fears, approaches that he can then apply outside. *See also* Anti-repression device.

Role reversal. Technique used in psychodrama whereby an auxiliary ego plays the role of the patient, and the patient plays the role of the other person. Distortions of interpersonal perception are thereby brought to the surface, explored, and corrected.

Role-training. *See* Role-playing.

Roll and rock. An encounter group technique that is used to develop trust in a participant. A person stands, with eyes closed, in a tight circle of group members and is passed around (rolled) from member to member. Then he is placed on his back on the floor, gently lifted by the group members, and rocked back and forth. He is then put back on the floor. After this exercise, the group members discuss their reactions.

Rosander anti-Negro behavior scale. A scale that measures white attitudes toward blacks by asking respondents what their behavior would be in various hypothetical situations involving black participants. The scale can be of aid in determining the degree of prejudice held by whites toward blacks and the influence of a group experience on such prejudices. *See also* Ford negative personal contacts with Negroes scale, Ford negative personal contacts with whites scale, Kelley desegregation scale, Steckler anti-Negro scale, Steckler anti-white scale.

Rosenberg self-esteem scale. A scale designed to measure a person's opinion of himself. Use of this scale gives the therapist a means of evaluating the effect a group experience has on a member's self-esteem.

Saboteur. One who obstructs progress within a group, either deliberately or unconsciously.

Sadism. A sexual deviation in which sexual gratification is achieved by inflicting pain and humiliation on the partner. Donatien Alphonse François de Sade (1740–1814), a French writer, was the first person to describe this condition. *See also* Masochism, Sadomasochistic relationship.

Sadomasochistic relationship. Relationship in which the enjoyment of suffering by one person and the enjoyment of inflicting pain by the other person are important and complementary attractions in their on-going relationship. *See also* Masochism, Sadism.

Satyriasis. Morbid, insatiable sexual needs or desires in men. It may be caused by organic or psychiatric factors. *See also* Nymphomania.

Schilder, Paul (1886–1940). American neuropsychiatrist. He started the use of group psychotherapy at New York's Bellevue Hospital, combining social and psychoanalytic principles.

Schizophrenia. Mental disorder of psychotic level characterized by disturbances in thinking, mood, and behavior. The thinking disturbance is manifested by a distortion of reality, especially by delusions and hallucinations, accompanied by fragmentation of associations that results in incoherent speech. The mood disturbance is manifested by inappropriate affective responses. The behavior disturbance is manifested by ambivalence, apathetic withdrawal, and bizarre activity. Formerly known as dementia praecox, schizophrenia as a term was introduced by Eugen Bleuler. The causes of schizophrenia remain unknown. The types of schizophrenia include simple type, hebephrenic type, catatonic type, paranoid type, schizo-affective type, childhood type, residual type, latent type, acute schizophrenic episode, and chronic undifferentiated type.

Schreber case. One of Freud's cases. It involved the analysis in 1911 of Daniel Paul Shreber's autobiographical account, *Memoirs of a Neurotic,* published in 1903. Analysis of these memoirs permitted Freud to decipher the fundamental meaning of paranoid processes and ideas, especially the relationship between repressed homosexuality and projective defenses.

Screening. Initial patient evaluation that includes medical and psychiatric history, mental status evaluation, and diagnostic formulation to determine the patient's suitability for a particular treatment modality.

Script. In transactional analysis, a complex set of transactions that are adaptations of infantile responses and experiences. The script is recurrent and operates on an unconscious level. It is the mold on which a person's life adaptation is based. *See also* Hamartic script.

Script analysis. The analysis of a person's life adaption—that is, his injunctions, decisions, and life scripts—and the therapeutic process that helps reverse the maladaptive behavior. It is the last phase in transactional analysis. *See also* Game analysis, Structural analysis.

Script antithesis. In transactional analysis, a therapeutic transaction designed to avert temporarily a tragic event in a script. *See also* Script, Script matrix.

Script matrix. Diagram used in transactional analysis to represent two parents and an offspring. It is useful in representing the genesis of life scripts. *See also* Script, Script antithesis.

Secondary process. In psychoanalysis, the mental process directly related to the functions of the ego and characteristic of conscious and preconscious mental activities. The secondary process is marked by logical thinking and by the tendency to delay gratification by regulation of discharge of instinctual demands. *See also* Primary process.

Sedative. Drug that produces a calming or relaxing effect through central nervous system depression. Some drugs with sedative properties are barbiturates, chloral hydrate, paraldehyde, and bromide.

Selective inattention. An aspect of attentiveness in which a person blocks out those areas that generate anxiety.

Self-analysis. Investigation of one's own psychic components. It plays a part in all analysis, although to a limited extent, since few are capable of sustaining independent and detached attitudes for it to be therapeutic.

Self-awareness. Sense of knowing what one is experiencing. For example, realizing that one has just responded with anger to another group member as a substitute for the anxiety felt when he attacked a vital part of one's self concept. Self-awareness is a major goal of all therapy, individual and group.

Self-discovery. In psychoanalysis, the freeing of the repressed ego in a person who has been brought up to submit to the wishes of the significant others around him.

Self-presentation. Psychodrama technique in which the patient plays the role of himself and of related persons (father, mother, brother, etc.) as he perceives them in a completely subjective manner.

Self-realization. Psychodrama technique in which the protagonist enacts, with the aid of a few auxiliary egos, the plan of his life, no matter how remote it may be from his present situation. For instance, an accountant who has been taking singing lessons, hoping to try out for a musical comedy part in summer stock, and planning to make the theatre his life's work can explore the effects of success in this venture and of possible failure and return to his old livelihood.

Sensation. Feeling or impression when the sensory nerve endings of any of the six senses—taste, touch, smell, sight, kinesthesia, and sound—are stimulated.

Sensitivity training group. Group in which members seek to develop self-awareness and an understanding of group processes rather than gain relief from an emotional disturbance. *See also* Encounter group, Personal growth laboratory, T-group.

Sensorium. Theoretical sensory center located in the brain that is involved with a person's awareness about his surroundings. In psychiatry, it is often referred to as consciousness.

Sensory-experiential group. An encounter group that is primarily concerned with the emotional and physical interaction of the participants. The experience itself, not the examination of the group process, is considered the *raison d'être* for the group.

Serotonin. A monoamine that is believed to be a neurohumoral transmitter. It is found in the serum and, in high concentrations, in the hypothalamus of the brain. Recent pharmacological investigations link depression to disorders in the metabolism of serotonin and other biogenic amines, such as norepinephrine.

Session leader. *See* Facilitator.

Sexual deviation. Mental disorder characterized by sexual interests and behavior other than what is culturally accepted. Sexual deviation includes sexual interest in objects other than a person of the opposite sex, such as homosexuality or bestiality; bizarre sexual practices, such as necrophilia; and other sexual activities that are not accompanied by copulation. *See also* Bestiality, Exhibitionism, Homosexuality, Masochism, Sadism.

Sexual drive. One of the two primal instincts (the other is the aggressive drive) according to Freud's dual-instinct theory of 1920. It is also known as eros and life instinct. Its main goal is to preserve and maintain life. It operates under the influence of the pleasure-unpleasure principle. *See also* Aggressive drive, Libido theory.

Shifting attention. A characteristic of group therapy in which the focus changes from one patient to another so that no one patient remains continuously in the spotlight. It is also known as alternating scrutiny. *See also* Structured interactional group psychotherapy.

Shock treatment. A form of psychiatric treatment with a chemical substance (ingested, inhaled, or injected) or sufficient electric current to produce a convulsive seizure and unconsciousness. It is used in certain types of schizophrenia and mood disorders. Shock treatment's mechanism of action is still unknown.

Sibling rivalry. Competition among children for the attention, affection, and esteem of their parents. The children's jealousy is accompanied by hatred and death wishes toward each other. The rivalry need not be limited to actual siblings; it is a factor in both normal and abnormal competitiveness throughout life.

Slavson, S. R. (1890–   ). American theoretician who pioneered in group psychotherapy based on psychoanalytic principles. In his work with children, from which he derived most of his concepts, he introduced and developed activity group therapy. *See also* Collective experience.

Sleep. A temporary physiological state of unconsciousness characterized by a reversible cessation of the person's waking sensorimotor activity. A biological need, sleep recurs periodically to rest the whole body and to regenerate neuromuscular tissue. *See also* Dream.

Social adaptation. Adjustment to the whole complex of interpersonal relationships; the ability to live and express oneself in accordance with society's restrictions and cultural demands. *See also* Adaptational approach.

Social configuration. Arrangement of interpersonal interactions. *See also* Hierarchical vector, Horizontal vector.

Social instinct. *See* Herd instinct.

Socialization. Process of learning interpersonal and interactional skills according to and in conformity with one's society. In a group therapy setting, it includes a member's way of participating both mentally and physically in the group. *See also* Interpersonal skill.

Social network therapy. A type of group therapy in which the therapist assembles all the persons—relatives, friends, social relations, work relations—who have emotional or functional significance in the patient's life. Some or all of the social network may be assembled at any given time. *See also* Extended family therapy, Visitor.

Social psychiatry. Branch of psychiatry interested in ecological, sociological, and cultural variables that engender, intensify, or complicate maladaptive patterns of behavior and their treatment.

Social therapy. A rehabilitative form of therapy with psychiatric patients. The aim is to improve social functioning. Occupational therapy, therapeutic community, recreational therapy, milieu therapy, and attitude therapy are forms of social therapy.

Sociogram. Diagrammatic portrayal of choices, rejections, and indifferences of a number of persons involved in a life situation.

Sociometric distance. The measurable degree of perception one person has for another. It can be hypothesized that the greater the sociometric distance between persons, the more inaccurate will be their social evaluation of their relationship.

Sociometric feedback. Information that people give each other about how much closeness or distance they desire between them. It is a measure of how social one would like to be with another. An example of sociometric feedback would be the answer by a group member to the question, "With what three members of this group would you prefer to spend six months on a desert island?"

Sociometrist. Social investigator engaged in measuring the interpersonal relations and social structures in a community.

Soliloquy. *See* Therapeutic soliloquy.

Somnambulism. Sleepwalking; motor activity during sleep. It is commonly seen in children. In adults, it is observed in persons with schizoid personality disorders and certain types of schizophrenia.

Splitting situation. Condition in a co-therapy group. A patient is often unable to express opposite feelings toward one therapist. The splitting situation allows him to express contrasting feelings—positive-love feeling and negative-hostile feeling—by directing one feeling at one co-therapist and the opposite feeling at the other co-therapist. *See also* Role-divided therapy.

Splitting transference. Breaking of an irrational feeling or attitude into its component parts, which are then assigned to different persons. For example, ambivalence toward a mother may be expressed in a group by reacting to one member as to a good mother and reacting to another member as to a bad mother.

Square interview. Occasional session in marriage therapy in which both spouses and each spouse's therapist are present. The therapists and sometimes the patients are able to observe, experience, and respond to the transactional dynamics among the four of them, thus encouraging a common viewpoint by all four people involved in marital therapy. *See also* Collaborative therapy, Combined therapy, Concurrent therapy, Conjoint therapy, Group marital therapy, Marriage therapy, Quadrangular therapy.

Square situation. *See* Quadrangular therapy, Square interview.

Squeaky wheel. Person who is continually calling attention to himself. Because of his style of interacting, he is likely to get more than his share of a group's effort and energy.

Status value. Worth of a person in terms of such criteria as income, social prestige, intelligence, and education. It is considered an important parameter of one's position in the society.

Steckler anti-Negro scale. A scale designed to measure the attitude of Negroes toward Negroes. It can be of use in ascertaining the degree of prejudice blacks have against their own race and in evaluating the corrective efficacy of group experience. *See also* Ford negative personal contacts with Negroes scale, Ford negative personal contacts with whites scale, Kelley desegregation scale, Rosander anti-Negro behavior scale.

Steckler anti-white scale. A scale designed to measure the attitudes of Negroes toward whites. It can be used to ascertain the amount of prejudice blacks have against whites and to evaluate the influence of a group experience. *See also* Ford negative personal contacts with Negroes scale. Ford negative personal contacts with whites scale, Kelley desegregation scale.

Stegreiftheater. *See* Theatre of Spontaneity.

Stekel, Wilhelm (1868–1940). Viennese psychoanalyst. He suggested the formation of the first Freudian group, the Wednesday Evening Society, which later became the Vienna Psychoanalytic Society. A man given to intuition rather than to systematic research, his insight into dreams proved stimulating and added to the knowledge of symbols. Nevertheless, his superficial wild analysis proved incompatible with the Freudian school. He introduced the word thanatos to signify death wish.

Stereotypy. Continuous repetition of speech or physical activities. It is observed in cases of catatonic schizophrenia.

Stimulant. Drug that affects one or more organ systems to produce an exciting or arousing effect, increase physical activity and vivacity, and promote a sense of well-being. There are, for example, central nervous system stimulants, cardiac stimulants, respiratory stimulants, and psychomotor stimulants.

Stress immunity. Failure to react to emotional stress.

Stroke. In transactional analysis, a unit of human recognition. Early in life, strokes must involve physical contact; later in life, strokes can be symbolic—such as, "Glad to see you!"

Structural analysis. Analysis of the personality into its constituent ego states. The goal of structural analysis is to establish and maintain the predominance of reality-testing ego states, free from contamination. It is considered the first phase of transactional analysis. *See also* Contamination, Ego state, Game analysis, Ogre, Script analysis, Transactional analysis.

Structured interactional group psychotherapy. A type of group psychotherapy, developed by Harold Kaplan and Benjamin Sadock, in which the therapist provides a structural matrix for the group's interactions. The important part of the structure is that a different member of the group is the focus of the interaction in each session. *See also* Forced interaction, Go-around, Up.

Studies on Hysteria. Title of a book by Josef Breuer and Sigmund Freud. Published in 1895, it described the cathartic method of treatment and the beginnings of psychoanalysis. It demonstrated the psychological origins of hysterical symptoms and the possibility of effecting a cure through psychotherapy.

Stupor. Disturbance of consciousness in which the patient is nonreactive to and unaware of his surroundings. Organically, it is synonymous with unconsciousness. In psychiatry, it is referred to as mutism and is commonly found in catatonia and psychotic depression.

Subjectivity. Qualitative appraisal and interpretation of an object or experience as influenced by one's own feelings and thinking.

Subject session. Group technique, used particularly in structured interactional group psychotherapy, in which a topic is introduced by the therapist or a group member and is then explored by the whole group.

Sublimation. An unconscious defense mechanism in which unacceptable instinctual drives are diverted into personally and socially acceptable channels. Unlike other defense mechanisms, sublimation offers some minimal gratification of the instinctual drive or impulse.

Substituting. Providing a nonverbal alternate for something a patient missed in his early life. Crossing the room to sit beside a group member who needs support is an example of substituting.

Substitution. An unconscious defense mechanism in which a person replaces an unacceptable wish, drive, emotion, or goal with one that is more acceptable.

Suggestibility. State of compliant responsiveness to an idea or influence. It is commonly observed among persons with hysterical traits.

Sullivan, Harry Stack (1892–1949). American psychiatrist. He is best known for his interpersonal theory of psychiatry. *See also* Consensual validation.

Summer session. In structured interactional group psychotherapy, regularly scheduled group session during the therapist's vacation.

Superego. One of the three component parts of the psychic apparatus. The other two are the ego and the id. Freud created the theoretical concept of the superego to describe the psychic functions that are expressed in moral attitudes, conscience, and a sense of guilt. The superego results from the internalization of the ethical standards of the society in which the person lives, and it develops by identification with the attitudes of his parents. It is mainly unconscious and is believed to develop as a reaction to the Oedipus complex. It has a protective and rewarding function, referred to as the ego ideal, and a critical and punishing function, which evokes the sense of guilt.

Support. *See* Mutual support.

Suppression. Conscious act of controlling and inhibiting an unacceptable impulse, emotion, or idea. Suppression is differentiated from repression in that the latter is an unconscious process.

Surplus reality. The intangible, invisible dimensions of intrapsychic and extrapsychic life. The term was coined by J. L. Moreno.

Survival. Game used in a professionally homogeneous group. It is designed to create awareness of one another's talents. An imaginary situation is created in which the members are no longer permitted to continue in their particular professions and must, as a group, find some other activity in which to work together meaningfully and profitably. *See also* Game, Hit-and-run game, Million-dollar game.

Symbolization. An unconscious defense mechanism whereby one idea or object comes to stand for another because of some common aspect or quality in both. Symbolization is based on similarity and association. The symbols formed protect the person from the anxiety that may be attached to the original idea or object. *See also* Defense mechanism.

Sympathomimetic drug. Drug that mimics the actions of the sympathetic nervous system. Examples of these drugs are amphetamine and epinephrine.

Sympathy. Sharing of another person's feelings, ideas, and experiences. As opposed to empathy, sympathy is not objective. *See also* Identification, Imitation.

Symptom formation. *See* Symptom substitution.

Symptom substitution. Unconscious psychic process in which a repressed impulse is indirectly released and manifested through a symptom. Such symptoms as obsession, compulsion, phobia, dissociation, anxiety, depression, hallucination, and delusion are examples of symptom substitution. It is also known as symptom formation.

Tachylogia. *See* Logorrhea.

Tactile hallucination. False sense of touch.

Tangentiality. Disturbance in the associative thought processes in which the patient is unable to express his idea. In contrast to circumstantiality, the digression in tangentiality is such that the central idea is not communicated. It is observed in schizophrenia and certain types of or-

ganic brain disorders. Tangentiality is also known as derailment. *See also* Circumstantiality.

Tardive oral dyskinesia. A syndrome characterized by involuntary movements of the lips and jaw and by other bizarre involuntary dystonic movements. It is an extrapyramidal effect occurring late in the course of antipsychotic drug therapy.

Target patient. Group member who is perceptively analyzed by another member. It is a term used in the process of going around in psychoanalytically oriented groups.

Task-oriented group. Group whose main energy is devoted to reaching a goal, finding a solution to a problem, or building a product. Distinguished from this type of group is the experiential group, which is mainly concerned with sharing whatever happens. *See also* Action group.

Tele. In psychodrama, an objective social process that strengthens association and promotes cohesiveness in groups. It is believed to function on the basis of transference and empathy.

Tension. An unpleasurable alteration of affect characterized by a strenuous increase in mental and physical activity.

Termination. Orderly conclusion of a group member's therapy or of the whole group's treatment as contrasted with a drop-out that is not advised by the therapist.

T-group (training group). A type of group that emphasizes training in self-awareness and group dynamics. *See also* Action group, Intervention laboratory, National Training Laboratories, Sensitivity training.

Thanatos. Death wish. *See also* Stekel, Wilhelm.

Theatre of Spontaneity (Stegreiftheater). Theatre in Vienna which improvised group processes and which was developed by J. L. Moreno, M.D.

Theoretical orientation. Alignment with a hypothetical point of view already espoused by a person or group.

Therapeutic agent. Anything—people and/or drugs—that causes healing in a maladaptive person. In group therapy, it refers mainly to people who help others.

Therapeutic alliance. Conscious relationship between therapist and patient in which each implicitly agrees that they need to work together by means of insight and control to help the patient with his conflicts. It involves a therapeutic splitting of the patient's ego into observing and experiencing parts. A good therapeutic alliance is especially necessary during phases of strong negative transference in order to keep the treatment going. It is as important in group as in dyadic psychotherapy. *See also* Working alliance.

Therapeutic atmosphere. All therapeutic, maturational, and growth-supporting agents—cultural, social, and medical.

Therapeutic community. Ward or hospital treatment setting that provides an effective environment for behavioral changes in patients through resocialization and rehabilitation.

Therapeutic crisis. Turning point in the treatment process. An example is acting out, which, depending on how it is dealt with, may or may not lead to a therapeutic change in the patient's behavior. *See also* Therapeutic impasse.

Therapeutic group. Group of patients joined together under the leadership of a therapist for the purpose of working together for psychotherapeutic ends—specifically, for the treatment of each patient's emotional disorders.

Therapeutic group analysis. *See* Group analytic psychotherapy.

Therapeutic impasse. Deadlock in the treatment process. Therapy is in a state of imminent failure when there is no further insight or awareness and sessions are reduced to routine meetings of patient and therapist. Unresolved resistances and transference and countertransference conflicts are among the common causes of this phenomenon. *See also* Therapeutic crisis.

Therapeutic role. Position in which one aims to treat, bring about an improvement, or provide alleviation of a distressing condition or state.

Therapeutic soliloquy. Psychodrama technique that involves a patient's portrayal—by side dialogues and side actions—of his hidden thoughts and feelings that parallel his overt thoughts and actions.

Therapeutic transaction. Interplay between therapist and patient or among group members that is intended to improve the patient.

Therapist surrogate. Group member who—by virtue of experience, intuition, or training—is able to be an effective group leader in the absence of or in concert with the group therapist. He is also known as a nuclear group member. *See also* Leaderless therapeutic group.

There-and-then. Past experience rather than immediate experience. *See also* Here-and-now.

Thinking. *See* Cognition.

Thinking compulsion. *See* Intellectualization.

Thinking through. The mental process that occurs in an attempt to understand one's own behavior and gain insight from it.

Third ear. Ability to make use of intuition, sensitivity, and awareness of subliminal cues to interpret clinical observations of individual and group patients. First introduced by the German philosopher Frederic Nietzsche, it was later used in analytic psychotherapy by Theodor Reik.

Thought deprivation. *See* Blocking.

Thought process disorder. A symptom of schizophrenia that involves the intellectual functions. It is manifested by irrelevance and incoherence of the patient's verbal productions. It ranges from simple blocking and mild circumstantiality to total loosening of associations, as in word salad.

Three-cornered therapy. *See* Co-therapy.

Three Essays on the Theory of Sexuality. Title of a book by Freud. Published in 1905, it applied the libido theory to the successive phases of sex instinct maturation in the infant, child, and adolescent. It made possible the integration of a vast diversity of clinical observations and promoted the direct observation of child development.

Tic. Involuntary, spasmodic, repetitive motor movement of a small segment of the body. Mainly psychogenic, it may be seen in certain cases of chronic encephalitis.

Timidity. Inability to assert oneself for fear of some fancied reprisal, even though there is no objective evidence of potential harm. In a therapy group, the timid person may make others fear the destructiveness of their normal aggression.

Tinnitus. Noises in one or both ears, such as ringing and whistling. It is an occasional side effect of some of the antidepressant drugs.

Tolerance. In group therapy, the willingness to put up with disordered behavior by co-patients in the group.

Too-tired-to-be-polite phenomenon. Phenomenon in a marathon group that stems from fatigue and results in the relaxation of the social facades of politeness. Some proponents of marathon groups have stressed the helpfulness of fatigue in breaking through the social games that participants play in the early stages of the group. *See also* Group marathon.

Totem and Taboo. Title of a book by Freud. Published in 1913, it applied his concepts to the data of anthropology. He was able to afford much insight into the meaning of tribal organizations and customs, especially by invoking the Oedipus complex and the characteristics of magical thought as he had discovered them from studies of the unconscious. *See also* Oedipus complex, Primal father.

Toucher. Someone who enjoys touching another person. When the touching is not of the clinging type, such a person in an encounter group usually helps inhibited people lose their anxiety about physical contact and closeness.

Traditional group therapy. Group therapy of a conventional type in which the role of the therapist is clearly delineated and the other participants are understood to be clients or patients who are attending the group meetings to overcome or resolve some definite emotional problems. *See also* Encounter group, Group psychotherapy, Sensitivity training.

Trainer. Professional leader or facilitator of a sensitivity training or T-group; teacher or supervisor of a person learning the science and practice of group therapy.

Training group. *See* T-group.

Tranquilizer. Psychotropic drug that induces tranquility by calming, soothing, quieting, or pacifying without clouding the conscious. The major tranquilizers are antipsychotic drugs, and the minor tranquilizers are antianxiety drugs.

Transaction. Interaction that arises when two or more persons have an encounter. In transactional analysis, it is considered the unit of social interaction. It involves a stimulus and a response. *See also* Complementarity of interaction, Forced interaction, Group stimulus, Structured interactional group psychotherapy, Therapeutic transaction.

Transactional analysis. A system introduced by Eric Berne that centers on the study of interactions going on in the treatment sessions. The system includes four components: (1) structural analysis of intrapsychic phenomena; (2) transactional analysis proper, the determination of the currently dominant ego state (Parent, Child, or Adult) of each participant; (3) game analysis, identification of the games played in their interactions and of the gratifications provided; and (4) script analysis, uncovering of the causes of the patient's emotional problems.

Transactional group psychotherapy. A system of therapy founded by Eric Berne. It is based on the analysis of interactions and on the understanding of patterns of transactions as they occur during treatment sessions. Social control is the main goal of therapy.

Transference. Unconscious phenomenon in which the feelings, attitudes, and wishes originally linked with important figures in one's early life are projected onto others who have come to represent them in current life. *See also* Countertransference, Lateral transference, Multiple transference, Rapport, Transference neurosis.

Transference neurosis. A phenomenon occurring in psychoanalysis in which the patient develops a strong emotional attachment to the therapist as a symbolized nuclear familial figure. The repetition and depth of this misperception or symbolization characterize it as a transference neurosis. In transference analysis, a major therapeutic technique in both individual and group therapy, the therapist uses transference to help the patient understand and gain insight into his behavior. *See also* Collective family transference neurosis, Dilution of transference.

Trend of thought. Thinking that centers on a particular idea associated with an affective tone.

Triad. Father, mother, and child relationship projectively experienced in group therapy. *See also* Nuclear family.

Trichotillomania. Morbid compulsion to pull out one's hair.

Tricyclic drug. Antidepressant drug believed by some to be more effective than monoamine oxidase inhibitors. The tricyclic drugs (imipramine and amitriptyline) are presently the most popular drugs in the treatment of pathological depression.

Tyramine. A sympathomimetic amine that is believed to influence the release of stored norepinephrine. Its degradation is inhibited by monoamine oxidase. The use of monoamine oxidase inhibitors in the treatment of depression prevents the degradation of tyramine. The ingestion of food containing tyramine, such as cheese, may cause a sympathomimetic effect, such as an increase in blood pressure, that could be fatal.

Unconscious. 1. (Noun) Structural division of the mind in which the psychic material—primitive drives, repressed desires, and memories—is not directly accessible to awareness. 2. (Adjective) In a state of insensibility, with absence of orientation and perception. *See also* Conscious, Preconscious.

Underachievement. Failure to reach a biopsychological, age-adequate level.

Underachiever. Person who manifestly does not function up to his capacity. The term usually refers to a bright child whose school test grades fall below expected levels.

Undeveloped potential. The behavior, feelings, and motivations of a person known neither to himself nor to others. It is the unknown quadrant of the Johari Window, a diagrammatic concept of human behavior. *See also* Blind self, Hidden self, Public self.

Undoing. An unconscious defense mechanism by which a person symbolically acts out in reverse something unacceptable that has already been done. A primitive defense mechanism, undoing is a form of magical expiatory action. Repetitive in nature, it is commonly observed in obsessive-compulsive neurosis.

Unisexual group. *See* Homogeneous group.

Universality. Total effect produced when all group members share specific symptoms or problems.

Up. The member who is the focus of discussion in group therapy, particularly in structured interactional group psychotherapy.

Up-tight. Slang term that describes defensive, rigid behavior on the part of a person whose values are threatened or who is afraid of becoming vulnerable and of experiencing painful emotions. Such a person frequently becomes a target for pressure in a therapy group.

Urine-testing. Thin-layer chromatography-testing for the presence of opiates, quinine, barbiturates, and amphetamines. Addict treatment programs use such testing to verify abstinence from illicit drug use.

Vector. An engineering term used to imply a pointed force being felt by the group. *See also* Hierarchical vector, Horizontal vector.

Verbal-deep approach. Procedure used in small groups in which communication is conducted exclusively through verbal means and is oriented to major goals. It is a technique used in analytical group therapy. *See also* Actional-deep approach, Actional-superficial approach, Verbal-superficial approach.

Verbal-superficial approach. Group therapy procedure in which language is the sole medium of communication and the therapeutic process is structured to attain limited objectives. It is a technique traditionally used in the treatment of large groups. *See also* Actional-deep approach, Actional-superficial approach, Verbal-deep approach.

Verbal technique. Any method of group or individual therapy in which words are used. The major part of most psychotherapy is verbal.

Verbigeration. Meaningless repetition of words or phrases. Also known as cataphasia, it is a morbid symptom seen in schizophrenia.

Verbomania. *See* Logorrhea.

Vertical vector. *See* Hierarchical vector.

Vienna Psychoanalytic Society. An outgrowth of the Wednesday Evening Society, an informal group of Freud's earliest followers. The new name was acquired and a reorganization took place in 1910, when the Society became a component of the newly formed International Psychoanalytical Society. Alfred Adler was president from 1910 to 1911, and Freud was president from 1911 until it was disbanded by the Nazis in 1938.

Visceral insight. *See* Insight.

Visitor. Guest who participates in discussions with patients in group therapy. In family therapy, members outside the nuclear family who are invited to the session are considered visitors. *See also* Extended family therapy, Social network therapy.

Visual hallucination. False visual perception.

Volubility. *See* Logorrhea.

Warming-up session. *See* Premeeting.

Waxy flexibility. *See* Cerea flexibilitas.

Wednesday Evening Society. A small group of Freud's followers who in 1902 started meeting with him informally on Wednesday evenings to receive instruction in psychoanalysis. As the society grew in numbers and importance, it evolved in 1910 into the Vienna Psychoanalytic Society.

West-Coast-style T-group. Sensitivity training or encounter group that is oriented toward the experience of union, intimacy, and personal awareness, with relative disregard for the study of group process. It is a style popular in California. *See also* East-Coast-style T-group.

Wild therapy. Group therapy conducted by a leader whose background may not be professional or whose theoretical formulations include widely deviant procedures when compared with conventional techniques.

Withdrawal. Act of retreating or going away from. Observed in schizophrenia and depression, it is characterized by a pathological retreat from interpersonal contact and social involvement, leading to self-preoccupation. In a group setting, this disorder creates a barrier for therapeutic progress.

Wittels, Fritz (1880–1950). Austrian psychoanalyst. One of Freud's early followers, he wrote a biography of him in 1924, during a period of estrangement, when he was under the influence of Wilhelm Stekel. Later, a reconciliation took place, and Freud conceded that some of Wittels' interpretations were probably correct.

Wolf-pack phenomenon. Group process in which a member or the therapist is the scapegoat.

Word salad. An incoherent mixture of words and phrases. This type of speech results from a disturbance in thinking. It is commonly observed in far-advanced states of schizophrenia.

Working alliance. Collaboration between the group as a whole and each patient who is willing to strive for health, growth, and maturation with the help of the therapist. *See also* Therapeutic alliance.

Working out. Stage in the treatment process in which the personal history and psychodynamics of a patient are discovered.

Working through. Process of obtaining more and more insight and personality changes through repeated and varied examination of a conflict or problem. The interactions between free association, resistance, interpretation, and working through constitute the fundamental facets of the analytic process.

Xenophobia. Fear of strangers.

Zoophobia. Fear of animals.

Contributors

Mark Kanzer, M.D.
Clinical Professor of Psychiatry and Past Director, Division of Psychoanalytic Education, State University of New York Downstate Medical Center, Brooklyn, New York

Harold I. Kaplan, M.D.
Professor of Psychiatry and Director of Psychiatric Education and Training, New York Medical College; Attending Psychiatrist, Flower and Fifth Avenue Hospitals; Visiting Psychiatrist, Metropolitan Hospital and Bird S. Coler Memorial Hospital and Home, New York, New York

Benjamin J. Sadock, M.D.
Associate Professor of Psychiatry and Director, Division of Group Process, New York Medical College; Associate Attending Psychiatrist, Flower and Fifth Avenue Hospitals; Associate Visiting Psychiatrist, Metropolitan Hospital; Assistant Attending Psychiatrist, New York State Psychiatric Institute, New York, New York

Emanuel K. Schwartz, Ph.D., D.S.Sc.
Dean and Director of Training, Postgraduate Center for Mental Health; Adjunct Professor of Psychology, Graduate School of Arts and Sciences, New York University; Clinical Professor of Psychology, Postdoctoral Program in Psychotherapy, Adelphi University, New York, New York

Alexander Wolf, M.D.
Associate Clinical Professor of Psychiatry, New York Medical College; Associate Attending Psychiatrist, Flower and Fifth Avenue Hospitals; Associate Visiting Psychiatrist, Metropolitan Hospital and Bird S. Coler Memorial Hospital and Home; Training Analyst, Division of Postgraduate Studies, Comprehensive Course in Psychoanalysis, New York Medical College; Supervising and Training Psychoanalyst, Postgraduate Center for Mental Health, New York, New York